Aboriginal Policing

Aboriginal Policing

A CANADIAN PERSPECTIVE

Bryan D. Cummins
McMaster University

John L. Steckley
Humber College

160201

Prentice
Hall

Toronto

National Library of Canada Cataloguing in Publication Data

Cummins, Bryan David, 1953–
        Aboriginal policing : a Canadian perspective

Includes index.
ISBN 0-13-040667-8

        1. Native policing—Canada. I. Steckley, John, 1949–. II. Title.

E78.C2C845 2002   363.2'08997071   C2002-900595-7

ISBN 0-13-040667-8

Vice President, Editorial Director: Michael J. Young
Acquisitions Editor: Sophia Fortier
Developmental Editor: John Polanszky
Marketing Manager: Toivo Pajo
Production Editor: Cheryl Jackson
Copy Editor: Craig Wilson
Proofreader: Lynne Hussey
Production Manager: Wendy Moran
Page Layout: Heidi Palfrey
Art Director: Julia Hall
Cover Design: Amy Harnden
Cover Image: PhotoDisc

1 2 3 4 5   07 06 05 04 03

Printed and bound in Canada

Bryan Cummins would like to dedicate this book to Tricia.

John Steckley would like to dedicate this book to his father,
Harold M. Steckley.

Contents

Preface

Aboriginal Policing: A Canadian Perspective was written to fill a void in the current literature. While the media and introductory sociology textbooks seem content to inform people that Natives are disproportionately represented in the prison system, that they clash with police, and that a number of miscarriages of justice against them have occurred, much more than that needs to be said. This text puts Aboriginal policing and justice issues into a deeper and broader framework, providing an overview of the cultural, historical, legal, and political bases for Aboriginal policing in this country. Our discussions on racism; differing cultural values, notions of sovereignty, and justice; the superficial stories and sensationalistic media opportunities; and the travellers' tales of non-Native journalist visitors to "Indian country" will help students to better understand Aboriginal policing in Canada.

We also wish to sketch in a face not often seen in the media's portrayal of and current literature about Aboriginal issues in Canada: that of the police engaged in Aboriginal policing. These officers are often either faceless or are unthinkingly portrayed as villains. It appears to us that most people engaged in Aboriginal policing are "good cops," but that the exceptions grab the headlines. It has been insufficiently considered that officers are put into situations, often volatile and life-threatening, that are not of their own making or choosing. They are often left to clean up the messes caused by others, both non-Native and Native. While doing the research for this book, we were greatly impressed by the sensitivity, compassion, good sense, and good humour that police officers, both Native and non-Native, bring to Aboriginal policing. We were also very impressed by the veteran RCMP officers with whom we spoke. As this book was going to press, one of these officers had volunteered for far northern duty so that he could again work with First Nations peoples. In his thinking, the non-monetary rewards of working with Natives in the Arctic outweighed those of working in southern Ontario.

It is true that, like the journalists and social scientists we often criticize, we tell a significant number of horror stories in this book. That cannot and should not be avoided, as Aboriginal policing has had a rough history and it can't be sugarcoated. However, as is the case with the better journalists who stick around after the deadline to find out more, and the sociologists who want to get past merely playing a numbers game, our wish is to present a balanced picture, and a hopeful one. We want to contribute to the solution, not just retell the problems.

To paint a truly national picture of Aboriginal policing in Canada, we have organized the book geographically. The book opens with a general introduction to Aboriginal policing followed by separate chapters on each of the larger provinces, the Atlantic provinces as a region, and the territories as a region. The concluding chapter is preceded by a chapter on field experience, which discusses challenges and strategies for both Native and non-Native officers.

We have also included several features to help students develop a deeper understanding of the issues being discussed: learning objectives, key terms with page references, and review questions. Key terms are defined in the glossary at the back of the book. Text boxes located throughout the book highlight important ideas and events associated with Aboriginal policing in Canada.

Acknowledgments

Both authors would like to thank Gina Antonacci, Program Coordinator of the Police Foundations Program at Humber College, for providing us with so much helpful direction at the beginning of this project. Also important at the beginning was Constable Jill Perry of the Royal Canadian Mounted Police, who put us in contact with some of the officers who shared their experiences with us. Without her kind and generous assistance, the book would have been much less complete. We would also like to thank all the officers who shared with us their experiences and their visions of Aboriginal policing.

The people at Pearson have been greatly helpful to us, from David Stover, Acquisitions Editor, to John Polanszky, Developmental Editor, Cheryl Jackson, Production Editor, and Craig Wilson, Copy Editor. Thanks as well to those at Pearson who worked on the project but that we did not get to meet or talk to.

We would also like to thank Native writers Gerald Alfred, Wally McKay, Mike Mitchell, Patricia Monture-Angus, Richard Wagamese and others, for giving us insights into Aboriginal policing that this book could not have been without.

Also worthy of acknowledgment are the owners and staff of the Toby Jug in Bolton, Ontario, who have maintained the proud tradition of the close relationship between writers and a local pub. We would especially like to thank the waitresses who reserved our corner table every Friday so we could plan the book in peace.

Bryan Cummins would like to give special acknowledgment to Mithra Dubey, B.A. (Hons.) who has been his research assistant for several years and has worked on a number of projects for him. As always, she worked quickly and ably to help with this book. A very special thank you is given to Tricia, who is always so supportive and encouraging.

John Steckley would like first to thank his wife, Angie. She makes his writer's journey possible. Also, he would like to thank Cosmo and Egwene, his dogs, who have keen insight as to how to keep a writer sane, even when they are driving him crazy.

Introduction to Aboriginal Policing

LEARNING OBJECTIVES

After completing this chapter, students should be able to:

1. Distinguish between individual and institutional(ized) racism.
2. Outline the significance of having a different culture of policing as a form of cultural difference.
3. Describe the various reasons why the rate of incarceration is so high among Native peoples.
4. Discuss how institutional racism in the justice system has typically influenced the treatment of Natives who have been drinking.

What is Aboriginal policing? What is this book about? It is about how non-Native peoples have policed and are policing Native peoples, some of the mistakes they have made, and some of the good practices they have used and are using. It is also about how Native peoples have policed Native peoples, some of the mistakes they have made, and some of the good practices they have used and are using. It is not easy to engage in Aboriginal policing, regardless of whether you are Aboriginal or not. There are traps to fall into that both Native and non-Native police officers need to be mindful of when they are involved in Aboriginal policing. There are unique traps as well for both groups.

This book talks about **racism.** Both "racism" and "racist" are words that are often thrown about carelessly, without much thought. We intend to begin with a little precision concerning our use of the term in this book. We will begin with the definition of racism found in Diana Kendall's book, *Race, Class and Gender in a Diverse Society: A Text Reader*:

> Racism is a system of beliefs and behaviors embedded in the power relations of a society whereby members of a subordinate racial-ethnic group are oppressed and exploited because they possess cultural, psychological, and/or physical characteristics that members of a dominant racial-ethnic group deem to be inferior. (Kendall, 1997: 300)

The essence of racism is captured in the following often-repeated equation: "racism = prejudice + discrimination + power" (Fleras and Elliott, 1999: 440). It is important to distinguish between two main kinds of racism. One is at the individual level of personal prejudice and more or less deliberate acts of discrimination, with a personal exercise of power (e.g., through a privileged personal link to the power of an institution). It is fair to say that *some* non-Native police officers have this kind of prejudice and commit these acts of discrimination. We will be relating some stories that reflect this prejudice, discrimination, and personal exercise of power. But it is the opinion of the authors of this book that this individual racism probably does not characterize most non-Native police officers. Certainly it has been our experience to encounter officers, in interviews and through various media, who are far from being racist.

More powerful and more difficult to identify and eradicate is **institutional** or **institutionalized racism.** As defined by Fleras and Elliott,

> Institutionalized racism involves an explicit set of discriminatory policies, priorities, and practices that openly deny and exclude minorities from full participation within the organization. (Fleras and Elliott, 1999: 437)

One of the best discussions of the concept of institutional racism is found in Stanley R. Barrett's book, *Is God a Racist?*:

> Institutional racism means racism that is intrinsic to the structures of society. It may be overt or covert, expressed formally in the laws of the land, or less visibly in patterns of employment and the content of school textbooks. What is significant about institutional racism ... is not only that different advantage along racial lines is embedded in society itself, but also that it perpetuates itself over time, for that is the nature of the institutional framework: independent of individual volitions, relatively unconscious and unmotivated, it reproduces itself. Effort is not required to maintain it; instead, effort is required to diminish it. In other words, institutional racism is almost synonymous with "the ways things are." (Barrett, 1987: 307–308, as quoted in Miller, Van Esterik, and Van Esterik, 2001: 297)

Both Native and non-Native police officers are sometimes made unwitting agents of institutional racism when the laws themselves are racist, or when politicians force them into confrontation even though good policing practice would caution that negotiation is a better plan.

Institutional racism meant that federal and provincial governments and policing agencies controlled Aboriginal policing long past the time (if there truly was such a time) when there was any realistic need for such outside control. In 1912, Royal Canadian Mounted Police (RCMP) Superintendent Deane recommended that Native peoples should have their own police force. In 1950, RCMP officers commanding Edmonton and Lethbridge subdivisions responded positively to Native chiefs and band councils who expressed a growing interest in policing their own reserves, by submitting a report to the commissioner of the RCMP recommending such a step. Institutional racism, however, would not let such a change happen. It would disturb the system too much.

Institutional racism can also harm the lives and careers of Aboriginal police officers. In Murphy and Clairmont's study of 1996, when 128 Aboriginal RCMP officers were surveyed concerning what they felt the shortfalls of their policing situation were, the following observations were recorded:

> By far the most frequent shortfall was considered to be discrimination and racism from non-aboriginal fellow officers and reflected in the policies and practices of the organization. It was widely contended that "native police officers are not recognized or treated equally." Officers frequently claimed that supervisors and middle management officers exhibited racism in their promotion practices and in the assignment of responsibilities. One member observed "white superiors use policy to go against native members yet they break policy and get away with it" while another claimed "the RCMP has a two tiered system, one for regular members in non-aboriginal positions while condescending to those in aboriginal positions." (Murphy and Clairmont, 1996)

THE CULTURES OF POLICING

We all readily recognize that different cultures have different ways of doing things. Members of a variety of cultures speak a variety of languages and eat a variety of foods. It is also relatively easy to see that these different ways of doing things are not better or worse; they are just different. English is not structurally a better language than Ojibwa, pasta is not a superior food to wild rice. It is more difficult to see that this kind of different-but-equal status also applies to other areas of life. Canadian business people trying to sign contracts in Asian countries need to learn that there are different cultures of business in these countries. If they try to get by with "business as usual," they will not sign many contracts.

The same applies to policing. There are different **cultures of policing**. The British police officer follows a different set of rules than his/her American counterpart. And this extends far beyond the well-known story of the traditional British "bobby" not carrying a gun, or the police announcing that someone is "helping us with our inquiries," which usually means in North American English that that person is a suspect.

It is a strongly held belief on the part of the authors of this book that Aboriginal policing needs to be part of a different culture of policing. This applies both to reserve policing and urban policing of Native peoples.

Murphy and Clairmont's 1996 study would appear to back up this position. When they looked at "Policing Role and Style Preferences," the statements that had the four highest "Strongly Agree" percentages were: (1) "talking to citizens is good police work" (74%); (2) "peace and order as important as catching criminals" (40%); (3) "police involved [with] community problems not just crime" (37%); and (4) "arrest not always best way to solve problem" (24%) (Murphy and Clairmont 1996). Compare these figures with the response to statements such as "enforcing law most important police job" (11%) and "police restricted to enforcing law/crime" (8%). While Murphy and Clairmont note that this is part of a general trend moving towards community policing, they conclude by saying that "These findings suggest philosophical broad agreement with non-traditional approaches to the policing role."

THE STATISTICS OF RACISM
A Cautionary Statement

In Métis/Coast Salish writer Lee Maracle's novel *Sun Dogs*, the Native heroine is Marianne, who, despite the fact that she is majoring in sociology, is critical of the typical sociological approach to her people. Concerning the sociological staple, statistics, Marianne says, "It shames me some to hear the statistics about us in class. The shame burns holes in whatever sympathy I may have for Indians, not my mom though" (Maracle, 1992: 3).

Before discussing the horrifying statistics that relate to Native peoples and the justice system, it is good to place the use of statistics when talking about Native peoples in proper perspective. Quantifying a problem is not a substitute for trying to address it. Early sociologists, the main proponents of using statistics in talking about Native peoples, often denied the influence of racism on the numbers they were obtaining. In an insightful chapter entitled "Controlling Society" in J. Paul Grayson's *Introduction to Sociology: An Alternate Approach*, John Alan Lee noted that

> The efforts of the legal establishment to maintain the fiction that Canadian law is blind to race are aided ... by the efforts of sociologists. For example, ... Bienvenue and Latif (1975) found that native/Indians were greatly overrepresented in 6000 sentences in Winnipeg courts, but argue that no discrimination existed. They suggest that Indians land in jail proportionately more often than whites because Indians prefer to go to jail. They consider it "a shared experience, a chance to rest ... get better food and meet old friends." Native Indians do not find this line of reasoning amusing. (Lee in Grayson, 1983: 515–516)

> Statistics do not explain themselves.

The Statistics

Native peoples today are greatly overrepresented in the justice system as offenders, victims, and inmates. This is particularly true in the western provinces, and especially so in Saskatchewan. In brief, of all the ethnic and racial groups in Canada, Aboriginal people have the highest rates of charges, arrest, and incarceration. As noted by James Frideres,

> In Canada, 17 percent of the prison population is Aboriginal even though they represent less than 3 percent of the population. Within federal prisons, Aboriginal people make up between 10 and 13 percent, while in provincial institutions the rate is much higher [e.g., 34 percent in Alberta, 49 percent in Manitoba, and 68 percent in Saskatchewan. See Frideres, 2002: 131]. (Frideres, 2002: 130)

The figures for female Native incarceration relative to non-Native women are even more striking. By the end of the 1980s, nearly half of the female provincial jail admissions were Native, with significantly more than half (68.4%) in Manitoba. At the same time, in federal correctional facilities Aboriginal women made up 14% of the female inmate population (Frideres, 1998: 190).

It is also worth noting that once in prison, non-Native inmates fare better than do Native inmates. A larger percentage of the latter are sentenced to two to ten years than are the former. Furthermore, the most desireable release from prison (i.e., full parole) favours non-Native inmates (54%) over Native (34%). The reverse is true for the least desirable form of prison release (i.e., mandatory supervision), with 29 percent for non-Aboriginals and 48 percent for Aboriginals (Frideres, 1998: 190; no specific year given for statistics).

Factors Contributing to the High Native Incarceration Rate

A number of different factors outside of guilt or innocence have negatively affected the Native incarceration rate. The Manitoba Aboriginal Justice Inquiry identified monetary reasons as constituting one of the key factors in the disproportionately high number of Aboriginals in prisons. Having to make bail, even if the figure set was only a few hundred dollars, was found to keep more Native inmates in prison longer. Non-payment of fines is also a cause of incarceration. In one provincial jail in Manitoba, up to 60 percent of the Native inmates in 1987 were serving jail terms because they were unable to pay fines (York, 1990: 145). This was true even though Manitoba at that time had a "fine-option" program, in which people could perform community work if they could not afford to pay a fine, something 3700 Aboriginals did in that same year in Manitoba (York, 1990: 144). This would seem to continue to be a problem. Frideres reports in 1998 (with no date attached to the figures) that nearly one-third of Aboriginal males and two-thirds of Aboriginal females were sentenced to jail because of fine defaults (Frideres, 1998: 188).

Once in court, Aboriginals are treated differently by the system. The Native Counselling Services of Alberta Courtwatch, for example, determined that 90 percent of Aboriginals plead guilty, compared to 75 percent of non-Aboriginals; 96 percent of Aboriginals are found guilty, compared to just over 80 percent for non-Aboriginals (Frideres, 1998: 187, 188; no specific date given for the figures).

One reason statistics such as these are seen relates to another factor—that, whether guilty or innocent, Native peoples are more likely to plead guilty. Frideres suggests that pleading guilty is a means of getting "the process over with." This would be a significant factor as doubtless a good number of Aboriginals felt that the non-Aboriginal judges and lawyers and other human elements in the justice system would find them guilty no matter what they pleaded. Other factors would include faulty advice from legal aid lawyers, an unfamiliarity with English (especially legal English), and possible differences in perceptions of the implications of the "guilty" plea (e.g., concerning the severity of the sentence).

A third factor accounting for the high Native incarceration rate is access to legal counsel, especially in more northerly or remote regions. Frideres (1998: 187) has noted that in these regions contact with one's lawyer does not begin until the actual court appearance. Furthermore, Native peoples contend that in these regions, particularly in fly-in communities, the convenience of the judges and lawyers is paramount, at the cost of the needs of the Native communities. They assert that cases are rushed through with little concern for the principles involved. Frequently, the judge and the attorneys have flown into the community with every intention of returning to their homes and families that same evening. Due process of the law has often been relegated to being a secondary concern.

ALCOHOL AND INSTITUTIONAL RACISM

A good example of systemic racism concerns Aboriginals and alcohol. One of the easy misleading stereotypes about Native peoples is that of the "drunken Indian." It should be pointed out how the justice system has contributed to that stereotype (while also being informed by it). Federal policy was informed by this misconception. Parts of the *Indian Act* once strictly restricted Aboriginal contact with alcohol. Prior to 1969, Section 94 of the Indian Act read as follows: "An Indian who (a) has intoxicants in his possession; (b) is intoxicated; or (c) makes or manufactures intoxicants off a reserve, is guilty of an offence and is liable on summary conviction to a fine of not less than ten dollars and not more than fifty dollars or to imprisonment for a term not exceeding three months to both fine and imprisonment."

Ojibwa author Wilfred Pelletier, writing in 1973, tells us about one of a number of different ways in which this law would contribute to the stereotype:

> There are still some reserves where drinking is against the law, so Indians go into town and buy a bottle or maybe two. They can't take it home and drink it, and it's against the law to drink in a public place. So what do they do? They go in a back alley or maybe in a men's can and they knock the whole bottle off real quick. So then there are some drunken Indians staggering around the town, because drinking that fast will knock anybody on his ass. (Pelletier and Poole, 1973: 90)

This discriminatory law held until the *Regina v. Drybones* case. Joseph Drybones, a Dene, had been charged under section 94b of the *Indian Act* for being intoxicated in a hotel bar in Yellowknife, Northwest Territories, on April 8, 1967. As section 94b differed significantly from the territorial Liquor Ordinance, Drybones' lawyers argued that this contravened the 1960 Canadian Bill of Rights. They won the case in 1969, liberalizing alcohol-related laws concerning status Indians across the country.

There is a long history of police treating Aboriginals who have been drinking differently than they do non-Aboriginals. Consider the following picture of "Crow Lake" presented by David Stymeist in his classic portrayal of this railway town in northwestern Ontario in the 1970s:

> Ontario Provincial Police cars park outside the entrance to the Crow Lake Hotel, the town's largest central pub, for an hour or so before and after the pub closes. The waiters will ask a drunk white man, who is perhaps a relative, friend or steady customer, if he wants to call a cab. The cab will arrive at the back door of the hotel and the man in question will leave unseen. Many Indians, however, are arrested as they leave the pub, and some have been arrested for public drunkenness as they were climbing the stairs to their rooms in the hotel. (Stymeist, 1977: 79)

Native people brought into a police station for drinking are also more likely to be charged and brought to court. A study by James Harding, published in 1980 ("Unemployment, Racial Discrimination and Public Drunkenness in Regina"), revealed that 30 percent of the Aboriginals arrested for drunkenness were charged and sent to court, while the corresponding figure was only 11 percent for non-Aboriginals (as reported in York, 1990: 148).

The Story of Minnie Sutherland: Death by Policing Stereotype?

Early on New Year's Day 1989, Minnie Sutherland, a 40-year-old Cree woman from Moose Factory, was struck by a car in downtown Hull, Quebec. The car hit her on one side of her head and then she hit her head again on the road. It was about 3:30 a.m. and Minnie and her cousin, whom we will call "Jean," along with a few hundred others, had been milling around the street, unwilling or unable to get home.

The car that struck her was driven by two off-duty nurses, who quickly stopped and got out of their car when they heard the bump and saw the woman fall. They checked her over a bit but could discern nothing amiss other than that her eyes showed she had severe eye trouble (she had been declared legally blind but could still see to get around with her glasses) and that her breath indicated that she had been drinking. Three male university students saw the accident and moved towards the scene to see if Minnie was okay. Two stayed with her while another went to call "911." Two young male police officers noticed the sudden stoppage of traffic and got out of the van they were driving to check on what had happened. One of the students told him, in English and in French, that the woman had been hit by a car. One of the officers asked Jean what had happened. Minnie's cousin wasn't sure (as she hadn't actually seen the accident), and just made reference to the fact that they had been drinking.

The officers then attempted to lift Minnie up to a sitting position. One of the students was upset by this, being aware that accident victims should, ideally, not be moved until medical help arrives, and shouted at the officers words to that effect. One officer told him to go and said that he would be arrested if he didn't keep quiet. Their confrontation continued on and off over the next little while.

The officers asked the nurse who had driven the car whether the car stopped was hers and then requested that she move it. The nurse didn't want to leave until she was certain that Minnie was okay and wondered at the casual attitude of the officer concerning an accident victim. According to John Nihmey, author of *Fireworks and Folly: How We Killed Minnie Sutherland,* who had access to the transcripts of the hearing that would follow, the attitude of the officer was that "They were perplexed by what seemed to be an overreaction to a drunk woman who had either slipped on an ice patch and fallen, or walked into a car that couldn't have been going very fast given all the traffic" (Nihmey, 1998: 82–83).

The officers first picked Minnie up and deposited her in a snowbank at the side of the road, then they asked Jean whether she and her cousin wanted them to call a taxi for them. Jean said "Yes." At about the same time, the third student returned, saying that Hull didn't have 911 service yet, so his attempt to get help had failed. Another one of the students suggested calling an ambulance, which sounded like a better offer than a taxi so Jean changed her mind, and told the police so. The officer radioed Hull Police Headquarters concerning the call for a taxi, saying "Cancel the taxi now. The squaw decided otherwise" (Nihmey, 1998: 84). The police then left, satisfied that the matter was finished.

The students and the two Cree women went into a restaurant. Minnie could not stand up without the support of her cousin and her three new acquaintances. The students, feeling that Minnie was looking a little better (although she was barely conscious), and wondering whether the police might be right in treating the matter lightly, left. Two men then picked up the two women and drove them to Ottawa. But seeing the state that Minnie was in, and not getting a positive response from Jean, they called 911 for them, and left.

A female police officer responded to the call. What she encountered was a Native woman with alcohol on her breath and another one who was passed out. The conscious woman said that they had been drinking. The officer tried to rouse Minnie to consciousness but failed. An ambulance pulled up, a paramedic checked Minnie over and just stated that the woman was drunk, suggesting that the officer take her to a detoxification centre. The ambulance left.

The officer took Minnie to the detox centre but they wouldn't admit her because of a policy of not taking non-ambulatory people. It was now about five o'clock. The officer then drove Minnie to her station and conferred with her sergeant. He checked Minnie over and seems to have concluded that he saw what he expected to see, a Native woman smelling of alcohol and passed out, in his view another drunk Indian. Still, he recommended that the officer drive Minnie to a nearby hospital.

Minnie arrived at the hospital at approximately 5:45 a.m. and stayed there until she died on January 11, of cardiac arrest, ultimately the result of a blood clot in the back of her brain caused by her accident. The doctors at the hospital had been unaware of the blood clot and hadn't felt her case was serious enough for an MRI (Magnetic Resonance Imaging) scan, new technology at the hospital, that had a long waiting list. On January 17, a doctor from the hospital sent the following letter to the Hull police:

> There is no doubt that the lack of information about the traumatic event was of great significance in making the initial diagnosis of the abnormality and in following this up to a logical conclusion which may have been able to prevent her demise. It is also unfortunate that Mrs. Sutherland received powerful antibiotics for her condition which would not have been necessary had this history been available. The antibiotics do have their own particular risks.
>
> In particular, if the allegations of the conduct of the Hull Police are correct, then a serious error of judgement has been made by the officers concerned and this should be investigated. (Nihmey, 1998: 163)

An investigation was held. A coroner's jury ruled in March that Hull police should offer compulsory courses to sensitize officers to the needs of visible minorities, but four out of the five jurors felt that racism was not a factor in the case. In 1990, the Quebec Police Commission also cleared its officers of racism charges.

THE IMPORTANCE OF KNOWING THE COMPLETE PEOPLE

In 1987, the very conservative Canadian Bar Association issued a fairly radical 119-page report, entitled *Locking Up Natives in Canada,* based on a two-year study and written by Professor Michael Jackson. This report became well known because of its suggestion that a separate, totally Native-run justice system might be one model for the future, a statement that ran into a lot of resistance from many non-Native individuals in the Canadian justice system. Jackson made an important observation concerning the inability of these people to consider such an option:

> Those in criminal justice typically see native people at the worst part of their lives. Police, sheriffs, judges and prison staff don't see native communities and their leadership solving their own problems. They see the people who have failed. They rarely come into contact with the native leaders responding to problems in positive, effective ways. From that viewpoint, the response is predictable: "How can native people do this [i.e., be effective leaders or professionals] when they can't stand up straight?" (Comeau and Santin, 1990: 132)

Likewise, Native people usually haven't seen non-Native police officers at their best, having contact with them almost exclusively in situations of arrest, not as whole people, members of a community.

KEY TERMS

cultures of policing (p. 3)   institutional racism (p. 2)   racism (p. 2)

REVIEW QUESTIONS

1. What is racism?
2. Distinguish between individual and institutional racism.
3. What is meant by the term "culture of policing"?
4. Name three factors not related to guilt or innocence that have negatively affected the Native incarceration rate.

chapter two

The Legal and Political Framework for Aboriginal Policing

LEARNING OBJECTIVES

After completing this chapter, students should be able to:

1. Discuss the significance of the *Indian Act*, treaties, and reserves for Native people in Canada.
2. Distinguish between the legal statuses of "Indian," "Inuk," and "Métis."
3. Identify the discriminatory nature of Section 12(1)(b) of the *Indian Act*.
4. Outline the legal basis and importance of treaties to Native people in Canada.
5. Describe the responsibilities of band councils and the restrictions placed on them.
6. Discuss the weaknesses of the position of "special constable."
7. Distinguish between Option 3 (a) and Option 3 (b).
8. Discuss the strengths and weaknesses of sentencing circles.

WHAT IS THE *INDIAN ACT*?

The *Indian Act* is a tool of a large federal bureaucracy created "to deal with" Indians. This bureaucracy predates Confederation by over a hundred years, going back to 1755.

Initially, the administration of Aboriginals was in the hands of the military, reflecting the role and importance of Native people in inter-European wars. Additionally, after the American Revolution and the War of 1812, there was a belief that Native people posed a potential threat to European settlement. Hence, their inclusion under military concerns.

In Upper Canada (Ontario), Native concerns remained in the hands of the military until 1830, when they were turned over to the Lieutenant-Governor of the colony and the reserve system was implemented to encourage Aboriginals to become farmers. Forcing them into an agrarian, Christian lifestyle was seen as the best means of "civilizing" Aboriginals.

In Lower Canada (Quebec), the military remained in charge of Native people until Lower and Upper Canada were united as the Province of Canada in 1840. At this time, all Native matters were transferred to the Governor General. It was not until 1860 that full control of Native matters was given to the colonies. The transfer of full control marked a change in the nature of Native-White relations. Until that time, Native people had retained a fair amount of autonomy. As long as Native matters had remained in the hands of the military and later the British Colonial Office (1840–1860), there had been little interference. The British Colonial Office was far away and could do little about colonial matters.

In 1867, section 91, paragraph 24 of the *British North America Act* (the piece of legislation that created Canada as a country) granted the federal government exclusive legislative jurisdiction over "Indians and Lands reserved for the Indians," essentially making them wards of the state. From 1867 to 1873 they were under the jurisdiction of the Secretary of State. In 1873 (the same year as the North West Mounted Police was formed), jurisdiction for Native people was transferred to the Department of the Interior. In 1880, a separate Indian Affairs Department was set up under the Minister of the Interior, John A. MacDonald, who was also the Prime Minister. Today it is called Indian and Northern Affairs Canada (INAC).

It is important to realize that the *Indian Act* of 1876, the tool with which the government controls Native people, was not a new piece of legislation. Rather, it was a consolidation of various pieces of existing federal and colonial statutes. The essential thrust of the legislation was to centralize and codify all legislation and to solidify the position of Aboriginals as wards of the state.

From the *Indian Act* come several terms that need to be understood to comprehend matters related to Aboriginal policing: Indian, reserve, band, band council.

Who Is Legally an Indian?

Not surprisingly, few issues have generated as much controversy as who gets to define who is and isn't "Indian." Native people contend, not without good reason, that they are the best determiners of "Indian" status. Conversely, because the federal government funds Native people, it feels that it has a right to determine who should get status. Being "Indian" in Canada, in the eyes of the federal government, has nothing to do with biology or culture. "Indian" in Canada is a legal/political classification, subject to the defining capacity of the *Indian Act*.

Government definition of "Indian" goes back to early legislation (1850) in Lower Canada (Quebec) which defined Indian in sweeping terms, including all persons of Indian ancestry, all persons married to Indians, anyone adopted by Indians and living in his or her adopted community, and finally anybody who was living with the band and was recognized as being Indian by the band.

Shortly thereafter (1851) the legal definition of who was "Indian" was amended to pro-
vide that to be an Indian you had to be of Indian blood or show that at least your father was
Indian. The law was also changed to provide that marriage only conferred status on non-
Status Indian women, not vice versa. This set a precedent. Section 12(1)(b) of the *Indian
Act* read as follows: "The following persons are not entitled to be registered, namely, ...(b)
a woman who married a person who is not an Indian ..."

Her children would likewise not have status, unlike the children of White women who
married status Indian men. Similarly, upon marriage a woman lost her band status and
became a member of her husband's band. These provisions violate notions of equality of
the sexes.

A fight ensued during the 1970s and early 1980s to end this discrimination. In 1985,
the discriminatory clause was removed with the passage of Bill C-31. However, the debate
was not a peaceful one and there are still bitter feelings within the Native community.
When the debate was being conducted, some Native leaders, especially male Native leaders, took the position that if Native women make the decision to marry non-Native men
they should be prepared to live with the consequences of that decision.

Perhaps the main cause of the anger had to do with the distribution of reserve and band
resources as well as the limited benefits of being a Status Indian, e.g., post-secondary education, a reserve home, etc. Some Alberta reserves have oil royalties which some leaders
feared having to share with those who had recently regained their status through Bill C-31.
The 1985 changes to the *Indian Act* allowed some Indian control over status. The federal
government decides whose names get on the Indian register. Bands may, however, by
majority vote, decide to take control of band membership and establish their own rules for
deciding who will be part of the band.

Who Is an Inuk?

Inuit (a plural term for which the singular is "Inuk") are not legally considered registered
Indians, although they do possess a legal status separate from that of other Canadians. As
will be pointed out in the Territories chapter, while the federal government assumed policing authority over the Inuit much earlier, it did not assume responsibility for the Inuit until
1939. When an official census was taken of the Inuit, each individual was issued a disk
with a number printed on it that identified who the person was officially. Carrying this
disk made a person legally Inuit. Other definitions have arisen that are used, but they vary
from jurisdiction to jurisdiction. In the 1975 James Bay Agreement, an Inuk living in
Quebec would be considered legally an Inuk if he or she possessed a disk number, had
one-quarter Inuit blood, or was considered an Inuk by the local community. In the 1978
agreement between the federal government and the Committee for Original Peoples
Entitlement (COPE), an Inuk was someone who belonged to any group known as Inuit,
Eskimo, or Inuvialuit who claimed traditional use and occupancy of the land. In
Newfoundland, the Inuit of Labrador have had a difficult time getting official recognition
because of that province's lack of recognition of special status of Aboriginals since it
joined Canada in 1949. Of course, Inuit living in the new territory of Nunavut have rights
not held by Inuit living in other jurisdictions.

Who Is a Métis?

The definition of who is to be considered a **Métis** is even more confused than that of who is an Inuk. The Métis are a people with a specific racial, cultural, and national history (see the chapters on Manitoba and Saskatchewan), primarily combining the Cree (and to a lesser degree Saulteaux) and the French (and to a lesser degree the Scottish and the English). In 1870, after the first Riel Resistance (named after Louis Riel, the Métis leader), the Métis had their rights to the land recognized through legal papers known as "scrip."

In Manitoba in 1871, there were 9800 Métis, 5270 of whom were French-speaking; the rest spoke English. In the same area, there were only 1600 Whites, and a greater, undetermined number, of Cree. That was to change with the western migration of settlers. With them came land speculators and government officials who were not above working out scams to cheat the Métis of their scrip. The laws relating to scrip changed 11 times over 12 years. Most Métis ended up moving west into what is now Saskatchewan and Alberta.

In the 1880s, the Métis found themselves in a similar situation to that which they had faced earlier in Manitoba. They again called upon Louis Riel, then living peacefully in Montana, to lead them in what would become known as the Second Riel Rebellion. They lost this time, thanks to the technology used against them (the new railroad, steamboats, and the precursors to machine guns) as well as Riel's personal reluctance to engage the enemy. Riel was hanged in 1885.

The Métis are still in an uncertain political position, with definition and recognition of rights differing from province to province. This is due, in part, to the fact that the term "Métis" can in some contexts refer to anyone of mixed Native and non-Native ancestry. Sometimes the name is written "métis" (i.e., not capitalized) to refer to these people. Some Métis in Alberta, descendents of the people who moved west from Manitoba, live in what are termed "colonies," developed during the 1930s. They have been fighting for royalties for the oil and gas extracted from their land. In that province, through the Métis Settlement Act, there are clear criteria for determining who is and isn't Métis. Saskatchewan uses similar criteria, but in Manitoba and Ontario, the only other provinces that have officially recognized Métis status, the definition is racially based, incorporating people who are Native but who for whatever reason do not have status as "registered Indians."

WHAT ARE TREATIES?

No discussion of the legal framework surrounding Aboriginals in Canada is complete without some mention of treaties. Why are there treaties? The simple legal answer is The Royal Proclamation of 1763. In 1763, King George III, following the Treaty of Paris (which concluded the Seven Years War with France), issued his Royal Proclamation. This dealt with a number of issues, including those pertaining to Aboriginals. It stated that any lands within the territorial confines of the new governments (which included present-day Quebec, Florida, West Florida, and Granada) that had not been ceded by the Indians "are reserved to them ... as their Hunting Grounds." The reason cited for this was that "whereas it is just and reasonable, and essential to our Interest, and the Security of our Colonies that the Several Nations or Tribes of Indians with who We are connected, and who live under our Protection, should not be molested or disturbed ..."

Also, the Proclamation dealt with land *not* within the limits of the new government. It reserved "for the use of said Indians, all Land Territories not included within the limits of our Said ... governments, or within the Limits of the Territory granted to the Hudson's Bay Company."

To prevent fraud, the Proclamation provided a way in which lands could be acquired for settlement. Indian lands "shall be purchased only for Us, in our Name, at some public Meeting of Assembly of the said Indians." This implies that all lands that had not been surrendered by the Indians to the Crown belonged to the Indians. It reserved all unsettled land for the use of the Indians as their hunting grounds. It provided that lands required for settlement had to be bought from the Indians and could only be bought by the Crown at a public meeting.

The Royal Proclamation became part of Canadian law, since under the Canadian legal system English laws became a part of the law of Canada on the dates when various colonial governments were formed. Without any specific law overruling such a law (which hasn't taken place), the Royal Proclamation is still valid.

What is a **treaty?** Generally, the Aboriginals involved in treaties would agree to give up their rights to a certain piece of land that was traditionally theirs. In return, they would have a much smaller area or areas reserved for their use. That is why the term **"reserve"** is used in Canada (as opposed to "reservation," used in the United States). Treaties 1 and 2 (see "The Numbered Treaties" section later in the chapter) provided for 160 acres per family of 5 and Treaties 3 to 11 provided for 1 square mile per family of 5. The title to the land, of course, remained with the government.

The people signing the treaty would also receive a certain amount of money. In that sense, treaties were somewhat like land sales. They were different, however, in that the Native people involved were not given access to the money. It was held for them "in trust" by the government. From 1818 onwards, treaties would also receive "annuities" or annual payments, typically involving a small sum per person. Monies were typically in the order of twelve dollars for every man, woman, and child upon signing and five dollars each year after. The "chief" typically received slightly more.

Treaties also often involved hunting and fishing rights, which, as we will see in the case of the Mi'kmaq treaties, can be problematic. An interesting example took place with the so-called Peterborough Bullfrog Incident (1977), in which two men were charged with taking bullfrogs out of season. This came under an 1818 treaty which makes no reference to hunting rights. However, the men contended that the right to hunt was given verbally to their ancestors at the time of signing. Subsequent research proved them to be correct. They were acquitted and the right to hunt and fish was recognized by the court.

There are legal limits on these rights. For example, the Migratory Birds Convention Act (which applies to geese and ducks) overrides any treaty rights. So does the Federal Fisheries Act. One case in 1962 involving the shooting of a mallard confirmed the supremacy of federal legislation over treaties.

The Mi'kmaq Treaties

The Mi'kmaq signed the Treaty of Portsmouth, New Hampshire in 1713. While it involved statements of "peace and friendship," as other treaties had before, it allowed the Native people "free liberty for Hunting, Fishing, Fowling, and all their other Lawful Liberties &

Privileges" (Dickason, 1997: 151). Statements to this effect were also included in the two treaties of 1725, the Mascarene Treaty and the Treaty of Boston. For years, all that was known about the conditions of those treaties was one aspect, the obligations of the Mi'kmaq and the Maliseet to keep the peace. In 1984, however, the other side of the Mascarene agreement was discovered in the public archives. It spelled out the obligations of the English to respect, among other things, the hunting and fishing rights of the people. This discovery would have a significant impact on how this treaty, and the 1752 treaty that followed it as a reaffirmation, would be legally interpreted. Prior to this discovery, in the 1929 County Court decision in *Regina v. Syliboy,* and in court decisions in 1958 and 1969, the treaties were not seen as guaranteeing Aboriginal rights. In *Regina v. James Matthew Simon* (1985), the Chief Justice recognized the supremacy of the 1752 treaty over provincial hunting laws.

In 1988, a Nova Scotia Lands and Forests officer arrested 14 Mi'kmaq, charging them with illegal hunting. The charges were dismissed after the Nova Scotia Court of Appeal ruled in another case that the people did have the right to hunt and fish for food and were exempt from provincial regulations when doing so. This still did not settle matters in terms of how that supremacy would be worked out regarding actual hunting and fishing. In 1989, the Mi'kmaq were allowed a special, limited hunting season but no formal recognition of their rights to hunt. They were allowed to hunt moose from September 24 to 29 and again from October 15 to 25, before and after the two-week season for non-Aboriginals.

As we will see in the chapter on Atlantic Canada, the reaction to this treaty being upheld was small compared to the reaction to the recognition of a treaty in 1760, which involved the Mi'kmaq and Maliseet in Nova Scotia and New Brunswick.

The Numbered Treaties

Much of Canada was publicly purchased through a series of large land transfers. The first of these were the Robinson Treaties of 1850, involving the land immediately to the north of Lakes Superior and Huron. The expansion of non-Native Canadian interests westward after the foundation of Canada and the purchase of land from the Hudson's Bay Company was the impetus for the numbered treaties, 1 to 11, signed between 1871 and 1921. These covered the territory from the eastern part of British Columbia and parts of Yukon Territory and the Northwest Territories in the West, the Prairie provinces, and most of northern Ontario. As was true of the Robinson treaties (which included land upon which mineral deposits had recently been discovered), there was a close connection between the federal government wanting something and the pressure for treaties to be signed. The settling of the Prairies by European farmers made imperative the signing of Treaties 1 to 7. The discovery of gold in the Klondike in 1897 resulted in Treaty 8 being signed in 1899. The building of roads and railroads to gain access to northern Ontario brought about Treaty 9. The provincial status of Alberta and Saskatchewan was followed by the signing of Treaty 10 in 1906, while the discovery of oil in Norman Wells was followed by Treaty 11 in 1921.

Later Treaties

Certain areas were neglected by treaty, most notably Quebec and British Columbia. Quebec had received the northern part of the province under the understanding that a treaty would be negotiated, but none took place. In 1975, following a confrontation between the Quebec government and the Cree stemming from the attempt to build a power dam on unceded Cree lands and waters, the James Bay and Northern Quebec Agreement was signed. In 1978, this was extended further into the north as the Northeastern Quebec Agreement. British Columbia was in a similar position to Quebec, as most of its Aboriginal land claims had not been settled. Recently, the Nisga'a, after over 100 years of struggle, were successful in obtaining their treaty.

Box 2.1	What Is a Treaty?

Recently, Chief Joseph Gosnell, writing about the Nisga'a treaty, gave the following meaningful, non-legalistic definition of what a treaty meant to him:

> What is it about a treaty? To us, a treaty is a sacred instrument. It represents an understanding between distinct cultures and shows respect for each other's way of life. We know we are here for a long time together. A treaty stands as a symbol of high idealism in a divided world. (Gosnell, quoted in Rose, 2000: 22)

WHAT IS A RESERVE?

With the treaties of the nineteenth and twentieth centuries came reserves. These small packages of land were "reserved" for Aboriginals after the treaties took away the majority of their lands. There are currently about 2284 such reserves. Their location was predominantly of the federal government's choosing, with thoughts of separation and keeping prime land for non-Native people primary in their decisions. Reserve land is not provincially held land. It is federal, held in common by the band and in trust by the federal government, allowing the latter to maintain a significant amount of control over what goes on.

In the Prairies during the late nineteenth century and early twentieth century, the reserves operated in some ways like open-air prisons. A pass system was instituted (one that impressed the Boers in South Africa so much that they adopted their own version of it with their apartheid), so that a Native wanting to leave the reserve would have to obtain a pass from the Indian Agent, a non-Native federal employee who wielded a great deal of power over the local band.

Reserves vary in size (from only a few hectares to one in Alberta that is 900 square kilometres) and in how many each band (see definition on pp. 17–18) has. In eastern Canada, there is typically one reserve per band, while in the West one band might have several reserves (Frideres, 1998: 133). British Columbia has a ratio of slightly over eight reserves per band, something that can make policing a Native community quite difficult (see the chapter on British Columbia).

One misleading assumption about reserves should be cleared up here. Usually when a reserve is portrayed in the media or even in some introductory sociology textbooks (see Schaefer et al. 1996: 193), the description is of a horrible place, overcrowded, with substandard housing, intense poverty, poor health conditions, violence, and substance abuse. Those conditions do exist in too many reserves, but that is far from being all that needs to be learned and understood about reserves. Students exposed only to those descriptions understandably ask the question "Why do they want to live in reserves if they are so horrible?" The answer can be seen in the following quotations from two Native writers. The first is Brian Maracle, a Mohawk writer who left his home reserve when he was five years old and then returned as an adult. His book *Back on the Rez: Finding the Way Back Home* describes his first year back on the reserve, the Six Nations reserve, near Brantford, Ontario. In the introduction to the book, Maracle discusses the importance of the reserve to the people. He links the homeland feel that people have for the reserve with their connection to the land and makes the important point of reserve as refuge:

> The reserves mean many things to the Onkwehonwe.[1] On one level, these postage-stamp remnants of our original territories are nagging reminders of the echoing vastness of what we have lost. On another, they are the legacy and bastion of our being. They are a refuge, a prison, a haven, a madhouse, a fortress, a birthplace, a Mecca, a resting place, Home-Sweet-Home, Fatherland and Motherland rolled into one. (Maracle, 1996: 3)

Noah Augustine wrote the following in a newspaper article entitled, "Indian Reserve a Haven from Racism":

> Living in Ontario where I wasn't known only opened my eyes to the extent of racism in this country. It troubled me greatly. I returned to the comfort and security of my home on the reserve. Others wonder why aboriginal people wish to stay on the reserves. It is no wonder to me. It was here where I was opened to the teaching of my elders, the power of the sweat lodge and the pride of my people. It is here where I found strength. (Augustine, 2000)

WHAT IS A BAND?

Prior to contact with Europeans, Aboriginals grouped themselves into various units, largely depending on the resources available to them. In southern Ontario and much of British Columbia, for example, where resources were rich (in the former case, crops of corn, beans, and squash; in the latter, the fish and shellfish bounties of river and ocean), there were communities or towns[2] with populations that could number 2000 or more. These communities would be linked into what anthropologists (but not the people themselves) and historians traditionally called "tribes." More typical of Canadian First Nations was the social organization of the Cree. Beyond the nuclear family, two groups were important to the Cree: the hunting group and the band. The hunting group, sometimes called by anthropologists the microband, was made up of several linked families, the population of the group ranging from approximately 10 to 20. Hunting groups would space themselves out according to the availability of resources in the area, often being 15 to 75 kilometres away from their neighbouring group. The hunting group would be together from late August until early June the next year.

From late spring through the summer, a number of these hunting groups would get together to form what anthropologists term "bands" or "macrobands" of perhaps 75 to 150, possibly more in some instances. While the food-obtaining reason for getting together was usually to fish at places where large number of fish could be found, this time served important social ends as well. It was a time to share vital information, to renew old acquaintances, and to pursue romance.

The legal (as opposed to anthropological) term **"band"** is defined by the *Indian Act*. In the apt words of Métis scholar Olive Dickason,

According to the Act, a band is a body of Amerindians for whom the government has set aside lands for their common use and benefit; for whom the government is holding monies for their common use and benefit; or who have been declared a band by the governor-in-council for the purposes of the Act. (Dickason, 2002: 264)

There are over 600 recognized bands in Canada today. It should be pointed out that not all band members live in the community on the reserve. In a good number of Native bands, many members live off-reserve, in part because of housing shortages and employment shortages on the reserve. As they have the right to vote in band elections, sometimes election results are divided along off-reserve/on-reserve lines. The authors know of one Ontario community that was divided in its proposal to have a casino. Those who supported the casino drew heavily on the off-reserve population. Those who opposed the casino were mostly those who lived in community.

What Is a Band Council?

As "band" and "reserve" are legal entities imposed on Native people, so is the **band council**. We will see that in the case of the Mohawk this imposition involved the police and violence (see the chapters on Ontario and Quebec). A band council is an elected body headed by a chief. The positions of chief and council are different from traditional Native positions of leaders. Canada's First Nations had a variety of political systems, involving leaders with varying degrees of authority, depending largely on the size of the grouping. One traditional figure that exemplifies the type of leadership many Canadian Native groups had is the Mi'kmaq **saqmaw**, a patrilineal position (i.e., reckoned on the father's side), typically inherited by the eldest son. A seventeenth century Jesuit missionary described the duties of the saqmaw (written as "sagamore"), although as a European he overemphasized somewhat the authority that the saqmaw had. He stated that they provided

> dogs for the chase, canoes for transportation, provisions and reserves for bad weather and expeditions. The young people flatter him, hunt, and serve their apprenticeship under him, not being allowed to have anything before they are married, for then only can they have a dog and a bag; that is, have something of their own, and do for themselves. Nevertheless they continue to live under the authority of the Sagamore, and very often in his company; as also do several others who have no relations, or those who of their own free will place themselves under his protection and guidance, being themselves weak and without a following. Now all that the young men capture belongs to the Sagamore; but the married ones give him only a part, and if these leave him, as they often do for the sake of the chase and supplies, returning afterwards, they pay their dues and homage in skins and like gifts. (Thwaites, 1959, vol. 3: 87–91)

Saqmaw leadership existed at various levels, from the small fall and winter groups, to the larger summer groups, to the district level, and finally the "kji'saqmaw" or "great chief." Mi'kmaq country, in the Maritimes and Quebec, was divided into seven districts. The responsibilities of the district saqmaw included assigning hunting territories according to changing family grouping size and local resource conditions, meeting to decide issues of war and peace, conferring with saqmaw of lesser standing, and making sure that everyone had enough. Generosity was a prized value, some district saqmaw giving away the best clothes and other possessions that they had (Miller, 1995: 354).

There are several key points to be made concerning this type of leadership. First, leaders typically exercised influence rather than power (defined as being the ability to bring about compliance whether the person wants to comply or not). A person with power can give orders or commands. A leader with influence must persuade, convince, demonstrate by example. The Huron language can help us understand this. In that language there are no words for "order," "command," or "obey." The strongest verb of this nature is "to request." The leaders of the seventeenth century Huron were typically referred to as "capitaine" or captain by the French. In the dictionaries the French Jesuits created in the Huron language, the word the Jesuits used most often to translate "capitaine" was "honenda, eracti," which can be literally translated as "they choose him as guiding principle or role model." Think of how different that term is from "commander," "governor," or "ruler."

This also points to the fact that although leadership often followed a particular line or lineage, there was likewise often a strong element of personal choice involved. In some traditional Native societies, if you did not like or respect the leader of one group or band, you joined another. If a leader lost the respect of the people, the people would choose to associate themselves with someone else. One of the necessary elements of a leader was the capacity to listen. The traditional Anishinabe or Ojibwa had the Crane clan provide its leader. One reason suggested for this is that the crane rarely spoke; therefore, it must be listening.

This is very different from the imposed structure and European-based political philosophy of the band council. There are two aspects of the band council worth noting. One is its relative powerlessness when it comes to dealing with the Department of Indian and Northern Affairs. This is clearly articulated in the following discussion by Frideres of the role of the band council:

> In a sense, the council acts like a municipal council. However, what differentiates it from a municipal-style government are its ill-defined and limited powers. Under the terms of the Indian Act, the council's powers have never clearly been delineated. Furthermore, the council normally operates with funds from a single source: Indian Affairs. And, Indian Affairs is capable of overriding all decisions made by council. Nevertheless, the linkage between the federal government and the band is so entrenched that councils may be viewed as the administrative arm of the Department of Indian and Northern Affairs. (Frideres, 1998: 433)

The other aspect is that it has significant power on the reserve, as it is often the main employer as well as the provider of housing, education grants, and other social benefits. The band council has responsibility for housing, education, health, and social assistance, with little legally mandated accountability to the people being governed concerning how money is handled or jobs and benefits allocated. As we will see in the chapters that follow, this is one of the difficulties in Native-run policing services.

The restrictions placed by band council power on the effectiveness of tribal policing was discussed in Anne McGillivray and Brenda Comasky's important book, *Black Eyes All of the Time: Intimate Violence, Aboriginal Women and the Justice System*. The authors demonstrated how band constables in Manitoba avoided dealing with domestic issues because of the local politics involved (McGillivray and Comasky, 1999: 92–93). In their study were allegations of a known abuser being hired by a chief and council to ensure that he avoided charges of domestic assault (McGillivray and Comasky, 1999: 93). Consider the following quotation from a woman who had been assaulted:

> [The band constables] took me to the nursing station. They made me stay there for a while. My head had bumps over it, and my forehead too. My chin was bruised. And they asked me to press charges, those Native cops. And I said, "no" and I told them I didn't want any trouble—kind of scary and I don't want him to go to jail. Maybe if the RCMP was there—you know how it is on the reserve ... Chiefs and councillors are helping him because he works for them. (McGillivray and Comasky, 1999: 140)

Of course, local politics and politicians having an influence on policing is not a problem unique to Native communities. The continuing debate in Ontario over the relative number and power of municipally and provincially appointed representatives on police services boards suggests this (see Stenning, 1996: 17–28). It wasn't until 1990 that the Ontario Police Services Act compelled all municipalities in the province that have their own police force to have a police governing authority dominated by provincial appointees. The debate continues as to whether this will take politics out of policing.

One of the negative effects of the imposed band council system is that it is fertile ground for the growth of factions, typically family-based groups whose disputes can readily divide a community. Elections can easily become battlegrounds between factions, with the "winners" taking home all the prizes (jobs, contracts, houses). It is difficult for police forces to be neutral, as the officers come from the disputing families and band councils have a lot of say in the police commissions. Band councils have the power to close down a policing service and return to policing by outsiders.

For these reasons and others, the band council system is unpopular among many bands across Canada, and for some time there has been discussion in some communities concerning returning to a system more in keeping with traditional governance. The thinking is that with a more consensus-based system, members of all factions will have input into governance. The present imposed "majority rules, minority suffers" system does not encourage this kind of input. One of the aspects of self-government many Native people are pushing for is a form of governance of their choosing, not one whose form is dictated to them by the federal government. Indian Affairs has historically been inflexible over the structure of government they deemed to be acceptable in Native communities; they have only accepted what they have devised. Until this is settled, Aboriginal policing of Native people by Native people will continue to be restricted in its effectiveness.

GOVERNMENT POLICIES

McNamara (1995, cited in Clairmont and Linden, 1998) notes three major policy eras in the development of the relationship between Aboriginal people and the criminal justice system. These are pre-1975, 1975 to 1990, and 1991 to the present. The pre-1975 period was one in which "little attention was paid in any official or programmatic way to the distinctive problems, needs, and participation of Aboriginal people in the criminal justice system" (Clairmont and Linden, 1998: 4). From 1867 to the 1970s, the Canadian government assumed a very paternalistic and institutionally racist role concerning Native people. Not surprisingly, there was little effort made to accommodate Aboriginals' specific needs and demands in terms of justice.

In 1969, the Department of Indian Affairs and Northern Development (DIAND) initiated a "Band Constable Program" that recommended that band councils hire **band constables** to administer band bylaws. This was permitted under Section 81 of the *Indian Act*, which allows that band councils can pass and enforce laws on matters such as regulation of traffic, observation of law and order, and the prevention of disorderly conduct and nuisances. The program was expanded in 1971 when DIAND issued **Circular 55**, which gave band councils the authority to create "**special constables**." The authority of these special constables was a far cry from the authority of a police officer. They were not permitted to carry firearms. Very little money was available for them, so they had very low salaries, were expected to provide their own vehicles, and sometimes did not even have uniforms (York, 1990: 147). In Murphy and Clairmont's 1996 survey of Aboriginal policing, band constables tended to speak of the shortfalls of their position in the following ways:

1. Low extrinsic job satisfaction (e.g., poor pay, poor infrastructure); one officer commented that "we are appointed as peace officers in Manitoba but the government treats us like security guards ..."
2. Frustration at the limits to their performing the police role; here several officers pointed to an "inability to perform at higher levels due to lack of training and essential skills."
3. Low prestige in the community and vis-à-vis other police; some officers echoed the views of one respondent who wrote of being "ridiculed by members of other police organizations" while others pointed to community disrespect, contending that "people always see us as a joke because of poor training and no equipment."

(Murphy and Clairmont, 1996)

In 1973, DIAND published its *Task Force on Policing on Reserves,* which put forward three options for the jurisdiction of Aboriginal policing: band council, municipal, and provincial. The last named option suggested two possibilities:

The first was that a separate Native Provincial Police Force be established to operate on its own, under the authority of the provincial attorney general, with its own form of police commission. The second option stated that Native policing could be conducted under the direction and control of existing provincial police arrangements, but would use Native people as special constables. (Seagrave, 1997: 255)

The first, **"Option 3 (a),"** would represent a real step toward Native self-government and has been discussed with some seriousness recently by Native groups in Alberta and Saskatchewan; however, it was never seriously considered by non-Native governments and policing agencies. What came to be known as **"Option 3 (b),"** with Native people in the familiar position of being controlled by outsiders, became the darling of policy-makers and police officials.

In 1975, the Solicitor General Canada and Justice Canada sponsored a National Conference on Native People. Following that conference, according to Clairmont and Linden,

[A]n agenda was set forth calling for the provision of better access to all facets of the justice system, more equitable treatment, greater Aboriginal control over service delivery, recruitment of Aboriginal personnel, cross-cultural sensitivity training for non-Natives, and more emphasis on alternatives to incarceration and crime prevention. Between 1975 and 1990 more than twenty government reports reiterated these types of recommendations. (Clairmont and Linden, 1998: 4)

Still, from the mid-1970s to 1990, through the Royal Canadian Mounted Police (RCMP; see pp. 24–25), the Ontario Provincial Police (OPP; see the chapter on Ontario) and the Sûreté du Quebec (SQ; see the chapter on Quebec), special constable programs were developed involving more but still limited authority, less than that of a regular officer. According to Geoffrey York, the regular officers would often use the special constables "merely as translators and intermediaries in their dealings with the Indian communities" (York, 1990: 148).

In the late 1980s, Native people were distinctly underrepresented as police officers in Canada. In 1988, the city of Calgary had two status Indians on its force of about one thousand (Comeau and Santin, 1990: 51) but a Native population of between thirty and forty thousand (Frideres, 1998: 241). In that same year in Ontario, just 26 of the roughly 4450 members of the OPP were Aboriginal. In Thunder Bay, a city in northwest Ontario in the middle of Native country, with about 10 percent of its population Aboriginal, only one of its 200 police officers was Native (0.5%) (York, 1990: 148).

If Native justice issues moved with glacial slowness prior to 1975 and started to trickle as a stream between 1975 and 1990, they flowed as a river during the 1990s. The Helen Betty Osborne and John Joseph Harper cases (see the chapter on Manitoba) had led to the Manitoba Aboriginal Justice Inquiry, published in 1990, while the Donald Marshall case (see Atlantic Canada chapter) led to The Report of the Royal Commission on the Donald Marshall Jr. Prosecution (Hickman, Poitras, and Evans 1990). These were followed by two major reports which, according to McNamara (1995, cited in Clairmont and Linden 1998) set the stage and agenda for the changes to come. Both were released in 1991. One was The Law Reform Commission's *Aboriginal Peoples and Criminal Justice,* the other was Manitoba's *The Justice System and Aboriginal People: Report of the Aboriginal Justice Inquiry of Manitoba.* Both served to focus attention on First Nations people and the justice system. That focus was magnified by the public awareness of Native justice issues with the dramatic confrontation at Oka in 1990.

Following the release of these two reports, the federal government began making changes to the way it dealt with Native people in judicial and legal matters. Among other shifts, responsibility for First Nations policing was transferred from DIAND to the Department of the Solicitor General. Within this department, the Aboriginal Corrections Policy Unit was created, while within the Department of Justice, the Aboriginal Justice Directorate was formed. These were both part of the Aboriginal Justice Initiative. As Clairmont and Linden state, "The mandates of these groups were to advance Aboriginal justice interests, improve the response of the conventional justice system and facilitate greater Aboriginal direction of, and innovation in, justice in Aboriginal communities" (Clairmont and Linden, 1998: 4).

Lending support to this movement was the massive final report of the Royal Commission on Aboriginal Peoples (RCAP) which emphasized the need to further promote Native autonomy and legal pluralism (i.e., a variety of forms serving Aboriginal justice).

FEDERAL POLICING INITIATIVES

An integral part of the federal government's Aboriginal justice initiatives is the First Nations Policing Policy (FNPP), the guiding force behind policing in First Nations communities today. It was initiated in 1991 "to provide First Nations across Canada with access to police services that are professional, effective, culturally appropriate, and accountable to the communities they serve" (Minister of Supply and Service, 1991: 1). It has been administered by the Department of the Solicitor General since April 1992 and operates on a principle of partnership involving the federal government, the provincial or territorial governments, and First Nations communities. These three enter into tripartite agreements for police services that meet the particular community's needs.

The FNPP has three broad objectives (Minister of Supply and Services, 1996: 3). One is to strengthen public security and personal safety, thereby ensuring that First Nations peoples enjoy a secure and safe life. This is to be achieved by access to policing that meets the particular needs of the community while also meeting acceptable standards in terms of the quality and level of service. A second objective is to increase responsibility and accountability, that is, "to support First Nations in acquiring the tools to become self-sufficient and self-governing through the establishment of structures for the management, administration and accountability of First Nations police services." These structures are set in place with the intent of trying to ensure independence from partisan political influence. The third objective is the building of a new sense of partnership, that is, the policy is implemented and administered in a manner intending to promote a relationship between Native and non-Native agencies "based on trust, mutual respect, and participation in decision-making."

Tripartite agreements provide that the federal government pays for 52 percent of the cost of First Nations policing, with the provincial or territorial governments picking up the remaining 48 percent. The First Nations will, wherever possible, be encouraged to pay the cost of maintaining their police services, particularly for enhanced services. This policy applies to all Native reserves, to certain other First Nations communities on Crown land, and to Inuit communities.

A number of criteria must be met for an agreement to take place (Minister of Supply and Services, 1996). First, all police officers in non-Native administered policing services must be Native, except where the First Nation agrees to and participates in the staffing of a non-Native person. This type of exception does take place, probably most often when Native and non-Native communities exist side-by-side,[3] although there is a disincentive for non-Native officers hired at the junior level as they are less likely than their Native peers to be promoted to more senior positions within the Native-run policing service. The duration of such staffing will be negotiated by the federal government, the provincial or territorial government, and the First Nation. Second, the First Nations police service must meet the standards of its home province or territory. Third, Native police officers must be properly appointed as peace officers and empowered to enforce all applicable laws. Finally, the police service must consult with and be accountable to the community it serves, through a police board, commission, or other advisory body.

The government's FNPP suggests a number of models eligible for federal funding under the tripartite agreements. These include a First Nations–administered police service organized on a band, "tribal," regional, or provincial basis, including arrangements providing for one First Nation to contract for the policing services of another. In Ontario, this type of model has been applied with the Anishinabek Police Services, which services a number of Anishinabe or Ojibwa communities, and the Nishnawbe-Aski Police Service, which services 46 Ojibwa and Cree communities. Another model provides for a special contingent of First Nations officers within an existing police service. This may include Native officers employed within a provincial or municipal police service with dedicated responsibilities to serve a Native community, or a group of Native police officers employed through a contractual agreement to provide a policing service to a First Nations community. In New Brunswick, the Buctouche and Indian Island communities have this type of arrangement with the RCMP. A third model is the "developmental policing arrangement," which is designed to smooth the transition from one type of policing arrangement to another.

The FNPP generally appears to be working. More than two-thirds of the targeted population has come under FNPP agreements. An independent review after the initial five years of the policy found it to be "relevant, sound and on-track" and that the federal and provincial/territorial governments, as well as most First Nations, believed the tripartite process to be the most effective way to address Native policing.

ROYAL CANADIAN MOUNTED POLICE INITIATIVES

Following a 1973 federal task force report recommending changes be made to on-reserve policing, the RCMP came up with the 3 (b) Option, which was implemented in all provinces except for Ontario (where authority over on-reserve policing was being transferred to the OPP), Quebec (where the Sûreté du Quebec had authority), and New Brunswick. This option created the position of "special constable," a position with limited authority but more than had existed earlier. The special constables were trained by the RCMP and were under the control of the local RCMP detachment rather than the local band council. By the late 1980s, more than 300 communities had had some experience with approximately 250 such officers. This program was terminated in 1990, as it was found to have a number of flaws. Aboriginal input was lacking. Special constables received lower salaries and less training than regular officers. And, according to Griffiths and Yerbury (1984), there was a reluctance on the part of Native people to become special constables owing to social isolation in, and even hostility from, their communities. In an inquiry into the deaths of five Blood or Kainai, a former special constable testified that he had had to put up with a constant barrage of racist remarks and anti-Native jokes from his fellow RCMP officers (York, 1990: 170).

In 1990, the Special Constable Program was replaced by the Aboriginal Constable Development Program, which was aimed at increasing the number of Aboriginal people eligible to become not Special but regular RCMP officers. Following shortly upon the lead of the FNPP, the RCMP developed the Royal Canadian Mounted Police First Nations Community Policing Service (RCMP-FNCPS), which "incorporates the principles and objectives of the First Nations Policing Policy including service levels equivalent to those of non-First Nations communities; compatibility and sensitivity to First Nations culture and beliefs; flexibility to accommodate local variations in policing needs; and a framework which allows for transition to an independent First Nations–administered police service where this is desired by the community" (RCMP First Nations Community Policing Service).

The RCMP-FNCPS handles Native policing under two separate agreements. One is a Framework Agreement between the province or territory and the federal government, outlining funding and other managerial arrangements. Another is a Community Tripartite Agreement between the Native community, the provincial government, and the federal government, outlining the specific details of the policing service. The elements of these agreements correspond very closely with those of the FNPP.

The RCMP also has a number of initiatives offered through its Aboriginal Policing Branch. The Aboriginal Cadet Development Program is operated through funding provided by Human Resources Development Canada (HRDC). This allows Aboriginals who are suitable candidates interested in a career with the RCMP but who do not meet basic entrance requirements, to upgrade their qualifications. Following a three-week assessment, candidates are sent to their home areas with a program designed to make up for their shortcomings. They are granted two years to meet the standards, whereupon they proceed to Regina to the RCMP Academy to undergo basic cadet training.

The Aboriginal Youth Training Program provides Native young people with 17 weeks of summer employment, beginning with 3 weeks of training in Regina. Once stationed at a detachment near their home community, they are under the supervision of a regular member of the RCMP for the remaining 14 weeks. Major funding for this program comes from the Department of Indian Affairs and Northern Development.

There is also the Commissioner's National Aboriginal Advisory Committee, whose mandate is "to provide a forum for the continuing discussion of recruiting, training and community relations with respect to Aboriginal peoples, intercultural relations and other related matters which may emerge from time to time." The committee consists of 13 Native people who convene in various communities across the country twice a year.

The RCMP is also involved with the Department of Justice in Community Justice Forums, which are attempts at restorative justice in Native communities. These are community-based programs which attempt to bring together everybody who has been touched by a crime to discuss the matter in an attempt to bring about a resolution.

NATIVE CORRECTIONS

Under the sponsorship of the Department of the Solicitor General Canada, new Native-based penitentiaries have been constructed for both men and women in western Canada, supplementing existing policies and programs of penitentiary liaison. The penitentiaries were developed in partnership with Native people and place an emphasis upon healing. The goal is to support and encourage Native communities to increase their knowledge of correctional issues and to assume greater responsibility for corrections.

An Aboriginal Corrections Policy Unit has been created, mandated to explore offender treatment in selected communities. This movement reflects a greater shift towards restorative and healing approaches to criminal behaviour.

Corrections Canada has also introduced Native-specific treatment programs, such as those for substance abuse. These have been added to pre-existing programs for First Nations inmates that addressed Native culture, spirituality, the use of Elders, and Native liaison worker programs. In western Canada, the National Parole Board has Elder-assisted parole hearings for Native inmates (Clairmont and Linden, 1998: 5).

Sentencing Circles

One of the most promising developments in the area of restorative justice comes in the form of what are variously called youth justice committees (when used with youth), community peacemaking circles or, more usually, **sentencing circles.** These provide alternatives to incarceration, through adaptations of traditional notions of restorative rather than punitive justice. They typically involve community members such as Elders, as well as Native social workers, lawyers, health care workers, and those affected by the crime, including both offender and victim(s) and their families. Guilt or innocence is not at issue; sentencing circles follow guilty pleas. The circles are more informal than traditional courts. People do sit in a circle, with no one above or at the head of the table. Usually, those involved sit while speaking, and personal names, rather than titles are used.

The participation in sentencing circles has been uneven in different parts of Canada. Yukon Territory had had, by the end of 1994, roughly 300 circle-sentencing experiences, more than the rest of all of Canada at that time, with about 100 in Saskatchewan, and a handful in Manitoba, British Columbia, and Quebec. The first case (1992) in Yukon was *Regina v. Moses,* in which an offender with a long history of substance abuse, violent acts, and incarceration had committed an assault with a bat on an officer, stolen an item, and breached his probation. The assault was a more or less spontaneous act of desperation.

Initial reports of the effectiveness of sentencing circles have been overwhelmingly positive, but during the last few years challenges to this good news have been made. Gordon Green, in the 1998 paper, "Community Sentencing and Mediation in Aboriginal Communities," expresses concern for the victims who are involved in the circles, especially in cases of domestic violence. He worries about how the emphasis on the healing of the offender might take away from supporting the victim, and whether or not there might be power imbalances between the victim's and the offender's "sides." The Native ideal is for there to be no such imbalance, but this remains a challenge that needs to be faced openly and honestly.

A more serious critique comes from Roberts and LaPrairie (1997). They suggest that the increased number of incarcerations among Native people in Yukon Territory and Saskatchewan from 1990 to 1995 indicated that sentencing circles might not be living up to their "extravagant claims." There are several responses to this critique. One is that the rate of incarceration might have gone up even more if not for the sentencing circles; it is difficult to tell. Second, such a radically new form of justice requires time to mature before its effectiveness can be truly measured. Third, there are other benefits that have to be brought into the picture in any measure of the effectiveness of these circles. Greater community participation in justice has clearly been demonstrated. What the long-term positive effects of this participation might be can only be imagined at this point; that positive effects will take place is difficult to doubt.

To illustrate the nature of this type of initiative, the following case study of a sentencing circle is presented.

The United Chiefs and Councils of Manitoulin Justice Project

The United Chiefs and Councils of Manitoulin (UCCM) Justice Project was first funded in 1994 by the federal Department of Justice and the Ontario Ministry of the Attorney General. However, it wasn't until January of 1998 that the UCCM Justice Project began diverting cases from the courts to justice circles. The objective of the Justice Project is "to contribute to building healthier communities by promoting Anishinabe values of healing, making amends and respect for self and others and encouraging the active participation of community members in justice and expanding aboriginal control of criminal justice" (*Tribal Council News,* vol. 2, issue 6).

From January 1, 1998 to the end of June 1999, the cases of 87 people belonging to seven different communities were diverted to justice circles. Seventy-seven justice circles were created, involving 110 members of the community. The kinds of cases involved were typically property offences (e.g., break and enter, theft, and vandalism) and relatively minor instances of assault. Not included were the more serious crimes of murder, manslaughter, sexual or spousal abuse, or impaired driving, which, in the words of a *Tribal Council News* article, "the government is intent on prosecuting" (*Tribal Council News,* vol. 2, issue 8).

The wording of articles written by the UCCM Justice Project for the *Tribal Council News* indicates the positive approach that the people involved have to their work. The individuals whose cases they are diverting are referred to as "clients" rather than "offenders," and their "sentences" are referred to as "plans of action."

These plans of action are tradition-based, but also creative and new. For instance, there are public apologies made by the clients, not only to the victims involved but to the police and others affected by their harmful actions. Some of the apologies have even been aired on a local cable television station.

In the words of one writer, "since healing the community is as important as healing the victim and client, the plans of action often require some form of community service" (*Tribal Council News,* vol. 2, issue 8). This community service has involved such activities as cleaning up the results of vandalism, painting a new detoxification centre, and participating in a walk held annually to raise awareness of violence against women.

Making amends is a key feature of the plans of action. This has even involved assisting victims with their traplines. In one case, a woman had assaulted another woman, a close neighbour whom she had known for a long time. Had she decided to fight the charge, which was her initial intention, she would probably have been put on probation and have been told to stay away from the victim. Instead, with the apology the two women have managed to remain on good terms. The benefits of this amends making were articulated by the client when she stated that "They don't resolve anything in court. It wouldn't have been right if we had hated each other. In court, I would never have got the chance to apologize" (*Tribal Council News,* vol. 2, issue 10).

The healing element has included referrals to drug and alcohol addiction treatment centres or mental health facilities, but has also entailed traditional activities. The intent of these activities is to heal the clients "by enabling them to learn more about themselves and their culture, thereby raising their self-esteem and sense of identity" (*Tribal Council News,* vol. 2, issue 8). Examples of the traditional activities recommended are helping to gather traditional medicines in the bush, participating in an arduous canoe trip around Manitoulin Island (the largest island in the world in a freshwater lake), and researching family ancestry. Some clients have done more than was required of them, as they felt rewarded by the activity.

An easy criticism of this system of alternative Native justice would be to say that the offenders get off lightly. In a *Tribal Council News* article, a client of the Justice Project spoke of how it was more difficult to face people he knew, rather than a judge and jury, "a bunch of strangers. Who cares what they think?" (*Tribal Council News,* vol. 2, issue 10).

There are difficulties. The staff of the Justice Project want to do more, but with only two lawyers on staff, along with three court workers, they are hampered by an extensive workload that has required them to cut back on the number of new cases that they handle. A lot of time is taken in putting together reports and proposals for the funding necessary to continue and to grow. Still, the outlook is positive. No one has had to return to the court for non-compliance with their plans of action, and 41 files have been formally closed.

NOTES

1. "Onkwehonwe" is a Mohawk version of an Iroquoian word that, according to Maracle, is literally translated as "real/first/original people." It is used as the equivalent of "Indian" or "Native/Aboriginal person" (Maracle, 1996: x).

2. The word "Canada" refers to one of those kinds of settlements in the language of the St. Lawrence Iroquoians, a people who haven't existed since the late 1500s.

3. The authors know of one case that meets this scenario, in the Mnjikaning Police Service, where the Mnjikaning and Orillia, Ontario communities exist side by side. There is a good working relationship between the Native policing service and the local OPP detachment.

KEY TERMS

band (p. 17)

band constables (p. 20)

band council (p. 18)

Circular 55 (p. 20)

Indian Act (p. 10)

Inuit (p. 12)

Métis (p. 13)

Option 3 (a) (p. 21)

Option 3 (b) (p. 21)

reserve (p. 14)

saqmaw (p. 18)

sentencing circle (p. 25)

special constables (p. 20)

treaty (p. 14)

REVIEW QUESTIONS

1. What is the *Indian Act*?
2. What is the role of Circular 55?
3. Identify the main problems with the relationship between band council and Aboriginal policing.
4. Discuss how policing initiatives changed during the 1990s.
5. What is a sentencing circle?

chapter three

Aboriginal Policing in British Columbia

LEARNING OBJECTIVES

After completing this chapter, students should be able to:

1. Describe the potlatch and discuss how it became a policing issue.
2. Outline the difficulties encountered by the Stl'atl'imx Tribal Police force.
3. Outline how a site is designated as sacred.
4. Discuss the arguments for and against the Gustafsen Lake site being called sacred.
5. Identify what the Native Youth Movement is.

NATIVE PEOPLES OF BRITISH COLUMBIA

There exists more diversity of Native populations in British Columbia than in any other province. Of the eleven language families or language isolates, eight exist in British Columbia: Algonquian (Saulteaux), Athabaskan (Beaver, Carrier, and Chilcotin) Salishan (Stó:lo, Squamish, Sechelt, Songish or Lkungen, Nuxalk or Bella Coola, Comox, Shuswap or Secwepemc, Okanagan, Lillooet, and Ntlakyapamuk), Tlingit, Haida, Tsimshian, Wakashan (Haisla, Heiltsuk, Kwakwaka'wakw (including the Kwakiutl), Nitinat, Nootka or Nuu'chah'nulth, and Kootenayan (the Ktunaxa or Kutenai).

POLICING THE POTLATCH

There is no single mainstream Western ceremony that can directly compare with the role of the **potlatch** for the peoples of the Northwest Coast. The potlatch is both sacred and a good time. It is like a combination of a Christmas mass, christening, confirmation and the Bible, a country's constitution and a legal contract, a movie based-on-a-true-story and live theatre, a drug- and drink-free rave, the ballet and an art exhibition, an old-style story teller and a mandatory course in local history. It is unique.

Potlatches are traditionally centred around hereditary names. They are religious ceremonies, often brought about by births, coming of age, marriages and deaths. They demonstrate that the individuals and groups hosting the potlatch are socially, economically, and spiritually worthy of such an important inheritance. Names are connected with specific stories, songs, dances, carved and painted images and the right to fish, hunt, or gather plants in a particular territory. Along with these rights come duties of passing down and performing well those art forms, conserving the life forms in their territory, and maintaining the strength and social unity of the group. The potlatch reinforces the values of those sacred duties.

The Banning of the Potlatch

Missionaries coming to the Northwest Coast tended to see the potlatch as "the enemy," or at least the competition. William Duncan, who worked with the Tsimshian, wrote in 1875 that the potlatch was "by far the most formidable of all obstacles in the way of Indians becoming Christians, or even civilized." The missionaries were supported in this view by government officials. The two groups pushed for and successfully achieved the banning of the potlatch in 1884. The law read as follows:

> Every Indian or other person who engages in or assists in celebrating the Indian festival known as the "Potlatch" or in the Indian dance known as "Tamanawas" [the Spirit Dance of the Salish] is guilty of a misdemeanour, and shall be liable to imprisonment for a term of not more than six nor less than two months in any gaol or other place of confinement, and any Indian or other person who encourages, either directly of indirectly, an Indian or Indians to get up such a festival or dance, or to celebrate the same, or who shall assist in the celebration of same, is guilty of a like offence, and shall be liable to the same punishment.

The US government was slower to act against the potlatch, waiting until the early twentieth century to do so. In Canada, the ban was extended to the Sundance of the Prairies in 1895. By 1914, Native peoples could not wear traditional clothing or perform dances, even at fairs or stampedes, without the written permission of the Indian Agent.

The people resisted. The potlatch went underground. For that and other reasons, the anti-potlatch law was difficult to enforce. In 1889, Kwakiutl Chief Hamasak was convicted and sentenced to the maximum sentence of six months. But Chief Justice Begbie discharged him on a technicality, noting that the law was imprecise.

James Sewid records the following almost comic situation concerning the potlatch that inducted him at the age of 16 into the very important Hamatsa Society. The potlatch had been reported. An RCMP officer was sent from Ottawa to investigate. He asked the people to show him what they did. According to Sewid,

He demanded to see it that night, so we put on a good show for him. The dances we did were all mixed together and not in the right way we had been doing them. I was dancing with a fool's mask on along with a group of [people wearing] masks. The mounted police was standing on one side of the house while the big dance was going on and one of our people was interpreting to him what it was all about ... (Spradley, 1969: 92–93)

At the conclusion of the ceremony, the RCMP officer declared the following:

"I'd like to see the young man that went through this thing. I'd like to see him dance for me tonight because I was sent here to investigate this young man. I want him to dance with everything he had on, all his masks and everything. I want him to do it just like the way he did it last week. (Spradley, 1969: 93)

James Sewid then heard from the village leaders that he would have to dance for the officer:

So I got all my stuff on and the others who were dancing my dances and came out started dancing. After I came out my masks came out and danced. At the end he got up and thanked the people and said, "It was a wonderful dance. I really enjoyed it. I can't see anything wrong with it." (Spradley, 1969: 93)

After that, the officer left for Ottawa.

But not all cases ended so positively. In 1921, 45 of the highest-ranking Kwakiutl were arrested. Twenty-two were sentenced to prison terms of two to three months. The tragedy was twofold. First, the leaders of a community were taken from them. Compare it with going to a small town and locking up the CEOs of the most successful businesses, the mayor and councillors, priests and ministers, police chief, fire chief, and teachers. Second, their sacred items were also taken. The condition of letting the others go was that the coppers, masks, and other objects that were integral parts of the ceremony had to be surrendered. Compare that with taking the company ledgers, the local law books, the Bibles and altars, and the textbooks and lesson plans. The comparison isn't completely fair, as the potlatch items were one of a kind. The items were dispersed as personal possessions of the Minister of Indian Affairs and to art collectors and museums.

In 1951, the potlatch ban was repealed (some 17 years after the Americans did it). In 1969, the people started negotiating for the return of their sacred things. In 1975, the National Museum of Man declared that it would return the items on the condition that they would be kept in museums. One opened in 1979, the Kwakiutl Museum of Cape Mudge, and the other in 1980, the U'mista Cultural Centre (u'mista means "a special return"). In 1988, the Royal Ontario Museum returned the items it had, and in 1993 the National Museum of the American Indian in New York repatriated some objects. Some items still remain to be recovered.

THE STL'ATL'IMX TRIBAL POLICE

On December 20, 1999, British Columbia received its first Aboriginal police service with full jurisdictional authority. The Stl'atl'imx (pronounced SLAT-lee-um) Tribal Police (STP) force is responsible for ten First Nations communities, comprising 3150 people in southern British Columbia. Nine out of the ten participating communities are of the Lillooet or Lil'wat ("Wild Onion") First Nation, whose Salishan family language is called Stl'atl'imx; the tenth is Shuswap, a closely related people.

The STP has five goals:

1. Our goal is a Police Service that values, protects, respects and is sensitive to our people and to our cultural heritage.
2. Our goal is a Police Service that considers itself part of the communities it serves, and therefore involves itself in community life, responds to community needs and is considered by the community as being trustworthy and approachable.
3. Our goal is a Police Service that directs its resources to protecting and ensuring the safety of all our people through proactive policing and crime prevention.
4. Our goal is a Police Service that functions in a positive work atmosphere with a sense of teamwork by our police officers and support staff.
5. Our goal is to have other police services consider our Police Service as professional in all respects and to consider it an equal.

(BC Police Commission, 1997: Appendix A)

The STP developed through a series of incremental steps to reach the stage it achieved in 1999. The history of the force dates back to 1988, when a Peacekeepers force was developed by a majority of the communities within the Lillooet Tribal Council. Four years later, the system became the STP. Each of the participating communities signed a Band Council Resolution enabling them to enter into a tripartite agreement, called a Tribal Police Pilot Project, with the federal and provincial governments. The agreement was signed on April 2, 1992, when the STP and the Stl'atl'imx Tribal Police Board (STPB) entered into a Memorandum of Understanding with the band councils of the participating communities and with the Attorney General of British Columbia and the Solicitor General of Canada. The STPB consists of ten members, one from each of the communities involved. The STPB has more responsibility for managing and leading the organization than is found in most municipal police departments.

The 1992 tripartite agreement included some dependence on the RCMP. The Native officers were recognized as special police constables under the RCMP's authority. The local RCMP detachment would provide assistance in the case of investigations of relatively serious incidents. The agreement was renewable upon expiration, but the ultimate goal was totally autonomous policing within the Aboriginal community.

The notion of a Native police service is a new one to non-Natives, and, unfortunately, can easily be interpreted by them as being threatening. What would be the reaction of local non-Natives when a Native police service is asked to give assistance to the RCMP off-reserve, as occurred with the STP? The local non-Native community of Lillooet early on expressed its concern regarding the jurisdiction of the STP off-reserve. On May 20, 1992, a member of the opposition party brought to the attention of the BC Attorney General, in a somewhat alarmist fashion, that "Over the past three months the Attorney General has received three petitions from some 493 residents of Lillooet regarding a very serious and potentially explosive situation in that community with the Stl'atl'imx tribal police unit allegedly harassing residents off reserve" (*British Columbia Hansard,* vol. 3, no. 9, 1995).

The issue seemed to have been resolved, as it was not again raised as an issue in the BC parliament.

By 1997, the STP was staffed mainly by Native officers. The exception was the chief constable, a non-Native with several years experience as a member of the RCMP. In addition to the chief constable, STP positions included a supervisor (vacant in 1997), three constables in Mount Currie, three constables in Lillooet, a constable in Seton Lake (vacant in 1997), and four civilian employees.

An audit or review of the STP undertaken by the British Columbia Police Commission in 1996 revealed a number of weaknesses and areas of concern regarding the force. These largely reflected funding problems and the expected growing pains of a new police service.

The problems with funding were not restricted to the limitations of the budget. Rather, while the provincial funding was timely, there were complaints by the police board that, at times, the federal government was tardy in making their commitment. This made it difficult for the STP to meet its financial deadlines. Restrictions of funding resulted in short-term officer contracts. Officers were issued one-year contracts only, increasing the difficulty of recruiting career-driven individuals. Furthermore, there was the perception that, due to the fiscal arrangement, the federal and provincial governments were trying to dictate the type of policing that the STP should provide, one that was not in keeping with traditional culture.

In terms of "growing pains," there appeared to have been a number of areas that needed attention, including more extensive training of police officers, clearer and written policy statements, and more effective communication among the communities, the board, and the police force.

The officers on the Stl'atl'imx Tribal Police Force received their initial training from the First Nations Tribal Justice Institute (FNTJI) and supplemental training from the Justice Institute of British Columbia Police Academy (JIBC). Training was especially important to the STP, as the majority of officers on the force did not have any policing experience or other training for their jobs. One of the major early problems with the STP has been the failure to attract experienced officers.

The 1996 audit revealed mixed reactions on the part of the officers to the training that they had received. Constables and civilian employees rated the training from "definitely unacceptable" to "good." The response to JIBC training differed considerably from that of FNTJI. Seven of the nine staff members questioned rated the JIBC training as "very useful" or "somewhat useful," a far better rating than the FNTJI received. Some of the negative staff comments regarding FNTJI included the following: "[It] should not be advertised as police training"; "[There was] a lot there that shouldn't be there"; and "[I] didn't think it was very good. [It] was organized very long for what you got out of it; [it] could be condensed down to four months" (BC Police Commission, 1997: 10).

As a consequence, both the police board and the staff of the STP had concerns about the FNTJI recruit training program. Most members of the police board did not believe that the STP officers had received adequate training generally (BC Police Commission, 1997: 77).

Another area of concern between the police board and the STP was in the area of what can be called a "clash of policing culture." The police board members were unanimous in wanting to provide the communities with a policing service based on the **"watchman"** system that was used by their ancestors. The "watchman" was respected for his decision-making. Trust was developed to the point that members of the community would feel comfortable in approaching him to hear their cases whenever they felt that someone had committed a transgression. The police board felt that they had adequately conveyed to the chief constable their views and positions concerning having police officers reflect that tradition, and that he, in turn, understood them completely. However, it was the majority view of the police board members that the officers of the STP were not applying this philosophy. There were concerns held by members of the police board that the majority of the police officers were reluctant to approach the community in a sincere attempt to develop a feeling of trust and respect. At the same time, the staff expressed the attitude that the board was not supportive toward them and that consequently a poor relationship exist[ed] between the two groups (BC Police Commission, 1997: ii and 13). The audit concluded by reporting that

> Ineffective communication between the Board, Constable, and members of the STP over the preferred style of policing has resulted in questions concerning the nature of the desired policing style, and how the STP can deliver such a service. The Board and the community are supportive of a community oriented policing style, while members of the police service are divided between those who support the cultural peacekeeper approach, and those who are focused on a more traditional [i.e., Western "traditional"] policing philosophy. (BC Police Commission, 1997: ii)

These are the major cultural challenges faced by all Native police services. To what extent do they reflect the culture of policing of the mainstream training they all receive (which, in this case, is more respected than more Native-driven training), and the mainstream policing experiences of those who early on take on positions of leadership in their police services? How free are Native police services to innovate if they are following traditional values? To what extent can they reflect their traditional culture in trying to work with and get the respect of other, more established mainstream policing services, and provincial and federal funding agencies?

The sheer expanse of the territory and number of communities covered by the STP was also seen as posing logistical problems. The distance between the three offices and the ten communities that comprise the STP had a profound effect on the overall communication and coordination of action within the organization, as well as adequacy of staffing. The position in Seton Lake was especially problematic because there was only one person stationed in that community. There was no immediate backup or relief. The police officer there had to wait a minimum of one hour for backup. As a result, there were high levels of stress experienced by the officer who had been stationed there and by the officer's family (BC Police Commission, 1997: 45). Furthermore, generally the STP was attempting to provide 24-hour per day coverage and yet there were no replacements for people absent due to holidays, illness, or training.

Leadership issues and a general low morale among the force were also problems revealed by the audit. The former was largely the result of an inability to attract a sufficiently experienced supervisor or experienced constables, the large responsibility for managing and leading assumed by a police board with few precedents to follow, as well as the heavy administrative responsibilities of the chief constable, who, like the board, is required to blaze trails rather than follow predictable paths. Still, staff members legitimately felt that they did not receive sufficient feedback from either the board or the chief constable concerning their jobs and that they did not receive sufficient support from the chief constable when dealing with complaints from the public. Interestingly, while five out of ten staff members rated morale as "poor" or "very poor," a majority still rated their job satisfaction as "good," despite the overall morale problem. They liked the challenge of day-to-day police work, working with the people in their communities, and enjoyed associating with their peers (BC Police Commission, 1997: 7–8).

Despite the problems and difficulties, the BC Police Commission noted that the board and the STP were conscientious and dedicated to improving the quality of the service. This must have served to good effect, for three years after the audit, as mentioned above, the STP moved ahead to assume full jurisdictional authority for the ten communities. As Chief Constable Harry McLaughlin noted in the BC Attorney General news release, "This occasion instills a new level of pride in our officers and a renewed sense of commitment to the Stl'atl'imx communities."

Box 3.1   The Sundance

For the Blackfoot, as with most other Native nations of the Prairies in Canada, the main traditional ceremony is the Okan (Blackfoot: "ceremonial pole") or **Sundance.** Traditionally it was initiated, sponsored, and presided over by a woman:

> The decision to hold a Sun Dance was made by a pure woman—i.e., a virgin or faithful wife—who had a male relative in danger of losing his life. A husband might be ill or a son may not have returned from a raid. The woman made a public vow that if the person's life was spared, she would sponsor a Sun Dance. Then, if her prayer was answered, she began preparations for the summer festival. (Dempsey, 1995: 392)

Sometimes, as a spiritual offering, young men inserted leather thongs through their chest or back muscles, the other end being attached either to a pole or to a buffalo skull. Then they would dance until the thongs ripped free. This was one reason given by the federal government for banning the Sundance in 1895. The following is a response by an anonymous Blackfoot:

> We know that there is nothing injurious to our people in the Sun-dance ... It has been our custom, during many years, to assemble once every summer for this festival ... We fast and pray, that we may be able to lead good lives and to act more kindly towards each other.
>
> I do not understand why the white men desire to put an end to our religious ceremonials. What harm can they do our people? If they deprive us of our religion, we will have nothing left, for we know of no other that can take its place. (Nabokov, 1991: 225)

The ban on the Sundance was lifted in 1951 when the *Indian Act* was changed.

STANDOFF AT GUSTAFSEN LAKE

Understanding the confrontation at Gustafsen Lake is made complicated by a number of factors. First, there is the lack of treaties and clarity surrounding Native land claims in British Columbia. The land that the confrontation was staged on was neither signed away nor considered legally owned by the local Native people, the Shuswap or Secwepemc. Related to this is the fact that fragile treaty talks were taking place in British Columbia at the time. Belief in that process could separate relatively conservative leaders from more radical elements impatient with receiving only words for so long. The intricacies of Native politics can influence the likelihood of a Native writer, commentator, or representative portraying the participants as "martyrs" or mere "outside agitators and criminals." Another complication comes from the fact that the issue relates to the Sundance (see Box 3.1). While sacred to the First Nations of the Plains in both Canada and the United States, the Sundance was not traditionally performed by the Shuswap. Further, the Sundance itself is a symbol of colonial oppression of Natives, as it was outlawed from 1895 to 1951. Fourth, the significance of the site was itself contested. The Sundance was held there because three different people had allegedly experienced visions on that site; local Shuswap Elders, however, did not feel that the site had any traditional sacredness to it. Finally, there is significant reason to believe that the RCMP, as the federal government had done in the Oka crisis, manipulated the media to villify the Native participants in the confrontation.

The Story

For six years, practitioners of the Sundance had been holding their ceremony on a privately owned ranch near Gustafsen Lake, 20 kilometres south of 100 Mile House in central British Columbia. Lyle James, an American who runs the property as a cattle ranch, had granted Natives permission to use the property for the purposes of the Sundance. The eight-day ceremony attracted dozens of Native people, about half from the area and the remainder from as far away as the American Northwest. According to the *Canadian Press (CP) Newswire* (June 22, 1995), problems dated back to 1992, when Sundancers complained about harassment from local ranch hands. As well, a tourist had been shot at in the area. Two people had been arrested and weapons were seized, although no charges were laid.

Then, on June 13, 1995, George Ostoforoff, a forestry worker, was shot at. He claimed that a rifle had been fired in his direction after he spotted two Natives near his truck by Gustafsen Lake. He believed that the shot was meant to frighten him away. Following this, after the annual June Sundance ceremony, a handful of people refused to leave the site, claiming that it was sacred ground (see Box 3.2 on sacred sites). Most were outsiders, either from the United States or were Canadian Aboriginals from outside Shuswap country. Their leader was a Shuswap, Jones William Ignace (whose Shuswap name meant "Wolverine"), 66, an organic farmer, and called by some an Elder.

During the trial that would follow a year later, it was alleged that Lyle James then ordered some ranch hands to serve a trespass notice to Percy Rosette, one of the group, telling the people remaining on the site that the ranch hands were going to hang some "red niggers." The presence of weapons was soon made obvious at the site. The standoff had begun.

Box 3.2	Sacred Lands, Sacred Sites

All four of the largest clashes between police and Natives during the 1990s—Oka, Gustafsen Lake, Ipperwash, and Oldman River—had at their heart not just land claims (as important as they are), but the issue of respecting the sacred sites of Native peoples.

What is the definition of a **sacred site**? What goes into establishing that a place is a Native sacred site? One of the

authors of this book, Bryan Cummins, co-authored with Algonquin Kirby Whiteduck an article, "Towards a Model for the Identification and Recognition of Sacred Sites" (Cummins and Whiteduck, 1998), based on work done in the winter of 1995 in an effort to establish sacred sites involved with the land claims of the Algonquins of Golden Lake First Nation. The authors wrote that a sacred site was, by definition, one which was in some way connected to the supernatural world. For example, it could be where religious rituals were performed or where religious art is depicted. While some archaeologists classify pictographs [paintings on rock] and petroglyphs [carvings on rock] separately, we included them under the classification of sacred sites, because it is generally agreed that they depict Native cosmology. Similarly, burials, by their very nature, imply a relationship with the supernatural. (Cummins and Whiteduck, 1998: 5)

As a result of that work, fifty-two sites within the land-claim area were deemed sacred; most were burial sites, six contained pictographs or petroglyphs, four were places where people had witnessed supernatural events, and two were traditional fasting sites.

Even given a definition, how can it be established that a given site is sacred? This involves recognition by the British-based Canadian legal system, which traditionally puts great stock in the written record, and dismisses "word of mouth" as hearsay. Native people are handicapped in such recognition, as theirs is an oral tradition. A few sacred sites have written documentation behind them, and burial sites can be readily identified.

However, for the most part the cultural outsiders who have the power to legally recognize that a site is sacred need to have the capacity to reach beyond their own culturally bound limits to "believe" in what experts without paper credentials and evidence have to say. It is a large step to take, as with the exception of cemeteries (which are legally protected), there are no sacred sites for mainstream Canadians in Canada.

Who are these experts whose word is to be trusted? For the most part, they are Elders. While there are some pretenders, most Aboriginal communities have a good sense of who their Elders are. These are not merely people who are old. In an important recent work entitled "In the Words of Elders," these key figures are defined as follows:

In traditional Aboriginal societies Elders were and still are evolved beings who possess significant knowledge of the sacred and secular ways of their people, and who act as role models, often assuming leadership positions in their communities. They are highly respected by the people. They are the teachers, healers, and experts in survival, guiding individuals' behaviour towards an understanding of the natural ways of Mother Earth. (Kulchyski, McCaskill, and Newhouse, 1999: xvi)

Making Distinctions

The operator of the ranch, and his wife, were quick to acknowledge that there had been no trouble in the past, stating that the Sundancers had "been pretty good." They had had no problems with them in the six previous years. They speculated that those involved in the standoff were "renegades ... from other places" (*CP Newswire,* June 22, 1995).

A similar distinction appears to have been made by Shuswap leadership. Mary Thomas, an intermediary for the Sundancers and the Caribou Tribal Council, is quoted as saying "The Sundancers' issues and concerns are different than [those of] the people who are holding and protecting the land" (*CP Newswire,* June 22, 1995). "Their policy [the Sundancers] is no violence, no lethal weapons. They attempt to settle everything in a peaceful manner." She denied that the militants were Sundancers, saying that the spiritual leaders of the Sundancers had tried to curb the militants, banning them from the ceremony. The purpose of the Sundance "is a spiritual purpose and it doesn't mix well with the politics that are taking place."

An editorial in the Alberta-based Native newspaper *Windspeaker* (September, 1995 vol. 13, no. 5), in part citing Caribou Tribal Council administrator Bruce Mack, spoke of Shuswap political leaders opposing the occupation and even supporting the police in their attempts to restore the land to the rancher. Over the four months of the occupation, the Caribou Tribal Council and other Shuswap political leaders would fail to convince the participants of the occupation to leave. Ovide Mercredi, Grand Chief of the Assembly of First Nations (1991–1997), would also fail in his negotiations. It was a time in his career when he was losing the support of many Native people in Canada. The only Native negotiator to which the occupiers would pay heed was Stoney religious leader John Stevens, from Alberta. According to Métis scholar Olive Dickason, Stevens was the one who finally persuaded them at the end "to give themselves up" (Dickason, 1997: 399).

Undaunted by their lack of local support, the Gustafsen group issued a press release under the name of Shuswap Traditionalists (they also called themselves Defenders of the Shuswap Nation). In it, they claimed that under constitutional law people on unceded and unsurrendered territory have the right to bear arms and to use force in resisting an invasion. To this end, they built foxholes, fences, and bunkers and posted signs saying "Indian land. No trespassing." They stated that they would never leave, unless it was in body bags (Dickason, 1997: 399).

Mountie Misinformation

The Canadian Broadcasting Corporation (CBC) ombudsman David Bazay wrote a report on the CBC's coverage of the standoff at Gustafsen Lake. In that report he spoke of how the RCMP commandeered unmediated access to CBC Radio by falsely claiming that a "hostage taking" was taking place, with lives at stake. According to Bazay, the RCMP control of information was such that "There was no way [for reporters] to confirm if the RCMP was giving the full story—or the degree to which it was sanitized or exaggerated— or if they were giving any part of the story at all" (cited in Hall, 2000). He further claimed that the RCMP later acknowledged that they had used "psychological warfare" whose aim was "to smear the reputations and to destroy the credibility of the protesters."[1]

How then can we know what happened? It is known that no serious injuries or deaths resulted from the occupation. There was gunfire on at least three occasions: August 11, August 27, and September 11. On the second date, two Mounties were shot but not hurt, although their bulletproof jackets sustained damage. In the trial that followed, it was alleged that the Natives had fired warning shots in self-defence at unknown intruders who, it turned out, were the Mounties in camouflage gear.

On September 11, there was a full-fledged firefight, with thousands of shots being fired during a forty-five minute battle. Involved were 400 RCMP officers, helicopters, and armoured personnel carriers. Six days later, after speaking with John Stevens, the Shuswap Traditionalists surrendered. Eighteen people were arrested, fourteen Aborginals and four non-Aborginals, thirteen men and five women. Together, they were charged with a total of sixty offences, including two charges of attempted murder. The operation cost an estimated $5.5 million, the most expensive police action in British Columbia's history.

The Trial

The case took one year to go to court, finally beginning on July 18, 1996. It lasted for 10 months, one of the longest and most complex cases in Canadian history. Courthouse security was extremely tight, like something out of a movie. Everyone entering the courtroom had to pass through a metal detector while the defendants sat behind floor-to-ceiling bulletproof glass.

The Crown contended that the case was straightforward: the defendants unlawfully occupied land belonging to Lyle James and shot at police officers (or aided and abetted those who did) while in the process of advancing a political agenda. The Crown stated at the onset that the issue was not one of land claims, that the trial was not a land claims hearing. Rather, it was about criminal actions on the part of the defendants.

The defence argued that this was not an ordinary trial. The defendants questioned James' right to the land. They believed that the land was theirs. They argued that the courts had no jurisdiction over disputes involving Native land that had never been ceded by treaty, that the case should be taken to the international courts. They further questioned James' right to request that the RCMP remove them from land that they deemed sacred, land upon which a religious ceremony had been held for a number of years. Shelagh Franklin, a defendant charged with mischief and possession of a dangerous weapon, summed up the group's position in the following way: "This is what Gustafsen is about: Who are the rightful owners of the land? American Lyle James and his cattle company, or the Shuswap people who have remained here since time out of mind?"

After nine long days of deliberation, the jury, consisting of six women and six men, reached its verdict. An editorial in *Maclean's* (June 2, 1997) described the rendering of the jury's decision:

> Choking back tears and holding an eagle feather, a sign of strength among aboriginal people, the jury foreman, himself of native ancestry, delivered the verdicts: a total of 39 acquittals—including the attempted murder charges—and 21 convictions. (*Maclean's*, June 2, 1997)

Wolverine was found guilty of mischief endangering life, weapons possession, discharging a firearm to resist arrest, and using a firearm in the commission of an indictable offence. Three other defendants were found guilty of mischief endangering life, as well as weapons charges. Twelve of the defendants were acquitted of the charge of mischief endangering life but were found guilty of the lesser charge of mischief to property valued over $5000.

Wolverine issued a statement to *Maclean's* through an intermediary: "We stood on constitutional and international law, which the judge refused to hear. We were wrongfully convicted. That's fraud, treason and genocide." He served his sentence until January 1999, when he was paroled.

Wishing to repair the damage to their relations with the local Shuswap, in September 2000, five years after the confrontation at Gustafsen Lake, the RCMP met with the Esketemc First Nation for a two-day meeting involving questions from both sides, a recognition ceremony, and traditional feasting. Inspector Howard Eaton, in charge of RCMP Aboriginal Policing in British Columbia, was positive about the experience: "From the RCMP perspective, we have a better understanding of the culture and the spirituality that is involved in a lot of these things, and I think that hopefully we'll handle these types of situations a little bit different in the future" (CBC Radio Regional News, September 20, 2000).

THE NISGA'A TREATY

In 2000, the Nisga'a Treaty was signed. In exchange for the Nisga'a people giving up their claims to 80 percent of their traditional land and their provincial tax exemptions, they received title to 1930 square kilometres in the Nass valley. It also gave them the right to make laws in several areas, including land use, employment, and cultural preservation. They will own the forest and mineral resources on their land (like a private owner would), but manage them, like other owners, within British Columbia's laws and standards. The treaty allows the Nisga'a to provide policing, correctional, and court services within their land, all pending provincial approval. The police service is to have the full range of police responsibilities, enforcing Nisga'a, provincial, and federal laws. The officers will be required to meet provincial qualifications, training, and professional standards.

For the Nisga'a to provide community correctional services, they would have to enter into agreements with either the provincial or the federal government. If a Nisga'a court is established, it would adjudicate prosecutions and civil disputes arising under Nisga'a laws and review the administrative decisions of Nisga'a public institutions (Rose, 2000: 30). The people will appoint their own judges, the method of selection subject to provincial approval. People facing imprisonment under Nisga'a law could elect to be tried in the British Columbia provincial court, and final decisions of the Nisga'a court could be appealed to the British Columbia Supreme Court.

THE NATIVE YOUTH MOVEMENT

The Native Youth Movement (NYM) was founded in 1990 in Winnipeg, but it seems that it is the British Columbia branch, formed in Vancouver in 1996, that has been getting the most press. They represent a sometimes confusing (to the outsider) mixture of elements. They have the Oka look, with camouflage outfits and scarves covering their faces, sometimes perform policing functions such as guarding Native fishermen from Department of Fisheries and Oceans (DFO) officers, carry handcuffs and police-issue batons, army knives, two-way radios, etc., and are trained in military techniques. They do not, however, carry or use firearms. They are educated and some are still in college or university.

In British Columbia, they have identified as "the enemy" the British Columbia Treaty Commission (BCTC). They refer to themselves as "the official opposition" to the BCTC, to chiefs and councils they feel are selling out the rights of future generations in order to receive money now, and even to the Assembly of First Nations (AFN; one NYM protester's sign read that AFN stands for "Another Financial Network"), which they feel are involved with the sellout.

The NYM has been engaged in civil disobedience without violence in a series of actions. In April 1997, they occupied the BCTC office for 40 hours. On January 30, 1998, they interrupted a meeting of top Native leaders. In April of that same year, they occupied the BCTC office again, this time for five days, with fourteen members being arrested. The charges were eventually dropped. On May 25, 1998, 43 NYM members occupied the Westbank Indian Band band office chanting "Sellouts, get the Hell out." Thirty-three hours later, 20 left voluntarily and 23 were arrested, again with the charges eventually dropped. In the summer of 1999, when the Cheam First Nation decided to disregard the ban on salmon fishing in their area, 20 NYM members were there. In the words of one member, named "Shrubs," "We have been invited here to show a political and physical presence."

Department of Fisheries and Oceans officers, trained by the RCMP and wearing bullet-proof flak jackets and carrying tear-gas canisters and semi-automatic weapons, tried to stop the salmon fishing by cutting and seizing Cheam nets, and by trying to arrest those whose nets were in the water or who had fish. Still, there were no arrests, and no violence erupted throughout that tense summer.

In the fall of 1999, the NYM received some bad press because of some small, photo-copied posters that appeared in Penticton. On the posters were written the words, "Get off our land or we will burn you out one house at a time." It was signed "Native Youth Movement." This seems inconsistent with the NYM approach, and was probably either the work of a single hothead or an attempt to discredit the NYM by their opponents, Native or non-Native. Monty Joseph, an NYM leader in Penticton, said that the NYM had nothing to do with the posters and that "This definitely is not the message I want to convey to the people of Penticton."

More recently (2001) the Native Youth Movement has been involved with opposing the further development and use of a resort, Sun Peaks, on Shuswap land. While the emotions have been high in this opposition, there has to date (the end of 2001) been no violent confrontation between the RCMP and the NYM and others involved in this protest.

NOTES

1. The lead defence lawyer, Bruce Clark, introduced as evidence an RCMP training video shot during the confrontation. In the video, RCMP officers openly used such words as "disinformation" and "smear campaign." The officers responded to the introduction of this evidence by saying that the comments were made in a joking manner and that they were not attempting to manipulate the media.

KEY TERMS

potlatch (p. 30)   sacred site (p. 36)
sundance (p. 35)   watchman (p. 33)

REVIEW QUESTIONS

1. How did the potlatch become a policing issue?
2. What were the difficulties encountered by the Stl'atl'imx Tribal Police force?
3. Why is it important for police officers to understand what makes a site sacred?
4. What were the justice institutions accorded the Nisga'a by their treaty?
5. What is the Native Youth Movement?

chapter four

Aboriginal Policing
in Alberta

LEARNING OBJECTIVES

After completing this chapter, students should be able to:

1. Discuss why the Cardston blockade took place and how it affected the Kainai's relationship with the RCMP.

2. Discuss the opposition to the Oldman Dam from the point of view of the Lonefighters, the chief of the Peigan, the RCMP, and the provincial government.

3. Outline the features of the trial of Milton Born With A Tooth that made it different from the trial of a non-Native individual.

4. Identify the weaknesses and flaws in the social and police services that contributed to the Connie and Ty Jacobs tragedy.

5. Outline and critically question the main criticisms of Native policing as described in the Cardinal Report.

There is a significant diversity of Aboriginal peoples living in Alberta, with languages coming from three language families: Algonquian, Athabaskan, and Siouan. The Algonquian peoples of Alberta include the three connected nations of the Blackfoot (Siksika, Peigan, and Kainai), the Cree, and the Métis. The Athabaskan peoples include the Tsuu Tiina or Sarcee, the Chipewyan, and the Dunne-Za ("Real People") or Beaver. The Nakota (also called Assiniboine and Stoney) are the sole Siouan group.

THE BLACKFOOT CONFEDERACY

Nineteenth century artist George Catlin referred to the Blackfoot Confederacy as "the most powerful tribe of Indians on the continent." Three nations traditionally made up the Blackfoot Confederacy: Siksika, Kainai, and Peigan. Historically, they shared language and customs, intermarried, and were military allies. Their collective name in their own language can be Sakoyitapix or "prairie people," Apikunipuyi or "speakers of the same language," or Nitsitapix or "real or true people," a term also used to refer to Native peoples generally (Franz and Russell, 1995: 135).

The Siksika or Blackfoot Nation

Siksika means "black foot." The name is derived from a man in the origin story who walked over the ashes of a prairie fire, making his moccasins black in the process. The English collective name for the allied nations, "Blackfoot" ("Blackfeet" in the United States) reflects the fact that White traders established first contact with the Siksika and does not indicate any special status of that group over the other two.

The Siksika Nation Police Service was established in 1992 and is developing toward full policing responsibility. It has 10 members who operate under a tripartite agreement between the Siksika First Nation, the Alberta government, and the federal government that will expire in 2002. In 1994, the Siksika Justice Commission signed a contract to provide community corrections programs and a courtworker program to members of their First Nation. In 1998, a courthouse on their reserve was set up as a circuit of the Drumheller Provincial Court, for approximately five days each month. Tried in this courthouse are local bylaw, child welfare, civil, criminal, traffic, and young offender offences.

The Kainai (Kainaiwa) or Blood Nation

The word "Kainai" or "Kainaiwa" means "many chiefs." In the origin story of the people, a traveller walked into a Kainai community and asked who the chief was. Many claimed to be chief. This First Nation's English name, Blood, comes from a name given to them by the Cree, a reference to their practice of sometimes covering their clothes with red ochre. The use of red ochre by eastern Native peoples to decorate clothing and skin led some early European travellers to North America to think that the people had red skin. The mistake stuck.

The Cardston Blockade

Section 35 of the *Indian Act* explicitly states that the federal government can expropriate reserve land at any time (see Kahnawake and Dudley George stories in the chapters on Quebec and Ontario, respectively). Band consultation or permission is not legally required. This has happened to the Kainai on more than one occasion. During World War I, they were one of several groups whose land was taken for "war production" farming and the program paid for with band funds. They protested, but with no result (Dickason, 1997: 300).

In 1928, the federal government expropriated Kainai land and turned it over to the CPR for grain elevators and other purposes that served the railroad. Early in 1980, a number of young Kainaiwa who felt that the people had been treated unfairly in these one-sided moves organized a "run" to Ottawa with a sacred bundle (see Box 4.1) containing land-claim documents and soil from their reserve. The run stretched from Blackfoot Crossing, where Treaty 7 was signed, to Ottawa. The young men who were the runners asked for a government response in two and a half months. When that time passed with no results, they formed a council and decided to blockade disputed land in Cardston adjacent to their reserve that had been expropriated in 1928. Early Monday morning, July 21, 1980, they erected a tipi on the access road to the grain elevators and bulk gas and oil stations. Their intent was to force the federal Minister of Indian Affairs to deal with their concerns.

Box 4.1   Medicine Bundles

An important component of the spiritual life of members of the Blackfoot Confederacy, other First Nations living in the Prairies, and to a lesser degree other First Nations in Canada, is the **medicine bundle.** It is difficult to compare it with any feature in European culture. One writer refers to it as a "portable shrine" (Friesen, 1997: 134). A medicine bundle traditionally contained sacred objects such as medicine pipes, feathers, bones, the talons of a hawk, or iniskim (literally, "buffalo stones," often fossils bearing spiral shells), wrapped up in hide. Often the items reflected messages sent in visions or dreams.

Medicine bundles were and still are important in Blackfoot ceremonies. The opening of the bundle, either at a Sundance or after the first thunderstorm, is a sacred moment in ceremony.

In the RCMP *Native Spirituality Guide,* first produced in 1993 by Corrections Canada and Elders in Manitoba, officers-in-training

> are especially urged to be careful with regard to the unauthorized handling of medicine bundles. If a bundle is touched by other than the designated person it can no longer be used in its uncleansed condition. The custodian must then perform purification rites to restore the bundle's sacredness. This process may take several days and involve the presence of additional spiritual elders. (Friesen, 1997: 238)

The Royal Canadian Mounted Police (RCMP) were alerted. They were advised by Dennis First Rider, a spokesperson for the group, that the protest was non-violent, with no alcohol or weapons allowed. Near the end of the day, the RCMP instructed them to take the blockade down. Seventeen Kainai were arrested for blocking the highway, the barricades were removed, and several vehicles belonging to the protesters were towed away. They were shortly released on their own recognizance, based on their agreement that they would not return to the site of the blockade. Almost all participants returned.

On the morning of July 23, two large earth-moving machines were brought in by the Kainai to form the blockade again. The RCMP were in a difficult position. The merchants whose businesses were blocked and the non-Native citizens of Cardston were beginning to resent the blockade. The Kainai protesters felt the same way about the federal government's lack of response. The regional Department of Indian Affairs and Northern Development (DIAND) representative came to the site and agreed to contact his superiors in Ottawa. The RCMP agreed to wait for Ottawa's response before taking any action.

One day later, the Minister finally made contact with the protesters, agreeing to meet and to discuss the issues. But his words were vague, lacking in any substantive promises. The Kainai had experienced that before, so they did not take down the blockade. The RCMP responded. A special tactical unit of the RCMP in Calgary was sent to Cardston. The orders were to take down the barricades. The protesters refused to leave the site. Numerous arrests were made on July 26 as the confrontation became more physical.

The third confrontation took place early on Sunday, July 27, when the Kainai who had been released again returned to the site. This time the confrontation was more violent. Police dogs were used and effected the dispersal. With this short-term gain for the RCMP came long-term pain. In the words of University of Calgary sociologist James Frideres, from whose publication most of the material quoted here was taken:

> this use of force coloured the Aboriginal perception of the police and changed their relationship with the RCMP for many years following. Aboriginal-police relations continue to be strained on the reserve. The Aboriginals and the community of Cardston have not resolved their differences, and neither seems to have forgiven the other for the role they played during the conflict. (Frideres, 2001: 337)

Frideres also noted that two decades later, the land claims are still not resolved, nor has there been any attempt by the federal government to deal with the underlying issues.

That same year (1980), the Blood Indian Police Commission was established. The Blood Tribal Police Service has had an uneven history since then. The service and the commission were scrapped for a while. An inquiry was published in 1991 examining the reasons for the failure: inadequate funding, poor and inadequate planning, and inadequate delineation of the roles and relationships of the parties involved, including the tribal council, the RCMP, provincial advisors and the chief of police (Stenning, 1996: 140). Fortunately, the Blood Inquiry resulted in the re-creation of the Blood Tribe Police, which now has full policing responsibility, one of only two Native police forces in Alberta to have it. Their tripartite agreement was signed in 1999 and lasts until 2004. The force has 20 members.

Box 4.2	Chief Crop Eared Wolf's Buffalo Skin: An RCMP Policing Initiative

On September 22, 1995, the RCMP made an important policing initiative. They returned a painted buffalo skin to the Kainaiwa. The skin dates back to the 1880s and recounts in pictorial form the life achievements of Chief Crop Eared Wolf, a Kainaiwa leader who led them through some of the most difficult times in their history, when they began reserve life and their population dropped drastically. The RCMP had owned the skin for 50 years, after it had been donated to the RCMP museum in Regina by a private citizen.

In return for this gesture, the Kainaiwa are providing the RCMP with a replica made by one of their artists. The replica will be used as a teaching tool in instructing RCMP cadets about the culture and heritage of the Kainaiwa.

Since 1990, there has been a 24-bed minimum security correctional centre on the reserve, run by the Kainai Community Corrections Society, which also runs a criminal courtworker program, an Elders program, and various crime prevention programs. See Box 4.2 for a discussion of a positive RCMP initiative toward the Kainaiwa.

The Peigan Nation

The name "Peigan" is derived from "Apikuni," variously translated as "scabby robes" or "poorly dressed robes." They were called that because in the Blackfoot origin story, the Peigan women had scraped the buffalo skins poorly, leaving pieces of meat and fur stuck to them.

The Lonefighters Society and the Oldman Dam

The Oldman River, which winds through Peigan land in southwestern Alberta, is as sacred to the Peigan as the Jordan is to Christians or the Ganges to Hindus. They named it N'api ("Old Man"), their name for the culture hero said to have created the first Peigan. The Peigan traditionally came to the river to pray, drink its water, and find medicine and food.

The Ni'taiitsskaaiks (literally, "lone-fight-plural") or **Lonefighters Society** can be traced back to at least the 1700s, when horses first arrived in Peigan territory. The society got its name from the occasion when one lone warrior fought against impossible odds without giving up. By the banks of the Oldman River, the Lonefighters buried their dead, performed the Sundance, held meetings, and prepared for war. The Lonefighters were expected to protect their land and their people to the last breath of the last warrior, earning them the respect of other Plains nations. They disappeared like the great herds of buffalo did.

The Lonefighters were resurrected in 1990 by Milton Born With A Tooth. The Peigan and the Alberta government had been fighting and negotiating for land around the river since 1976. At the centre of the conflict was a government-proposed dam on the Oldman River. Roughly 30 to 40 Lonefighters (ranging in age from 20 to about 45 years) were involved in the protest against the dam.

On August 2, with the dam mostly completed, the Lonefighter society took action. Armed with a bulldozer, the Lonefighters started diverting the river in an attempt to sabotage the project. The plan was to cut a diversion ditch on Peigan reserve land, reconnecting the river to its natural creek bed, which had been blocked in the early 1920s. This would divert water away from the waterworks system managed by the provincial government, rendering the highly sophisticated and expensive dam useless.

The provincial government responded by obtaining a court injunction the next day, declaring the diversion illegal. Milton Born With A Tooth countered by saying that the provincial government had broken the law because it had allowed construction of the dam without a proper environmental assessment study being conducted. In an interview at the Lonefighters' encampment, he told reporters that what they were doing was "re-healing" the river, and that the RCMP were not bothering them because they were aware that no laws were being broken.

The 2300 Peigan of the local reserve were split concerning the tactics of opposition. Chief Leonard Bastien told reporters that the Lonefighters Society did not have the backing of the chief and council, and that they intended to meet with federal and provincial negotiators to try to bring about a peaceful resolution to the situation. Nonetheless, Bastien made it very clear that he understood the reasons for the protest. "Personally, I am against the Oldman River Dam because of the cultural genocide on our people," he told Jackie Red Crow from *Windspeaker* (August 17, 1990).

The crisis at the Oldman River climaxed on September 7 and 8, 1990. A Lonefighter runner spotted 16 RCMP cruisers and vans, along with Lethbridge Northern Irrigation District officials. They had with them heavy equipment and were proceeding toward the weir. The runner sounded the alarm to the rest of the Lonefighter camp. The Lonefighters then assumed predetermined defensive positions and built bunkers. The RCMP began flying helicopters over the camp.

As the RCMP began to close the distance between the two groups, the Lonefighters began to yell at them, warning them off Peigan land. After some time, a number of the Lonefighters began to throw rocks at the advancing police. Then, Milton Born With A Tooth fired at least two warning shots "that sent the RCMP scurrying for cover" (Woodward, 1990).

Following the initial outburst of gunfire, the Lonefighters claimed a number of small victories. The RCMP removed the heavy equipment. They also complied with two Lonefighter demands. Some of the Lonefighters felt that Ray Gauthier, an officer from the Pincher Creek detachment, was unduly biased against them. When they asked that he be taken away from the front lines, it was done. They also asked that the helicopter not fly in "Peigan air space." The RCMP again complied.

At the same time, the Peigan closed ranks. While initially, according to Chief Bastien, about 76 percent of his community was opposed to the diversion, the majority subsequently came around to the Lonefighters' position. The band council passed a resolution that day, stating that the RCMP was trespassing. The resolution was read to the officers by Chief Bastien. Three days later, chief and council voted nine to one to pass another resolution supporting the diversion. The Lonefighters said that they were proud of the band and council, adding that "They literally threw away a promise of hundreds of thousands of dollars (from the government) to support the diversion."

On September 7, the RCMP sealed off the area and dug in for a siege, setting up a roadblock and constructing an observation tower. The Lonefighters heard that the Mounties were moving a tactical squad, riot police, and an ambulance into position. Police-squad leaders were seen poring over a map, and a helicopter was again flying overhead.

There was a lighter side to the conflict as well. Traditional prairie Native practice was to "count coup" (pronounced as "coo") on enemies by sneaking into their camp unarmed and touching them with a coup stick. During the night, one Lonefighter touched the sleeve of an officer. Some of the Lonefighters would give praise to some of the RCMP, who they saw as being unwitting federal tools of a provincial government. Raymond Crow Shoe, who had had a shoving match with some officers, had good words to say for RCMP Superintendant Owen Maguire who had ordered his men to back away, adding that Maguire had "reasoned with me in a friendly manner." Lonefighter spokesman Glenn North Peigan would say in front of a group of officers that there were many good police.

However, the situation worsened on September 8, 1990. Overnight, the RCMP tightened their position around the Lonefighters' camp. A warrant was issued for Milton Born With A Tooth, but the Lonefighters refused to surrender their leader. Harsh words were exchanged when Glenn North Peigan encountered officer Ray Gauthier, who had supposedly been withdrawn from action the day before.

After a tense, 33-hour standoff, Milton Born With A Tooth was arrested. He was denied bail on the basis of the "public interest" and spent over three months in jail, some of it in solitary confinement. The Alberta government attempted to charge him with civil contempt for violating their court injunction of August 29, 1990 preventing attempts at diverting the Oldman River. Judge Roy Dewell threw out the application, saying that it lacked detail and was deficient. Born With A Tooth was released on bail on December 18, only to have weapons charges laid against him. He was ordered to return to his home on the Peigan reserve. He was found guilty on seven charges ranging from pointing a firearm to obstructing police officers, and was sentenced to eighteen months in jail.

But there was evidence that racism was at play in this decision. When the verdict was appealed, the Alberta Court of Appeal quashed the seven convictions and ordered a new trial. In the opinion of the court, the presiding judge in the original case, Justice Laurie MacLean, had cut short cross-examination designed to raise doubt about police intentions and had unjustly deemed much of Peigan culture and traditions "irrelevant" to the case.

Justice MacLean was eventually reproached by the Canadian Judicial Council in 1993. The council's judicial conduct committee concluded that the record of the case was "filled with examples of how a judge should not conduct himself during the course of a high profile trial involving sensitive and cultural issues." The matter had been brought to the attention of the council by the Canadian Alliance in Solidarity with Native People, which accused the judge of having "displayed an insensitivity to cultural and religious differences" during the trial (*Western Report,* vol. 10, no. 3, 1995). They claimed that Justice MacLean had said that "Native spirituality is as irrelevant as Satanism," and that he had used the word "fantasy" in reference to Native spiritual beliefs.

The new trial had difficulties from the beginning that also appeared to have had a racial taint to them. The defence tried unsuccessfully to have the trial moved out of Fort McLeod, alleging that there was significant prejudice against First Nations people there and that the community had vested interests in the dam. Chief Justice Kenneth Moore of Alberta's Court of Queen's Bench had instructed that half the jurors at the retrial be Aboriginal. However, the trial judge, Willis O'Leary, dismissed that order, claiming that it was incompatible with Canadian judicial practice and that no provision exists for "tailor made" juries based on race. He did, however, let Born With A Tooth take a traditional Blackfoot oath, involving the burning of sweetgrass and the touching of a sacred pipe, allowing that it was just like taking a biblical oath.

On March 14, 1994, after deliberating for four hours, the jury found Milton Born With A Tooth guilty of seven weapons charges. When the judge polled the jurors to see whether they had concurred, a Native woman broke down, sobbing. The judge ordered the jury back to its chambers. They returned an hour and a half later, with the woman accepting the verdict. The defence attorney, Karen Gainer, suggested that the woman might have been pressured into compliance.

Milton Born With A Tooth suggested that the police were responsible for much of what had happened: "They should have sent a couple RCMP officers down to the camp that day; instead they sent an army" (*Windspeaker,* October 9, 1994). Milton Born With A Tooth received a 16-month sentence.

By 2000, the Peigan had discussed policing options, but no change had been put into place. The RCMP has established on-reserve Aboriginal policing detachments in their community. The Lonefighters have been disbanded.

The Connie and Ty Jacobs Story

The Native people in this story are Tsuu T'ina ("earth people" or "many people") or Sarcee (a Blackfoot term), a people whose language belongs to the Athapaskan family. The Tsuu T'ina used to live farther north, until the eighteenth century when they split from the Tsatine ("beaver people") or Dunne-za ("real people") and moved south to join the Blackfoot Confederacy. Around 1800, Alexander Henry wrote, "These people have a reputation of being the bravest tribe in all the plains, who dare to face ten times their own numbers, and of this I have convincing proof during my residence in the country" (Friesen, 1997: 127). Today, the Tsuu T'ina have one community just east of Calgary.

In this story, two people are killed in a preventable tragedy. If it were a play we would say that the victims of this tragedy died not so much because of what the players did, but because of the unfinished construction of the stage on which the players stood. Native child welfare agencies and the Native police services that work with them are far from completed structures. The problems they are created to deal with will not go away simply because these agencies are created. Merely having Native-run organizations means little until the organizations are allowed to mature. To do this they need both equality with and distinctiveness from their counterparts in non-Native communities: equality in training, funding, planning, and experience, distinctiveness in drawing upon the unique cultures they serve (just like their counterparts).

The positive aspects of this story are twofold: (1) it led to recommendations that were badly needed; (2) it demonstrates the valuable role that can be played by Native judges in handling potentially explosive interracial policing matters. The story unfolded as follows.

On March 22, 1998, Connie Jacobs, aged 37 years, and her husband, Hardy, were at home on the Tsuu T'ina First Nation reserve with their four children, who ranged in age from four months to nine years, as well as two grandchildren (referred to as nieces in some reports) aged four and one year. They had been drinking heavily the night before. Connie and Hardy got into an argument. She threw a plate at him, opening a 10-centimetre gash over his left eyebrow. Hardy left to seek medical attention and was followed by his wife and their nine-year-old son, Ty. They found Hardy passed out alongside the road a short distance away from their home.

Ty set out to find a neighbour with a telephone to call for medical attention. A cousin, Barry Otter, picked him up en route, and subsequently called "911." The 911 dispatcher called Calgary Emergency Medical Services (EMS), which, in turn, called the local fire chief, Chris Bigplume. Paramedics came to the house, along with Chris and his wife, Tanya. A call was also made to the RCMP, advising them that the injury had been the result of a domestic dispute but that their assistance was not needed. This all transpired between roughly 3:00 and 3:50 pm.

The Bigplumes noted that Connie and Hardy Jacobs both appeared intoxicated and that broken glass, clothes, beer cans and other garbage littered the floor of the house. Connie and her husband seemed unaffected by their recent fight and even joked about it. Before leaving with Hardy, an ambulance attendant asked Connie whether she wanted RCMP assistance. She replied that she did not.

Chris Bigplume, feeling that the children appeared to be hungry and neglected and therefore at risk, advised his mother, Sally Simeon, who was the Chairperson of the Tsuu T'ina Child and Family Services, about what he had seen.

Like its counterparts in many other communities, the agency was underfunded, under-staffed, overworked, and was hampered by a bad match between employee responsibilities and their qualifications and experience. Lorraine Duguay, the director, did not have any front-line experience as a case worker, nor did she have a degree or diploma in social work. Child welfare worker Connie Bish had experience in child apprehension, but she lacked formal qualifications and training and did not have designation allowing her to conduct emergency apprehensions under the Child Welfare Act. Pat Whitney had been recently hired but lacked both training and qualifications. Another employee had been a front-line supervisor but had been let go less than two weeks before because of lack of funds.

Bish and Duguay had dealt with the Jacobs before, having conducted a prior child apprehension in February 1997. At that time, Connie and Hardy had undergone alcohol counselling and treatment. Based on that experience, the two child welfare workers sensed that the situation might be urgent. They contacted the RCMP in Okotoks and stated that they wanted their help in a child apprehension. The officer at the time advised them that coverage was short in the area and that he was going off duty shortly and would be replaced by another officer. Constable Dave Voller, a 17-year veteran, arrived at work just prior to 6 p.m. and by 6:20 p.m. was on his way to Tsuu T'ina Child and Family Services. He was familiar with the community, having worked at the reserve for more than two years.

Bish, unhappy with the first officer's response, attempted to contact the Tsuu T'ina Tribal Police Services (TTTPS). Regrettably, they referred her back to the RCMP.

It is important to understand the state of the TTTPS on the reserve. It was in a transition phase, two years into its first five-year tripartite agreement. It lacked a secure, stand-alone police station. Instead, it operated out of a small office above a gas bar and commercial centre on the reserve. It also lacked such basic police facilities as holding cells for prisoners and standard policing computer information services. On this particular weekend, it was even more understaffed than usual. One officer had recently resigned and another had been injured as a result of a motor vehicle accident that also caused damage to the police vehicle.

Bish then called Constable Tammy Dodginghorse of the Tribal Police, who was at home, to ask for assistance. Constable Dodginghorse had just finished her shift and was beginning her days off. She was a relatively inexperienced officer, recently having completed her training. She had also been placed under a "Notice of Shortcomings." Consequently, she was required to consult with both the chief of the TTTPS and her supervisor with the RCMP for permission to assist any outside agency. This she did, being advised by her RCMP supervisor to wear her uniform and take her equipment. As she lacked a police vehicle, she travelled with Connie Bish to the Jacobs house, followed by Lorraine Duguay in her vehicle.

They got out of their cars and approached the house. Bish had a "Notice of Apprehension" form in her possession, but, as was noted in the subsequent Goodson inquiry, "the two child welfare workers and the tribal police officer did not prepare a game plan and as a result each was unsure of her role in the operation."

An unclothed four-year-old boy answered the door, revealing a house in disarray as he opened the door. Blood was on the doorframe and on the floor and walls of the house. The house temperature was low, the children were inadequately dressed, and beer cans and clothes were strewn on the floor. Nine-year-old Ty Jacobs was hiding under blankets in a closet. Connie Jacobs appeared to be intoxicated and to have passed out while breast-feeding a baby. It took some effort by the child welfare workers to wake her up.

Constable Voller had made contact with Lorraine Duguay on her cellphone. He had asked to speak to "Connie," meaning Ms. Jacobs, but instead the phone was passed to Connie Bish, who advised him that the situation was under control and that his services were not needed. He was also told that Constable Dodginghorse was there. He then started back to Okotoks.

When she finally regained consciousness, Connie Jacobs was quite agitated and told Bish, "You are not taking my fucking children." Her sister later said that she feared that her children would be abused if they were taken by social services and put into foster homes. Constable Dodginghorse sensed that the situation was getting worse and contacted the RCMP, requesting backup. Constable Voller turned his vehicle around, but his progress was slowed by rising wind and increasingly heavy snowfall. In the meantime, Connie Jacobs had picked up a broom and was following Bish about the house. Constable Dodginghorse removed the broom and asked the child welfare workers to leave the house, whereupon Ms. Jacobs started rounding up the children and moving them to the basement.

Constable Dodginghorse positioned herself so that she could see inside the house and also watch for the arrival of Constable Voller. Through a mirror on a back wall, she could see activity in the kitchen, where the door leading to the basement was located. At approximately 7:00 p.m., she noticed the Mountie's car entering the subdivision. Glancing back to the house, she caught a glimpse of movement in reflection in the mirror. She approached the house only to see Connie Jacobs aiming a rifle at her at a distance of about 2.5 metres. She yelled, "Gun, gun," jumped down and retreated around the corner of the building. Bish and Duguay, sitting in their car, heard the yell and looked to see the rifle now aimed at them. They advised Constable Voller of the situation when he pulled his car alongside theirs.

Constable Voller looked up to see Ms. Jacobs step onto the landing of the house holding a rifle about 16 metres away from him. He crouched down behind his vehicle and unholstered his handgun. Ms. Jacobs shouldered her rifle. As Constable Voller shifted positions behind his car, Connie Jacobs followed his movement with her rifle. Thinking that his 9 mm handgun was too powerful for the situation, that he might injure innocent people in the house should he have to fire, Voller reached into his vehicle for his RCMP shotgun. He later testified that he did not know that Ty was standing as close to his mother as he was, although the Mountie was aware that there were six children in the house (*NativeNews*, October 13, 1999). He then ordered Duguay and Bish to leave. He shouted to his colleague, Constable Dodginghorse, but received no response.

Connie Jacobs then stepped forward and pointed the rifle at the officer. He twice told her to put the gun down, but she fired at him, missing. She lowered the rifle and appeared to be reloading, so Constable Voller again ordered her to put the weapon down. She said something unintelligible except for the words "my babies." She then brought the rifle up to her shoulder, at which point Constable Voller fired one shot from his shotgun, "aiming at center of mass" (Goodson, 2000). This occurred at approximately 7:27 p.m.

Of the twelve 32-calibre pellets fired from the shotgun, five hit the door frame. Three pellets hit the woman in the chest, one penetrating her heart. Two struck Ty, who had been standing slightly behind and to the side of his mother—one in the jaw, the other penetrating his aorta (the main valve leading to the heart). It is believed that both died in less than a minute and that no amount of medical help, regardless of how quickly administered, could have saved them.

The Mountie knew that he had hit the woman with his shotgun fire, but because of a number of factors affecting visibility, he did not know the outcome. He radioed for backup and medical personnel. Then he and Constable Dodginghorse, who had made her way back to Constable Voller, drove away from the scene.

Officers from the Turner Valley detachment of the RCMP, as well as canine officers from Calgary, arrived within the next 40 minutes. Emergency Response Team (ERT) officers from the RCMP would arrive later. Eventually, there were over 30 police officers on the scene. It was not until after 11:00 p.m. that the ERT began approaching the Jacobs residence. They found Connie Jacobs lying partially on top of her son, an 1889 Winchester .303 beneath her. The gun had been found on the reserve in 1997 by Hardy Jacobs, his brother Harry, and a friend. It had allegedly been hidden, along with five bullets, by Harry Jacobs in the basement in September of that year.

Subsequent investigation found three live shells on the floor in a fan shape around the body of Ty Jacobs, who, according to later testimony from the surviving children, had loaded the rifle for his mother (*Edmonton Sun,* October 20, 1999). One shell was in the hand of Connie Jacobs. There was a spent shell in the firing chamber and gunshot residue on the face and hands of Connie Jacobs. A child's bloody footprint near Ty's body suggests that one of the other children had approached the dead bodies. An autopsy revealed that Connie had a blood alcohol level of 310 milligrams per 100 millilitres of blood.

The Investigations

The RCMP conducted its own investigation, but Tsuu T'ina Chief Roy Whitney and Assembly of First Nations (AFN) Grand Chief Phil Fontaine called for an independent inquiry with an Aboriginal judge who had an understanding of First Nations communities. Chief Whitney exonerated the child welfare workers and tribal police of any wrongdoing, stating that they had been following department procedures in dealing with the incident (*Windspeaker,* April 1998).

At the request of Alberta Justice, the British Columbia Ministry of the Attorney General conducted an independent review of the case. Former Justice Robert Allan Cawsey concluded that Constable Voller "had seconds, or at the most, minutes to decide on a course of action ... no criminal charges should be laid in this matter." The review also concluded that racial bias did not play a role in the shooting (*Edmonton Journal,* October 22, 1998).

Native reaction to the inquiry was negative. Rumours and hard feelings abounded. Cynthia Applegarth, Connie's sister, said that she was not surprised that no charges were laid and that she had been informed by the BC team that had Constable Voller been charged, he would have been acquitted. The family wanted another investigation, claiming that the BC team did not have all the evidence.

Assembly of First Nations Grand Chief Phil Fontaine claimed that the review was flawed because it had been conducted by "seven white males," and that the AFN's own investigation had "reveal[ed] [that] there are too many unanswered questions." Fontaine also promised a broader inquiry into what he referred to as the violent history of conditions between Aboriginal people and the RCMP (*Edmonton Journal,* October 22, 1998). Jean LaRose, AFN spokesperson, stated that in the previous 20 years 43 percent of the people shot and killed by the RCMP had been Native, raising questions about how the force dealt with First Nations communities.

A more thorough inquiry under Native judge Thomas Goodson was then held. Originally scheduled to last eight weeks, it eventually ran from February 1, 1999 to March 16, 2000. Very early on in the inquiry, the Native community became receptive to the process, in part because it was presided over by a Native judge and was held mostly on the Tsuu T'ina reserve (it was moved to Calgary in the later stages).

By October 1999, much of the early harsh criticism Natives had levelled at Constable Voller had dissipated. Darryl Slade, writing in the *Calgary Herald* on October 19, 1999, observed that: "Initially, many residents on the reserve were critical of Const. Voller for shooting Ms. Jacobs, 37, and her nine-year-old son. But numerous witnesses have praised Const. Voller as an officer generally and for his handling of the event on the night in question."

The same day, the *Calgary Sun* reported that Brian Lambert, Connie's brother, didn't anticipate difficulty encountering the Mountie personally in the light of the tragedy, noting that "it's one of those things you have to deal with." The next day, following the officer's testimony, Lambert was reported as saying that "through the evidence that's coming out he's just doing his job. What else could he have done?" (*Canadian Press,* October 19, 1999).

Judge Goodson assigned primary blame not to the specific people involved but to the general context, stating that "I doubt if the characters involved (including Connie Jacobs) had much to do with the events that transpired." He made important, sweeping recommendations aimed at lessening the possibility of repeating this tragedy (Goodson, 2000).

Concerning "Tribal Police Forces," the recommendations stressed developing equivalence of tribal police forces with other police services. Specifically, they stated that

> First Nations that are setting up police forces need to have the police service established with a secure stand alone and properly equipped police station and be staffed with properly equipped, trained and experienced police officers ready to operate along with the assistance of the RCMP and to retain the assistance of the RCMP as long as required.

For staffing, the recommendations required as a minimum standard that there be a police chief, a senior experienced officer, and one or more junior officers in training. There were statements that the training and pay of a "tribal police officer" should be equivalent to that of an RCMP officer or member of the Calgary/Edmonton Police Service, the latter "to obviate the defection of trained and experienced officers to other forces for monetary reasons."

Concerning "Police Relations with Outside Agencies," Judge Goodson recommended that "All police forces should develop policies, procedures and systems to be employed when assisting outside agencies such as bailiffs, public health workers or child welfare workers, and training in this area should be a standard requirement of police training."

The recommendations stressed that sharing of information such as "prior child apprehensions, criminal records, and the existence of firearms or other weapons within the residence" was of critical importance.

Alberta Justice's "Annual Summary of Aboriginal Justice Programs and Initiatives 2000" recorded that in the year 2000 the Tsuu T'ina Nation Police Service shared on-reserve office space with the Tsuu T'ina RCMP detachment and had 7 members, with two officers working out of a satellite office. Their five-year tripartite agreement ends in 2001. The Tsuu T'ina Nation Court, with jurisdiction over offences that have taken place on the reserve, first sat on October 6, 2000. In this court, the judge, Crown prosecutor, judicial clerks, and "peacemakers" are all Native people who are qualified for their positions.

The Assiniboine, Nakota, or Stoney Nation

These people have been known by a number of names: one English, one Cree and one in their own language. The word "Assiniboine" is derived from a Cree term meaning "those who cook with stones," giving them their English name "Stonies." This refers to their traditional method of cooking, which involved lining a hole with rawhide, filling it with water, then placing heated rocks inside to cook meat and vegetables in a stew or soup. Today, the Assiniboine prefer to be known as "Nakota" (also spelled Nakoda), a term in their own language. In Alberta, the Nakota live in the three reserve communities of Bearspaw, Chiniki, and Wesley, in southern Alberta not far from Calgary.

The Nakota are policed by the RCMP, although more independent options have been discussed. They share a corrections society with their Tsuu T'ina neighbours. Since 1992, the Tsuu T'ina Nation/Stoney Corrections Society has provided community corrections services, including probation supervision, courtworker services, and a crime prevention program. As with other Aboriginal-run corrections societies, the culture and traditions of the people are emphasized.

The Cree Nation

There are a number of policing situations among the Cree of Alberta. Leading the way in terms of independence and breadth of services are communities such as the Louis Bull and Alexis First Nations. The Louis Bull Police Service, which came into existence with Special Constables empowered under the Alberta Police Act in 1987, was the first fully autonomous First Nation police force in Alberta. It signed a tripartite agreement in 1995. In 1996, the force consisted of eight constables and was governed directly by the First Nation (Stenning, 1996: 140–141). By 2000, the number of members had been reduced to four.

The Louis Bull Police Commission comprises three members, all of whom are appointed by the First Nation government. There are no stipulations regarding whether or not a commissioner may hold an elected office, and there is a bylaw allowing for an increase in the number of commissioners when appropriate and necessary. The commission has a number of advisory, support, and inquiry—as opposed to executive—functions. It has the authority to inquire into any issues pertaining to the conduct or performance of duty by a member of the force, and extends its authority to internal disciplinary matters, grievances, and public complaints against police force members.

The Alexis First Nation signed a tripartite agreement in 1997. In the words of Chief Roderic Alexis, "This agreement is of historical importance in terms of the way it will provide culturally-sensitive justice and protection for our First Nation. I believe this agreement will help restore our peoples' confidence in justice and public security, and that in doing so, unity in our community will result" (www.sgc.gc.ca/release/319970205.htm, consulted July 24, 2001).

They are developing toward full policing responsibility, but now their chief of police is the Mayerthorpe RCMP detachment commander. The Alexis First Nation Police Service has three members at present.

The community has also formed the Alexis Justice Committee. According to the 2000 annual report of Alberta Justice, the committee is often used as a sentencing resource to augment pre-disposition or pre-sentence reports. The committee identifies the unique cultural resources available on the reserve (sweats, Elders, addiction monitors, etc.) ... [and] monitors the probation of some offenders and provides the court with "reviews" of the probationers' compliance. These reviews are usually carried out in court at three month, six month and 12 month intervals.

The Alexis First Nation is working toward the development of a sentencing circle, one which "anticipates the judge, prosecutor, defence lawyer and police officer as possible participants," the judge stepping back into a judicial role to possibly impose the sentence arrived at by consensus in the sentencing circle.

Representatives of the Alexis First Nation, together with those from Alexander, Enoch, O'Chiese, and Sunchild First Nations, formed the Yellowhead Tribal Community Corrections Society (YTCCS). Under contractual agreement with Alberta Justice since 1991, the YTCCS is responsible in the five communities for young offender and adult probation services, crime prevention, and a courtworker program, all emphasizing Cree cultural and spiritual traditions.

On June 20, 1995, the establishment of the Lesser Slave Lake Regional Police Service was announced, Alberta's first Regional Police Service. It was formed in a tripartite agreement with the Lesser Slave Lake Indian Regional Council, and the provincial and federal governments, and was actively supported by the RCMP. Eight Cree communities were involved, with a collective population of about 2,500. They are found north of Edmonton roughly in the centre of Alberta. Chief Walter P. Twinn, who has the Justice Portfolio on the council said of the agreement:

> As a result of this agreement, our reserves will have their own police service. This will help improve the living conditions of our people on their reserve lands. We hope to achieve law and order on our reserves and security for our people and property. Now, in addition to federal laws, our band bylaws will also be enforced (www.agc.gc.ca/release/e19950620.htm, consulted June 2, 2001).

THE CARDINAL REPORT

In July 1997, the Conservative government of Ralph Klein in Alberta, through the Minister of Justice and the Attorney General, initiated a review of First Nations policing in the province. The objective was to assess the effectiveness of Native police services and to make recommendations concerning any weaknesses that were identified during the review. Officers from the RCMP, First Nations chiefs, and community leaders were consulted. One year later, a discussion paper, "First Nations Police Services—Review," was prepared and circulated to all stakeholders for their comments. A final report, prepared by Mike Cardinal, a Métis and veteran Conservative MLA for Athabasca-Wabasca, was submitted in November 1998.

The Cardinal Report was critical of Native policing in Alberta, stating that "the participants in this review have come to the conclusion that First Nations police services in Alberta are in some cases not providing a satisfactory level of policing to meet the needs of their communities" (Cardinal, 1998: 13). Among other general criticisms, the report maintained that, in some cases, policing programs could not fulfill their mandates properly because of "high attrition rates, low morale, inferior leadership/management, and an array of organizational problems within the police services themselves" (Cardinal, 1998: 13). Furthermore, in some instances, reserve residents generally were not satisfied with, and lacked confidence in, First Nations police services and individual officers. While acknowledging that some First Nations police services had developed "adequately" and were "performing without significant difficulties, such cases were "not generally the norm."

The report identified a number of areas of concern, including:

1. lack of available qualified on-reserve candidates;
2. inadequate selection standards;
3. insufficient basic recruit training and virtually non-existent in-service training;
4. inadequate leadership and management practices;
5. inappropriate use of police funding;
6. local political interference;
7. low salaries, limited benefits and career mobility;
8. difficulties in policing home reserves;
9. inadequate facilities;
10. inability of officers to adequately investigate criminal offences and prepare and present cases for prosecution;
11. low community satisfaction and confidence regarding police officer knowledge, skills, abilities, fairness, and impartiality;
12. lack of effective crime prevention;
13. uncertainty and ambivalence regarding program objectives, roles, responsibilities, and accountability; and
14. disagreement and uncertainty regarding appropriate funding levels.

Significantly, it was not the relevance of First Nations policing that was criticized. Criticism was levelled, rather, at the way that First Nations policing was being handled. Cardinal summed up the report with the following: "The road to providing truly effective policing in First Nations communities is still being paved. Although there are bright and promising sights along the road, it remains a long way from completion" (Cardinal, 1998: 23).

The Cardinal Report should be viewed in a much larger context. One element in this, of course, is its political context. Cardinal is a provincial cabinet minister in a government that has a history of conflict with some of the Native groups whose police services were being assessed. Although the person who headed the review is Aboriginal, there was nothing specifically Native about the way the police services were assessed. They were judged as if they were police services like any other. That might not have been insightful or fair.

Further, the analysis was somewhat superficial. Beyond merely identifying problems, for the police services to improve there is a need for the problems to be put into separate categories, such as the following (not an exhaustive list):

1. those problems that can also be found among mainstream police services and require broad, systems-wide solutions;
2. those problems that are due to the newness of Native police forces and will probably disappear with greater experience;

3. those problems that would be resolved by more equitable and more stable long-term funding;

4. those problems that would be resolved by giving Native police services more authority; and

5. those problems that come from the federal government-imposed political structures of the bands, where chief and council are given a level of power that can easily be abused.

KEY TERMS

Lonefighters Society (p. 46)

medicine bundle (p. 44)

Section 35 of the *Indian Act* (p. 43)

REVIEW QUESTIONS

1. Identify weaknesses of the Blood Tribal Police Service during the 1980s.
2. Why is the gift of Chief Crop Eared Wolf's buffalo skin an important police initiative?
3. Why do you think that the band members and band council changed their views of the Lonefighters' position regarding the Oldman Dam?
4. What are some of the weaknesses and flaws in the social and police services that contributed to the Connie and Ty Jacobs tragedy?
5. What criticisms might be made of the Cardinal Report?

chapter five

Aboriginal Policing
in Saskatchewan

LEARNING OBJECTIVES

After completing this chapter, students should be able to:

1. Identify the distortion of the image of the Mountie in the Piapot story.
2. Outline how the relations between Native and non-Native people in the 1870s and 1880s influenced the actions of Almighty Voice in 1895.
3. Discuss the positive and negative aspects of the Saskatoon Police Services work with Aboriginals.

Saskatchewan is a Cree word meaning "it flows fast," a name that refers to the Saskatchewan River. The Aboriginal people of Saskatchewan come from six different nations. There are Cree who speak two different dialects of their language, Plains Cree and Woods Cree. Related linguistically and culturally are the Saulteaux and the Métis. Coming from different languages and cultural traditions are the Siouan-speaking Dakota Sioux and Nakota or Assiniboine, as well as the Athabaskan-speaking Chipewyan.

Saskatchewan and Manitoba have the highest number of treaties in Canada. Different Saskatchewan Aboriginal groups have signed Treaties 2 (1871), 4 (1874), 6 (1876 and 1889), 8 (1899) and 10 (1906). This has relevance to Aboriginal policing, as there has been some talk of organizing police forces according to treaty number.

Aboriginals have a particularly high profile in Saskatchewan, partially because of historical events such as the second Riel Resistance (see Box 5.1) and also because of numbers. About 14 percent of the population of Saskatchewan is of Aboriginal heritage (Kerr, 2000).

Box 5.1 | **Louis Riel**

In 1670, the Hudson's Bay Company (HBC), a business run by English traders, was given by King Charles II a trade monopoly in the lands drained by the waters that flow into Hudson Bay. He also gave them the land. It amounted to most of Quebec, a good piece of Ontario, all of Manitoba and Saskatchewan, and a major part of Alberta.

In 1867, the year of Canadian Confederation, the new country began negotiating with the HBC for their land. People moving out to the West at that time included "Canada Firsters," who arrogantly declared to the Métis that the future in the West belonged to them and not the "half breeds." Tension was heightened when outsiders began surveying land that had been held by the Métis for generations. In 1869, the Métis took action. A 25-year-old college-educated man named Louis Riel emerged as their leader. They formed a provisional government and blocked the entry of the Canadian governor at the US-Canada border. The provisional government had the support of most people, but they made the unfortunate mistake of imprisoning and eventually executing an especially obnoxious White, Protestant Ontarian by the name of Thomas Scott.

In 1870, most of the proposals put forward by the provisional government were put into legal place by the Manitoba Act. The Métis had their rights to the land recognized through legal papers known as "scrip." Land speculators and government officials were not above working out scams to cheat the Métis of their scrip. The laws relating to scrip changed 11 times over 12 years. Most Métis ended up moving west into what is now Saskatchewan and Alberta.

Riel was officially exiled by the federal government, but time and again he was elected to parliament by the people of Manitoba, Métis and non-Métis alike.

In the 1880s, the Métis were back in a familiar situation of being treated as second-class citizens by the federal government. They again called upon Louis Riel, then living peacefully in Montana, to lead them in another act of political resistance. They would lose this time, thanks to the technology used against them (the new railroad, steamboats, and the precursor to machine guns) and due to Riel's reluctance to fight. He would be hanged in 1885, largely because of his authorization for executing Thomas Scott years earlier.

THE RCMP IN SASKATCHEWAN

The Royal Canadian Mounted Police (RCMP) are the provincial police in Saskatchewan. By 2000, 40 First Nation communities in the province had signed 29 tripartite agreements involving the Mounties (F Division). These agreements specify that the First Nations communities must be policed by Aboriginal members, making necessary 86 officers. In

2000, there were 92 such officers serving in F Division; as not all were placed in First Nations communities, there was a need for more. In order to meet that need, and in order to increase the 8 percent Aboriginal officer complement to the 14 percent that would match the Aboriginal population of the province, a full troop of 20 was graduated in May 2000 in Regina.

There is debate in the Aboriginal communities in Saskatchewan concerning having their own province-wide police force.

THE IMAGE OF THE MOUNTIE AND THE INDIAN IN THE PLAINS

Story Number One: The Mountie Confronts Piapot

One of the few relatively distinct images of western Canada's past is that of the "Mountie and the Indian." It flatters the Mountie, but is not complimentary to "the Indian." As Daniel Francis describes in his excellent work *The Imaginary Indian: The Images of the Indian in Canadian Culture* (Francis, 1992), an important aspect of the image is the portrayal of the Mountie as the saviour of the drunken Indian victimized by the unscrupulous American whisky trader at places such as Fort Whoop-Up, near present-day Calgary. While there is some truth to the fact that the North West Mounted Police (NWMP, formed in 1873) did act bravely in taking on the often well-armed traders, the image of the drunken and helpless Indian is an exaggeration and contributes to a negative stereotype.

Similarly negative is the often-repeated story of "the confrontation," with the Mountie facing down the "wild savage." It is part of the "always gets his man" mystique of the NWMP, and later their descendant group, the RCMP. Again, it contributes only to negative stereotyping of the Aboriginal. Further, it can be an exaggeration, even outright fiction. Such is the case with one story about the Plains Cree leader, Piapot.

Piapot (c. 1816–1908) was a Plains Cree leader who rose to prominence in the last half of the nineteenth century. In 1874, he signed Treaty 4. In that treaty, the leaders had been promised that they could choose their reserve lands. In 1879, he was one of a group of leaders who requested reserves side by side, which would allow the Cree to continue to hunt the remaining buffalo in southern Saskatchewan. The federal Indian Commissioner didn't agree with this plan. The people would be harder to control if they settled there. They might cross the paper border into the United States. Further, the railroad was going through that area, and the federal government did not want any interference with this hallmark of "progress."

Rather than negotiate with Piapot and the others, the Indian Commissioner then reneged on the treaty promise of choice of reserve and declared that Piapot and his people had to move north, near Regina. He enforced this policy by not providing the food rations that the people needed in the transition time between buffalo hunting and learning another way to obtain food. Piapot resisted, in part because some of his people died from the diet of fatty and salty bacon that could not replace the more nutritious buffalo meat, and partially because he knew that what he was being forced to do was not in the agreement. Eventually, Piapot was forced to give in, but not by military might or Mountie bravery. He believed in keeping his word. Because of that, he did not join the Riel Rebellion of 1885.

Piapot's leadership, honesty, and loyalty were not well-recorded in most of the history books produced in the next century. Instead, a fictitious story was composed by the journalist William Fraser, first printed in 1899, and was often reproduced in well-read histories of the RCMP. It became part of the "Mountie mystique" in later history books. It was about a confrontation between a brave Mountie and a Native leader, the fictional stuff of the Canadian Wild West.

Piapot and his people were camped by the CPR (Canadian Pacific Railroad) lines refusing to leave. Two Mounties (one by the name of William Wilde) were sent to defuse the situation. In Francis' rendition of the story,

> When Piapot refuses to move ... Wilde pulls out his watch and tells the Indians they have fifteen minutes to clear out. As the minutes slowly pass, Indian braves try to intimidate the Mounties by bumping their horses and firing guns into the air. Finally, when the time is up, Wilde calmly gets down from his horse, walks over to Piapot's tent and kicks down the lodge pole, collapsing the tent in a heap. He proceeds to knock over another tipi, and then another, until Piapot gets the message and shamefacedly orders his braves away. (Francis, 1992: 66–67)

It is important to make mention of the image of the "Mountie and the Indian" because both the RCMP officers and Aboriginals are aware of this image. It has contributed to an atmosphere of confrontation that has existed between the groups. Trust is hard won between the two.

Story Number Two: Almighty Voice

Kahkeesaymanetoowayo, "Voice of the Great Spirit," known in English as "Almighty Voice," has attained a place of notoriety in Canadian history. When the tragic story of this Saskatchewan-born Plains Cree was over, three police officers, two Aboriginals, and a civilian volunteer would be dead. And it was all over a dead cow.

Almighty Voice was born in 1874. He grew up on the One Arrow Reserve, named after his grandfather, who was sympathetic to Riel during the 1885 Resistance, and who, in his seventies, spent three years in jail for that sympathy. The White people knew Almighty Voice as Jean Baptiste, the name by which he was "registered" with the federal authorities. When Almighty Voice became a teenager, the NWMP were keeping a close eye on the Plains Cree, fearing another "uprising" following the Resistance of 1885. They didn't have anything negative to say about the young Cree man in those days, but that changed in 1895.

In June of that year, Almighty Voice killed and butchered a cow for food without first asking the permission of the Indian Agent. Indian Agents were non-Native federal officials who had tremendous discretionary power over Native people on reserves, controlling, among other things, the **pass system,** by which people needed a "pass" to leave the reserve for any purpose.[1]

There are various alleged reasons why Almighty Voice killed the cow (see Horwood and Butts, 1984: 209). Some have said that it was because his wife was sick and starving; others that it was to feed his brother's starving child. Regardless, by the strict letter of the law, it was a government cow on loan to the Cree for breeding purposes.

At first there were no repercussions. Nobody seemed to have noticed the missing cow until four months later, when it was brought to the attention of the authorities. The Mounties arrested Almighty Voice and took him to Duck Lake, where he was jailed. The sentence was one month. It has been suggested that a constable hinted the sentence might be changed to hanging (MacEwan, 1971: 195), a suggestion challenged by Horwood and Butts (1984: 2101). Almighty Voice would have remembered the hangings of November 17, 1885, when eight Natives, most of them Cree, were hanged at the same time. The White man's law would seem arbitrary enough to him that it wouldn't have taken much for him to suspect the worst.

Almighty Voice managed to escape, and ran 10 kilometres, crossing the cold October waters of the Saskatchewan River, and then travelling another 21 kilometres to his mother's lodge. He stayed for a day or two, gathered some supplies, and took his wife with him as he fled, a fugitive of a system of law that did not make a lot of sense to him.

The NWMP officer in charge of bringing Almighty Voice back was Sergeant Colebrook, who had initially arrested him. On October 29, 1895, one week after the jail-break, he and a Métis scout named François Dumont were tracking the fugitive when they heard a rifle shot. Riding over to investigate, they found a young woman holding the reins of a pair of horses, while her companion was picking up a prairie chicken he had just shot. It was Almighty Voice and his wife, Pale Face.

Officer Colebrook, according to MacEwan (1971: 196), was "a good and courageous officer," and with "typical Mounted Police firmness" approached the young Cree, telling him to surrender. Robin (1976: 72) claims that Colebrook spoke to Almighty Voice in English, whereas Horwood and Butts say that Colebrook used Dumont to translate his words. Almighty Voice raised his rifle and told Dumont to tell Colebrook to back off. Three times the Cree man asked the officer to leave. In MacEwan's version of the events, Colebrook "heard the call of duty above the warnings and did not pause" (1971: 196). Horwood and Butts, less inclined to put a Hollywood face on the story, stated that Coleman had no intention of turning back and telling his superiors that he had retreated "because a lone savage waved a rifle at him" (1984: 210). Pale Face was crying, and Almighty Voice started to move back toward the trees as Colebrook rode his horse toward him. The police officer had his right hand up and opened, as a gesture of peace, while his left hand was in his coat pocket, where he kept his revolver. All the while, Dumont kept pleading with Colebrook not to advance or the young man would shoot. At a distance of about eight metres, Almighty Voice shot the Mountie through the heart. Dumont fled.

Following the shooting, Almighty Voice disappeared. Rumours about where he was abounded. Some had him as far away as the United States, while others, more imaginative, had him living in a specially constructed shelter beneath his parents' house. The Cree weren't telling. For a year, the police could not find him, despite a five hundred dollar reward, big money in those days, being put up for his capture.

In May 1897, Napoleon Venne, a Métis rancher and tracker, saw three people butchering a cow near the One Arrow reserve. He recognized Almighty Voice's brother-in-law and his 14-year-old cousin and assumed the third person was Almighty Voice. He took the news to the NWMP, who had previously received information that the fugitive was in the area.

Venne and Corporal Bowridge, of the Batoche police detachment, returned to where the three Cree had been seen. As they approached, two young men came into view, one of whom bolted for the trees. As they came closer, shots rang out, and Venne was hit in the shoulder. They retreated and went for reinforcements.

The next day, a large group of police officers and civilians surrounded the three Cree and cordoned them off in a five-acre stand of trees. Almighty Voice's family (including his mother, Spotted Calf) and friends came and watched the unfolding events, despite being warned not to by the police.

Both sides demonstrated courage. Sergeant C.C. Raven had penetrated 50 metres into the underbrush when he was shot twice, being hit in the thigh and the groin. He returned fire and shouted for Inspector Jack Allan, who rode forward and was shot in the arm by Almighty Voice. When the Mountie fell from his horse, the Cree man approached him and demanded his gun belt. Allan refused. Before Almighty Voice could shoot Allan again, the police drove him back with gunfire, picking up the two officers. The police threatened to burn them out, but this was an empty threat. The Cree knew the wood was too green to burn. However, they had no food, water or horses, and had limited ammunition. The sensible thing for the officers to do would have been to wait them out, but Corporal C.S. Hockin, now in charge, decided to rush them, probably fearing an escape during the night. Hockin was shot leading a charge. A constable, J.R. Kerr, and Ernest Grundy, the postmaster from Duck Lake, were killed. Hockin died hours later. On the other side, it is believed that Tupean, Almighty Voice's brother-in-law, was also killed (Horwood and Butts, 1984: 215) at this time, shot in the head. It was discovered later that the fugitives had used a knife to dig out a rifle pit one and one-half by two and one-half metres. It is thought that the three men had used this cover to allow the attackers to come very close, where they could be shot at with considerable accuracy (Robin, 1976: 81).

Reinforcements arrived, including two dozen Mounties, amounting to about one hundred heavily armed men, equipped with seven- and nine-pound cannons. The two remaining Cree had little chance of surviving. On May 30, the cannon bombardment began. Spotted Calf chanted a death song for her son.

At dawn, May 31, the barrage that Assistant Commissioner McIllree would call "most excellent practice" (Horwood and Butts, 1984: 216 and Robin, 1976: 90) continued, with only an occasional shot in response. It lasted for four hours. When all was silent in the woods, the police advanced. Almighty Voice and his cousin were lying together in the rifle pit, killed by shrapnel wounds. A piece of Almighty Voice's skull, removed by cannon fire, is preserved in a glass case in a museum in Prince Albert (Horwood and Butts, 1984: 217).

SASKATOON POLICE STORIES

Box 5.2	Quotable Quotations: Saskatoon Aboriginal Policing

Mayor Jim Maddin (a former police officer):

> You have a segment of the population afraid of the police ... and a segment of the police afraid of the population.

Craig Neurf (Saskatoon Police Service's Aboriginal Liaison Officer):

> An Aboriginal kid in Saskatoon today stands a better chance of ending up in the criminal justice system than finishing high school.

Ernie Louttit (Cree officer, Saskatoon Police Service):

> You hear native groups say, "We need this or we need that" ... Yeah, we need them to come down here and do something. We, as natives need strong leadership, we need elected leadership, we need to take care of our own problems—stop our own people from drinking and stop our own people from hurting each other.

SOURCE: Stackhouse, 2001: F2-F4.

Saskatoon Policing Profile

The Native population of Saskatoon has grown incredibly over the last 50 years, from an official figure (always a conservative number) of 48 in 1951, to 1070 in 1971,[2] and a combined total (single origin and multiple origin) of 22 165 in the 1991 census (Frideres, 2001: 148). The census of 1996 listed 7.9 percent of Saskatoon residents as Native, the greatest proportion of any city in Canada (Regina being second with 7.1 percent). It is estimated that approximately 15 percent of Saskatoon's more than 200 000 people, or more than 30 000 people, are Native.

This Native population is overrepresented in two crucial and interrelated areas: poverty and crime (see Box 5.2). The 1996 census identified 64.9 percent of Saskatoon Aboriginals as being poor, as compared with 19.2 percent of non-Aboriginals in that city, meaning that 22.5 percent of Saskatoon's poor are Aboriginal. During the period 1980–1989, 19.9 homicides per 100 000 population in Saskatoon were suspected to have been committed by Aboriginals, 1.1 per 100 000 by non-Aboriginals. The victims of homicide had a similar profile, with 12.9 and 1.0 the Aboriginal and non-Aboriginal rates, respectively.

However, Natives have been underrepresented in the police force. In 1992, the Saskatchewan Indian Justice Review Committee reported that despite the fact that there was a stated intent of commitment to increase the complement of Aboriginal staff, less than 1 percent of police officers in Saskatoon were Aboriginal (compared with likewise disproportionately low figures of 5 percent in Prince Albert and 2 percent in Regina) (Saskatchewan Indian Justice Review Committee 1992, cited in Satzewich and Wotherspoon, 1993: 202). The percentage has increased since then—18 of the 94 constables hired since 1996 are Native (Stackhouse, 2001: F4), but the overall population (34 out of 328 staff) is still lower than the Native percentage of the Saskatoon population (34 out of 328 staff), especially at the level of senior staff. To be fair, it is difficult to get Native staff, in part because of the "enemy" image, in part because potential recruits would be financially better off if they worked for the RCMP or for the city police in Calgary or Edmonton[3].

Starlight Tours in Saskatoon

In 1997, Brian Trainor, a veteran police officer, wrote a column entitled "Tales from the Blue Lagoon" for the weekly newspaper the *Saskatoon Sun* that told a story about one night on the beat for two "fictional" officers, "Hawk" and "Gumby." In the story, they pick up a loud, abusive drunk and take him on what is known as a "**starlight tour**," driving him outside of the city. The column ended as follows:

> Sensing that this wasn't the way home, the drunk began to demand he be taken to the highest power in the land. A few quick turns and the car comes to an abrupt stop in front of the Queen Elizabeth II Power Station. Climbing out and opening the rear door, he yelled for the man to get out, advising him that this was the place he had asked to go to. Quickly gathering his wits, the drunk tumbled out of the car and into the thickets along the riverbank, disappearing from view. One less guest for breakfast. (Kossick, 2000)

Something similar happened to Darrell Night. From the night of January 27 to early morning on January 28, 2000, 33-year-old Darrell Night got drunk. He was an unemployed bricklayer with a criminal record, a big, sturdy man at six feet, three inches and

240 pounds. During his binge, he saw two officers in a police car and, according to the officers, lunged at their vehicle, flashed an obscene gesture at them, swore, and hit their car with his free hand. They arrested him for causing a disturbance, handcuffed him, and put him in the vehicle. Then they started driving him out toward the country rather than heading for the police station. Night feared for his life and begged to be released. Finally, the officers took him to the Queen Elizabeth II Power Station south of the city. According to later officer testimony, they wanted him to take the long walk into town to sober up and calm down. But he was wearing no coat, just a denim jacket, and the temperature was about twenty-two degrees below zero Celsius. After they left him, Night realized he had to act quickly. He went to the power station and got a night watchman to call him a cab. That may have saved his life.

Night did not tell his story to anyone in legal authority for a while. He was Cree, and the officers were White. Who would be more likely to be believed? Hearing other stories finally made him tell his.

The day after Night's ordeal, Rodney Naistus was celebrating a reunion with his brother and cousin at a local bar. He was a 25-year-old Cree man with a muscular build, newly released from prison. Not much is known about the course of events that night. It is not clear when he became separated from his relatives. His body was found later in the Holiday Park industrial area, a short distance away from the power plant where Darrell Night had had the close call the night before.

The day after Naistus' ordeal, Lawrence Kim Wegner, a popular 30-year-old Saskatchewan Indian Federated College Cree student studying social work, went on a drug binge with his new roommates. He left his shared apartment between 8:00 and 10:00 p.m. after shooting up a mixture of morphine and synthetic cocaine. The young man who left with him had collapsed within an hour of leaving Wegner's place and was taken by his family to a hospital. Some time between eleven o'clock and midnight, Wegner showed up banging on the door of the apartment of some distant relatives of his, yelling "Pizza, pizza." One of the relatives called the police, to be informed that someone else had called about him earlier.

A passerby, an army veteran, says that he was out driving near midnight that night and saw two police officers shoving a man matching Wegner's description into the back of their cruiser. Wegner's body wasn't discovered until February 3, 2000, in a wheat-stubble field by the power plant. February 4, when the discovery became public news, Darrell Night built up his courage and went to the Saskatoon police station to make a complaint.

The Investigation

The Saskatoon Police Service began investigating the matter after Darrell Night's complaint. The next week, two veteran officers involved in Darrell Night's "starlight tour" were suspended with pay. Police Chief Dave Scott stated that he suspended them in order to maintain public trust and the trust of the Aboriginal community but that he didn't feel that the officers were connected with the deaths of Naistus and Wegner. Scott was quoted as saying:

> Is this widespread? Are there reasons for me, as chief, to be concerned about the activities of our police officers? At this time I have no indication of that ... I would ask first that you have confidence in me as the chief of police and the leader of this police service, to ensure that a complete investigation will be done properly and I can assure you it will be. (Zakreski, 2000)

On February 16, the RCMP took over the investigation with a special task force of 16 RCMP officers (not including support staff), making it the largest investigative unit it had ever deployed in Saskatchewan.

By March 10, the Saskatoon Police Commission suspended without pay the officers who admitted to dropping off Night. It was stated that this was necessary in order to restore public confidence in the Saskatoon Police Service. The Saskatoon Police Association protested this. In the words of its president, Al Stickney, "They're on their own. These are two guys with families and no paycheque, who have not been convicted of any wrongdoing" (Perreaux, 2000).

About a month after their suspension without pay, the two officers were charged with "unlawful confinement and assault." They would receive back pay until the date of the charge.

The investigation added three more cases to the list. It came to include Neil Stonechild, who was found dead from exposure in Saskatoon's north industrial area in 1990. It had been twenty-eight degrees below zero Celsius the night before. Neil was 17 years old and on the run from a young offenders home with a warrant out for his arrest. A witness had seen him last in police custody, and heard him claim that he felt that the police were going to kill him. The two other cases were those of Lloyd Joseph Dustyhorn, found dead outside an apartment building on January 19, 2000, and D'arcy Dean Ironchild, found dead in his bed in February that same year.

In an official press release dated July 3, 2001, Acting Police Chief Wiks said,

> In light of a recent article in the *Star Phoenix,* that alleges wrongdoing and involvement of members of the Saskatoon Police Service in the death of Rodney Naistus, I find it necessary to respond.
>
> I have recently been in contact with the RCMP in Regina. I received assurances from them, that not only is there no basis for any criminal charges, there is absolutely no indication or evidence of any involvement by members of our Police Service or anyone else in relation to this death.
>
> I am confident that the inquest ordered by the Justice Ministry will confirm this with the disclosure of all the facts of the investigation. (Wiks, 2001)

On September 20, 2001, the two officers who took Darrell Night on his starlight tour were acquitted of assault but were convicted of unlawful confinement. Hours later, they were fired by the Saskatoon Police Service. Jim Mathews, interim police chief, stated in a news conference that, "The nature of their actions caused harm and damaged the reputation of the Saskatoon Police Service, locally, provincially and nationally and has done a disservice to all police officers" (*Globe and Mail,* September 21, 2001: A17).

On October 31, 2001, it was announced that the two officers had asked for a sentencing circle. In the words of their lawyer, "This community has a rift in it. There is a rift between the white community and the Aboriginal community ... It is certainly our hope that a sentencing circle may help to heal that rift by allowing input from the Aboriginal community and the white community" (*Toronto Star,* October 31, 2001: A3).

John Stackhouse, in a recent (2001) *Globe and Mail* article, described the request as "so bizarre that it prompted laughter in the courtroom and anger on the part of natives, who felt they were being mocked" (Stackhouse, 2001: F2). The request was denied.

The Other Side of the Saskatoon Police Service

In 1994, the Saskatoon Police Service (SPS) created the Aboriginal Liaison Officer position. On the official Web site of the SPS, it is stated that "the position is meant to bridge relations between the police service and the Aboriginal community" (www.city.saskatoon.sk.ca/ police/pprograms/liaisons/index.asp#peace, consulted October 2001). Through this office, the SPS works with the Saskatoon Tribal Council, the Métis Nation of Saskatchewan, and the Federation of Saskatchewan Indian Nations. In 1995, the SPS won the National Ivan Ahenakew Award for efforts in employing Aboriginal officers and in the development of cultural programs.

A number of good programs have been developed to attempt to construct bridges linking the two groups. There is an Annual Native Recognition Night, in which a $500 scholarship is awarded to an Aboriginal student who has completed grade 12 in Saskatoon and is attending a post-secondary education program. There is a nine-week Aboriginal Justice and Criminology Program Practicum administered by the Department of Sociology's Aboriginal Justice and Criminology Program University at the University of Saskatchewan. The practicum "places students on a police shift with officers rotating through various units. The students obtain first-hand knowledge of the Police Service and police duties. Upon completion we request a constructive critique of their experience."

Perhaps the most intensive and successful aspects of SPS and Aboriginal community bridging is done through the Peacekeeper programs, which put Aboriginal at-risk youth (many of them sent from the Saskatoon Tribal Council's "Youth Circles" diversion program) and officers together. According to the SPS website,

> The programs are an extension of the circle process and allow youth to better understand negative behavior, the law and to develop positive relationships with police. These programs also serve a purpose for the Saskatoon Police Service, as outlined in the mandate of the Aboriginal Liaison position, to break down barriers that not only exist on the Aboriginal side, but on the police service side. (www.city.saskatoon.sk.ca/police/pprograms/liaisons/index.asp#peace)

The programs incorporate a wide variety of expected activities (e.g., attending boxing matches, hockey and football games, and a basketball tournament) and also innovative activities. Included in the latter group is Project Firewood/Rocks. In this program, Aboriginal youth and SPS officers travel to northern Saskatchewan to load a truck trailer with firewood and rocks to be taken to Saskatoon to the Elders. The Elders will use the wood and rocks in sweat lodge ceremonies (see Box 5.3), some of which will involve both the youth and officers as participants.

Other programs include summer canoe trips with 20 adults and 20 youth. Incorporated into these trips are Native cultural teachings and ceremonies, as well as the development/enhancement of wilderness and survival skills. Similar activities are the 2-day, 40-kilometre Grey Owl hike in Prince Albert National Park and a Cultural Awareness Winter Camp including 60 youths, officers, and Elders and members of the Saskatoon Tribal Council. Activities include Elders holding talking circles, sweat lodges, and educational sessions.

In September 2001, the SPS placed a full-time officer in Saskatoon's only Aboriginal high school.

Box 5.3	The Sweat Lodge

The following is taken from a generalized description of the **sweat lodge** as it used by the Ojibwa or Anishinabe peoples in the context of a vision quest. It should be pointed out that sweat lodges differ both within the traditions of the Ojibwa peoples and between them and other Aboriginal peoples. The purpose of this piece is just to give the reader a little familiarity with the sweat lodge:

> The Sweat Lodge is constructed of 16 overlapping willow poles. It is shaped to resemble the sky world above that covers the earth like a dome. The entrance must face the east as this is where all birth takes place, starting with sunrise. During the course of the day, the sun moves into the western sky, sinking below the horizon only to be reborn again the next day. All life works in this cyclical manner.
>
> A pit is dug inside the centre of the lodge where the grandfathers are received and where they meet mother earth. The grandfathers are stones, the oldest elements in creation. As such, they hold the mysteries of the ages. Before the grandfathers are brought into the lodge, they are first placed at the bottom of a sacred fire in front of the lodge. Here they are heated until they become white hot. How long the Vision Quest seeker plans to sweat will determine how many stones will be called upon to guide him in the Sweat Lodge. Between the Sweat Lodge and the sacred fire is a pathway of cedar. Once this path is made it may never be crossed.
>
> When the Sweat Lodge and sacred fire are prepared, the Elder calls the participants to the fire. They then throw sacred tobacco into the fire and pray. This is how the people give thanks to the creator. The Elder then tells how the Sweat Lodge came to be, a story which describes how a little boy was sent to the seven grandfather spirits in the star world during a time of great sickness and was given the gift of the Sweat Lodge to bring back to his people for healing. A water drum is placed inside the Sweat Lodge close to the entrance. This drum is called the Little Boy Drum in remembrance of the little boy who brought back the teachings. The participants greet the drum as they enter. It has seven stones that surround the top, representing the seven grandfathers who first gave the little boy the teaching. When the Sweat Lodge is occupied, the Elder sings the ceremonial songs that have been handed down from generation to generations.
>
> The grandfathers are then brought in to the lodge and placed in the pit. The Elder throws water onto the grandfathers, and the steam makes the lodge quite hot (Rice and Steckley, 1997: 226).

Regina Police Service Officer Greg McNabb

In 1999, Regina Police Service Constable Greg McNabb was 29 years old (Wood, Demont, and Geddes, 1999). He came from a mixed Aboriginal heritage. His father was Dakota Sioux and his mother Métis. His father died when he was two years old. When his mother remarried, he moved out of a Native community and into a White community. Although he was not raised in Native traditions, his uncle, a respected elder, was able to teach him as a young man about the sweat lodge and other important traditions. His becoming a police officer is due in part to the influence of his Cree stepfather, who was a special constable with the

RCMP. When he was 14 years old, his stepfather put McNabb to work washing police cruisers, and generally provided a role model showing that an Aboriginal could be an officer.

When he was 19 years old, Officer McNabb entered the RCMP training academy in Regina. After homesickness led him away from a posting in Alberta, he joined the Regina Police Service in 1993, one of the 29 Native people in the 319-officer-strong Regina Police Service, a proportion close to the Aboriginal population of the city and a significant increase from their 2 percent of the force in 1991. He was assigned the tough, north central area of town, an area that in some ways amounts to being a Native ghetto. Regina itself can be a tough posting, at 14 785 crimes for every 100 000 people (it has a population of a little over 180 000), the highest crime rate in the country (Wood, Demont, and Geddes, 1999).

The Aboriginal population of Greg McNabb's beat both strengthen and challenge him. The youngest and oldest do the former. In his words, "It's nice to sit down and talk with other native people in the area once in a while, especially the older people—they know the score. And younger children are always friendly" (Wood, Demont, and Geddes, 1999). Aboriginal offenders offer a special challenge: "I hear 'traitor' and I get, 'Why are you doing this to your own people?' ... But I consider who is saying it: someone who is resorting to name-calling instead of dealing with a problem" (Wood, Demont, and Geddes, 1999).

NOTES

1. The pass system was an influence on the development of South African apartheid.
2. This growth in 1971 was a major reason why an important sociological study of Natives in Saskatoon was undertaken by Edgar J. Dosman (*Indians: The Urban Dilemma*, 1972).
3. The Calgary Police Service recently toured northern Saskatchewan reserves looking to recruit Aboriginals. They offered pay that was 10 percent higher than that offered by the Saskatoon Police Service (Stackhouse, 2001: F4).

KEY TERMS

pass system (p. 61)   starlight tours (p. 64)   sweat lodge (p. 68)

REVIEW QUESTIONS

1. Why might the non-Native and Native view of the RCMP be different?
2. How might the relations between Native and non-Native people in the 1870s and 1880s have influenced the actions of Almighty Voice in 1895?
3. How were the Saskatoon police officers able to justify their "starlight tours"? Why do you think non-Native people were not given the same treatment by the Saskatoon officers?
4. In what ways has the Saskatoon Police Service acted to make positive connections with the Native community?
5. What difficulties face Aboriginal officers who police urban Aboriginals?

chapter six

Aboriginal Policing in Manitoba

LEARNING OBJECTIVES

After completing this chapter, students should be able to:

1. Describe the traditional form of policing in the Métis bison hunt.
2. Assess the early weaknesses of the Dakota Ojibway Police Service.
3. Identify the role racism played in the initial police investigation of the Helen Betty Osborne case.
4. Discuss how stereotyping of Native people affected the J.J. Harper and 911 cases.

Native peoples in Manitoba constitute the Métis, the Dakota, and the Saulteaux (a branch of the Ojibwa) in the south, and the Cree and Chipewyan in the north.

TRADITIONAL POLICING: THE MÉTIS

The First Nations traditionally had little need for police forces as we know them now. However, as is the case in all societies, there were traditional, socially recognized means of maintaining peace within the group. Generally speaking, when the population of Native groups got larger, there arose a greater need for a more concerted effort at maintaining peace. Among the Plains nations, such as the Blackfoot, the warrior societies (see the Lonefighter Society in the chapter on Alberta) were responsible for maintaining the peace at the large summer gatherings. Perhaps the best-documented example of what may be called Native policing comes from the Métis summer bison hunts in Manitoba.

The Métis were formed as a people during the eighteenth century. During that period, the fur trade was extending west into the Prairies. The move west was personified by the French voyageurs who manned the big canoes and who married Plains Cree women. Such marriages were practical for both cultures, and their children learned from each people. The Métis language, Michif, was part French (mostly nouns) and part Cree (mostly verbs).

From the Native culture came techniques for engaging in the buffalo hunt and preparing pemmican[1] from buffalo meat, which became the staple food for those involved in the fur trade. European culture gave the Métis farming techniques, the Catholic Church, and the big ox-drawn carts with which they carried large loads of pemmican from the hunt to their homes.

By the beginning of the nineteenth century, there were several thousand Métis, most of them around the southern area of present-day Manitoba. The Métis bison hunt was firmly established by 1820. It provided the Métis with an impressive organizational structure and was important in shaping them as a formidable military and political force. At the time, there was no comparable military or commercial activity in western Canada. The hunt required the organization and movement of hundreds of men, women, and children, as well as their horses, oxen, and carts, often hundreds of kilometres. A successful hunt might take several days or even weeks. In 1840, one hunt involved 1630 people and 1240 oxen carts. The community travelled 250 miles in 19 days before seeing any bison. When they did and completed their hunt, the Métis had over one million pounds of meat to take home and be distributed among the Métis themselves, fur traders, and White colonists. This particular hunt began in early June and did not finish until August 17, 1840 (Purich, 1988: 29–31).

Foster (1986: 388–392) and Purich (1988: 29–32) provide good descriptions of these bison hunts. In the Red River area, people would leave their river lots in the late spring and travel south to Pembina, near the American border, for a rendezvous with other Métis. Only the sick, the very old, and the disabled would remain behind. Once at their destination, the hunters met in a general assembly to select officers and to establish the basic rules of the hunt. French military terms were used for the different positions. Ten "capitaines" would be appointed. These, in turn, would choose ten "soldats." The foremost of the "capitaines" was the hunt leader, also referred to as "le President." Added to these were ten guides, usually hunters past their prime.

Rules reflected the importance of ensuring the well-being of the group. It must be remembered that the purpose of the hunt was to gather meat for the entire community and to supply food (in the form of pemmican) for the fur trade. The rights of the individual had to be curtailed somewhat to ensure the success of all involved.

At one historic meeting, the following basic rules and reprimands were established (Purich, 1988: 30). No hunting was allowed on Sundays. Nobody was allowed to range ahead, lag behind, or break off from the group. No firing of guns was allowed until the order was given. Each captain and his soldiers would establish night patrols to guard the camp. There was a sliding scale of punishments for violating these rules. The first violation resulted in the offender's saddle and bridle being cut up. A second offence resulted in his coat being cut up. A third resulted in a public flogging. Theft was punished by public humiliation. The thief was put in the middle of the camp and publicly called a thief three times.

Evidence of the essentially egalitarian nature of Métis social structure can be seen in the fact that during the buffalo hunt, each captain and guide commanded for one day. Thus, over a 10-day hunt all of the guides and captains would have had their turn at command. During the actual hunt, the soldiers and even the captain were under the command of the guides. At night, however, the carts were placed in a circle, the tents were set up, and the captains were in charge (Purich, 1988: 30).

The hunt was orderly. Each morning, a hunt flag was raised above a guide's cart, indicating that the cart's owner was in charge for the day. Once camp was struck, carts loaded, and the livestock put under control, the hunt started. The camp headed out, two or more carts abreast in the direction determined by the guide for the day. The day's captain organized his soldiers so that they were ahead, to the side, and to the rear of the line of carts. Throughout much of the nineteenth century, the Métis were at war with the Dakota Sioux, so the soldiers were on the alert not only for bison but also for enemies (Foster, 1986: 389 and Purich, 1988: 31).

Soldiers always rode together in twos. The Métis had a recognized code for indicating the presence of bison or enemies. By riding away from or toward each other at a gallop, the two men could signal to the hunt group whether bison or Dakota had been spotted (Foster, 1986: 389). When one or the other was spotted, authority shifted from the guide and captain of the day to the hunt leader. If there were enemies with which to contend, the carts were circled and joined with interlocking shafts to corral the livestock and prepare for battle. If the presence of bison had been signaled, the hunt began.

The hunt was a mixture of incredible skill and nerve on the part of both the mounted hunters and their horses, and a significant amount of danger. Given the inherent dangers of "running the buffalo," it was imperative that strict control be maintained, with captains, soldiers, and guides all performing the duties dictated by Métis tradition. It was a policing system that worked well.

THE DAKOTA OJIBWAY POLICE SERVICE

While the Royal Canadian Mounted Police (RCMP) are responsible for the bulk of Native policing in the province, the Dakota Ojibway Police Service (DOPS) provides policing services for four (originally eight) southern Manitoba communities. It is one of the oldest First Nations policing services in Canada, originally established in 1977.

The DOPS has its headquarters in Brandon. Officers are sworn peace officers within the province of Manitoba and have jurisdiction throughout that province. There are twelve members employed at one of the four detachments as well as three administrative officers located in Brandon. In addition, each detachment employs a clerk/typist. The Brandon headquarters has three support staff who maintain administrative, investigative, and CPIC files. Further, the DOPS employs guards, matrons, and maintenance personnel in each of the communities for which it provides policing services.

Each detachment of the DOPS is under the supervision of a corporal, who has complete control of all operations of the detachment. The corporal is required to meet with the chief and council of the community, as well as with the local police committee, to ascertain local policing needs and concerns. Members have either successfully completed the RCMP recruit training program or a recruit training program from a major city, such as Winnipeg or Calgary. Additional, in-service training is provided by the Canadian Police

College in Ottawa, the Brandon Police Service, the RCMP, and the First Nations Chiefs of Police Association.

The goals and objectives of the DOPS demonstrate a commitment to making the policing service one that not only achieves the goals of "regular" policing services, but also meets the unique needs of Aboriginal policing. These goals and objectives include:

1. To reduce crime and introduce crime prevention, proactive policing, high visibility, and community involvement.
2. To maintain the community-based structure originally initiated upon the department's incorporation in 1977.
3. To attract and retain suitable First Nations people as police officers in order to provide policing services to the DOTC [Dakota-Ojibwa Tribal Council] communities.
4. To enhance and improve the quality of life within the community by providing a police service of credibility and accountability to all community members.
5. To reduce the number and costs to the taxpayers of correction services and prison terms of First Nations people.
6. To ensure the criminal justice system addresses the concerns and needs of the First Nations communities.

(DOPS Web site, www.dops.org)

Given its history as one of the initial First Nations police services in Canada, it is not surprising that the DOPS has been at the forefront of policing initiatives. Members below the rank of Deputy Chief, for example, belong to the Manitoba First Nations Police Association (MFNPA), which they formed in 1993. This was a pioneering move in Canada for First Nations police services. It allows for collective bargaining between members of DOPS management and members of the MFNPA.

Similarly, Frank McKay, a Chief of Police for DOPS, was a founding member of the First Nations Chiefs of Police Association (FNCPA), established in 1992. The primary objective of the FNCPA is for stand-alone First Nations police services to cooperate on different projects, develop training methods, and share information.

The DOPS is given direction by the Dakota Ojibway Police Service Commission (DOPSPC), which consists of one member from each of the local police committees. These committees are established in each community served by the DOPS and consist of a chairperson and three or more representatives chosen by the community. The emphasis is on local policing and, to that end, the local police committee identifies local policing concerns and needs, develops community-based strategies to meet them, and maintains liaisons with the local DOPS corporal. (See Box 6.1 for a discussion of a community-based approach to a serious problem in a Saulteaux community.)

The DOPSPC has been evaluated twice, in 1980 and in 1988. The first evaluation was quite critical. Among the criticisms of the commission were: (1) failure to clarify its established policy objectives through an operational definition; (2) excessive involvement in operational matters beyond the commission's mandate; (3) undermining the authority of the chief of police by ignoring and reversing his recommendations and decisions; and (4) inadequate recognition by First Nations members of the commission of the distinctions between their roles as chiefs and their roles as commission members (see Stenning, 1996: 148). The second evaluation was somewhat more positive, noting that replacing the band chiefs on the commission with councillors had been a step toward depoliticizing the DOPSPC.

Box 6.1	The Hollow Water Community Holistic Circle Healing Program

Hollow Water First Nation is a Saulteaux community of about 600, situated on the east side of Lake Winnipeg, some 190 kilometres north of Winnipeg. What they developed in their community, the Community Holistic Circle Healing (CHCH), has become a useful model for other Native communities interested in developing sentencing circles.

The birth of CHCH goes back to 1984, when a group of people in the community involved in providing health and social services got together to discuss how they could bring about a more positive future for the youth of the community. They soon focused on ending the sexual abuse that had a negative impact on most of the people in their community, young and old. They developed a circle composed of a team of people, mostly women, involved in child protection, community health, nursing, policing, and spirituality, so that their approach would be holistic, not divided into separate aspects of the self.

The team devised a 13-step program promoting a kind of healing justice for sexual-abuse "victimizers." The first two steps are especially important. The first is Disclosure, where the offence is admitted by the victimizer. For the team to work to support them, the victimizer must enter a plea of guilty, rather than taking the case to court, and must express a willingness to accept full responsibility for what he or she has done. Rupert Ross noted in his brief 1993 study of CHCH that virtually all those accused of sexual abuse had requested the team's support in this matter, so that trials were rare.

The second step is the Healing Contract, designed by people who had been affected by the offence. These people have to make their own commitment to the healing process, both that of the victimizer and themselves. This contract is meant to last for more than two years. Special attention is placed on the feelings and thoughts of the victim(s), the non-offending spouse, and the families of both victim(s) and victimizer. The team puts together a Pre-Sentence Report that assesses the victimizer's chances of rehabilitation and what will be required to effect that rehabilitation. An action plan is put together based on this report and on the Healing Contract. Upon completion of the Healing Contract, a Cleansing Ceremony is held to "mark a new beginning for all involved" and to "honour the victimizer for completing the healing contract/process" (Ross, 1993).

A 1993 position paper provides some interesting insight into how the attitudes of those working for the CHCH have changed concerning the need for incarceration of individuals whose cases might be considered "too serious" for the CHCH process:

> In our initial efforts to break the vicious cycle of abuse that was occurring in our community, we took the position that we needed to promote the use of incarceration in cases which were defined as "too serious." After some time, however, we came to the conclusion that this position was adding significantly to the difficulty of what was already complex casework. (Cited in Ross, 1993)

They have come to believe that

> Removal of the victimizer from those who must, and are best able to, hold him/her accountable, and to offer him/her support, adds complexity to already existing dynamics of denial, guilt and shame. The healing process of all parties is therefore at best delayed, and most often actually deterred. (Ross, 1993)

THE HELEN BETTY OSBORNE CASE

Beginning in the 1970s, a number of cases involving Aboriginal people focused attention on police-Aboriginal relations in Manitoba. The first of these was the Helen Betty Osborne case, which attracted attention because of the senseless brutality involved, the 16-year delay in bringing about the conviction, and the underlying racism that emerged from the subsequent public inquiry.

Helen Betty Osborne was a Cree woman from Norway House, Manitoba. The oldest of 12 children born to Justine and Joe Osborne, she was 19 years old at the time of her death in 1971. She had moved to The Pas to attend high school. The Pas (from the Cree word "W'passkwayaw," which translates as "like a wooden narrows") has been home to First Nations people for over 5000 years. Non-Native people slowly began moving into the area after a fort was built there in 1749.

The Aboriginal Justice Inquiry (AJI) determined that The Pas in 1971 was essentially composed of two separate communities—Native and non-Native—that rarely interacted in any meaningful, positive way. The White community excluded the Natives from their midst, yet their businesses depended on the more than 2000 members of the Native community as customers. Invisible but effective lines were drawn in public places. Each group sat on its own side of the movie theatre. In at least one of the local bars, Native people were only allowed in certain areas. In the high school cafeteria, the two groups ate apart from each other.

Violence, while not common, was not unknown. White men often chased after and assaulted Native men. Gang fights between the two communities took place. The AJI referred to the "northern, brawling, almost frontier-like atmosphere that prevailed in The Pas at the time" (Aboriginal Justice Inquiry Web site, www.ajic.mb.ca, consulted July 26, 2001).

The RCMP, responsible for policing both the reserve and the town, were more part of the non-Native community than they were of the Native community. They socialized with non-Native people but would only go to the reserve on police business. They would randomly stop Native youths for little or no apparent reason, but did not apply the same practice to White youths.

On the night of Friday, November 12, 1971, Betty Osborne had been out with a number of different friends. While she had drunk some beer, it was clear from her actions that her judgment and behaviour were scarcely affected by the alcohol. A long-time friend, Rebecca Ross, saw Osborne walking away from a dance hall at 2:15 a.m., November 13. That was the last time any friend or family member would see her alive.

That same night, four young men were "cruising" for Native women. The stereotype was that First Nations women were readily available for "partying" and sex. In the view of the AJI, the RCMP were well aware that young White men "cruised" but ignored it. They did nothing to prevent it or to caution Native families, especially women, of the dangers the practice presented.

The four young White men were 18-year-old Lee Colgan, 23-year-old James Houghton, 25-year-old Norman Manger, and 18-year-old Dwayne Johnston. Colgan was a student who lived with his parents and worked part-time. Houghton, too, lived with his parents, across the street from Colgan. Manger had had a troubled life. His mother, who was Native, had died when he was two years old, and he never saw much of his father while he was growing up. He had been unemployed for a year, and was drinking heavily. By his own admission, he was "a bum" (www.ajic.mb.ca).

Dwayne Johnston was the hardest case of the four young men. He was a high school dropout who worked for the Canadian National Railway. Because his parents had separated, he boarded with a local family. Johnston was a member of a local motorcycle gang that had had run-ins with the law. He was also a racist. He hated Native people so much that his friend Colgan stated that he had "never seen anybody hate Native people so much in my life" (www.ajic.mb.ca). Considering where they both lived, that was saying a lot.

After they had drunk some beer and some stolen wine, the four young men, driving in Colgan's father's car, spotted a single Native woman walking along Third Avenue. Houghton pulled alongside Ms. Osborne and tried to persuade her to "party" with them. She was not interested, so Johnston got out of the car and pushed her in. Houghton then drove 24 kilometres to his parents' cabin. Crammed in the car between Johnston and Colgan, Ms. Osborne was physically and sexually assaulted as the men ripped her blouse and grabbed at her breasts. When they reached the cabin, she was hauled from the car and beaten by Johnston while the others drank and watched. At one point, Colgan assisted Johnston while he beat her.

Fearful that her anguished cries might attract attention, the men forced Osborne back into the car and drove her to a pump house in the vicinity of the Guy Hill Residential School. Colgan later testified that Johnston alone hauled Ms. Osborne from the car and started beating her again. The others remained in the car, drinking. According to Colgan, they could hear banging against the side and rear of the car. This persisted for five to ten minutes. Houghton at this point got out of the car. With the help of the car's dome light, Colgan could see that Ms. Osborne did not have many clothes on. In fact, she may have been wearing only her winter boots. Johnston returned to the car, retrieving a screwdriver from under the front seat, while Houghton stayed outside with the young Cree woman. Colgan then climbed from the back seat to the front, turned the car around and called for the others. Somebody replied, "Just a minute," and soon after, Johnston and Houghton returned to the vehicle. One of them said, "She's dead." They headed back to town, wiping off the screwdriver and throwing it away as they drove. Colgan washed blood off the back of the car the next day, and, while doing so, noticed a small stain on the back seat. The four agreed not to speak about the murder.

Ms. Osborne's body was found the next day, 23 metres into the bush adjacent to the pump house at Clear Lake. Evidence indicated that she had first lain to the west of a mound of earth 12 metres from the edge of the bush and had then been dragged into the bush where the body was found. Her clothing, with the exception of her boots, had been removed and then hidden over 30 metres away, below some rocks. Her boots had been removed at some time and then put on again.

She had been viciously beaten and stabbed, apparently with a screwdriver, more than 50 times. Her face had been smashed beyond recognition, leading the AJI to conclude that whoever did it acted during "the venting of some unimaginable fury or with the intent of making her identification impossible" (www.ajic.mb.ca). The details of the autopsy indicated that her skull, cheekbones, and palate had been broken, her lungs and one kidney damaged, and her body extensively bruised. This was in addition to "well over" 50 stab wounds. It was impossible to determine exactly at what time during her beating and stabbing she died. She had not been raped.

Thirty-one people, including residents of the reserve and the man with whom Osborne was lodging in The Pas, tried and failed to identify the body. It was only after fingerprints had been taken from one of her school books and matched with those of the body that a definite identification was made.

Initially, the RCMP concentrated their investigation on friends and acquaintances of Ms. Osborne. Among those interviewed were her boyfriend, Cornelius Bighetty, and her close friend, Annaliese Dumas, both of whom "were treated as actual suspects." The AJI was critical of the way the police handled this first part of the investigation, noting that much of it involved "conscious racism." In their words, "The manner in which the police pursued their initial investigation by rounding up and questioning only Aboriginal students was motivated, at least in part, by racism." Furthermore, the police did not obtain the consent of the parents of the Aboriginal students questioned, nor did they advise them after questioning had taken place. "This was discriminatory in light of the courtesies shown to the families of Colgan and Houghton," two of the actual perpetrators. Remarkably, Bighetty told the AJI that "he had no complaint about the way he was treated by the police." However, he did say that "he would not allow the police to treat his own children the way he was by the RCMP in 1971" (www.ajic.mb.ca).

In May 1972, the police received an anonymous letter, implicating Colgan, Houghton, and Manger. It was later determined that the letter had been sent by Catherine Dick, who had been told of the murder by Colgan shortly after it happened. The police seized the car and searched it, revealing traces of hair and blood as well as a piece of a brassiere strap. After the seizure of the car, an informant told the police the name of the fourth man, Johnston, responsible for the crime. At this point, the lawyer for the four men, D'arcy Bancroft, advised them not to speak with the police. Despite numerous attempts and a variety of strategies designed to break the silence of the four men, nothing worked. The RCMP felt that they lacked sufficient evidence to lay a murder charge against any of the four suspects. Rumours circulated throughout the town as to the names of those involved. An unidentified woman would later testify that at a drinking party held not long after the killing, Johnston stood up, made stabbing motions with his hand, and say, "I picked up a screwdriver and I stabbed her, and I stabbed her, and I stabbed her."

The decade between October 1972 and 1983 was one of relative inactivity in the case. Occasional interviews were held with Colgan and Manger, and the case was infrequently reviewed. Colgan told the AJI that during these years, the police would occasionally send him screwdriver drinks in the bars of The Pas, a not-so-subtle reminder that they were watching him and were aware of his suspected role in the death of Helen Betty Osborne. But few real steps were taken to solve the crime. All this changed in 1983.

Constable Urbanoski Takes Up the Case

In July 1983, Constable Bob Urbanoski of the Thompson, Manitoba detachment of the RCMP began an extensive review of the case. He interviewed the officers who had worked on the original investigation and two original informants. The latter didn't prove too help-ful, as one was unable to recollect anything, even under hypnosis, and the other claimed he recalled nothing of what he had told the police in 1972. Still, by the end of 1984, Constable Urbanoski submitted a proposal to work full-time on the case.

Urbanoski knew that the four men still talked about the crime with their friends and acquaintances, so he used wiretaps. This resulted in the questioning of 38 people. Subsequent statements from informants, including Colgan's ex-wife, led the RCMP to place a notice in the local weekly paper requesting more information. The RCMP implied that a number of people had come forward with information, which was not really the case. The ruse worked. Four more people offered themselves to be interviewed.

By December 1985, Constable Urbanoski was able to seek permission to lay charges against Johnston and Colgan. These were authorized in August 1986. Colgan was arrested on October 3, Johnston on October 27. Colgan would eventually offer to give testimony in return for immunity from prosecution, an offer that was accepted. As a result of that deal, Houghton was arrested on March 15, 1987. In November, Manger was located and the RCMP convinced him to testify at the trial of Houghton and Johnston.

One hundred and four prospective jurors were considered for the trial. Twenty of these were Native, but they were rejected by the lawyers. In December 1987, 16 years after the murder, Dwayne Johnston was convicted of murder and sentenced to life in prison. James Houghton was acquitted. Lee Colgan had received immunity from prosecution and was set free. Norman Manger was never charged because he had claimed to have been too drunk to remember anything that happened that night.

The AJI, in its concluding statements, asserted its belief that it was not just one man that was involved in the assault, that Colgan was "not fully forthright and honest in his tes-timony before us or at the trial of Houghton and Johnston," that he "withheld facts from his testimony about his and Houghton's actions that night."

Four men had been in the car that picked up Helen Betty Osborne, abducted her, ter-rorized her, and eventually brutally murdered her that night in The Pas in 1971. Only one of them would be punished for the crime. After serving 10 years in prison, Dwayne Johnston was released from prison on full parole in October 1997. There was considerable protest from Native peoples across Canada.

The case leaves us with several important questions. Why did it take so long for the case to come to court? How different would the case have been had Native men killed a White woman? Why were the initial suspects Aboriginal, when "cruising" for Native women was a well-known local practice of young White men? Was the systemic racism against Native people so strong that it could only take the extraordinary diligence of one RCMP officer, rather than the normal functioning of the justice system, to resolve the issue?

THE SHOOTING OF J.J. HARPER

Fifteen months after Dwayne Johnston was sentenced to prison for killing Helen Betty Osborne, Manitoba was again faced with a case that focused attention on Aboriginal-police relations. On March 9, 1988, John Joseph Harper, a fairly prominent Cree leader, was shot to death by a Winnipeg police officer in the very early hours of the morning. There were no witnesses to the shooting. The case is tragic for a number of reasons, not the least of which is that an innocent, unarmed man was killed by a police officer. In the weeks and months that followed, a police officer would commit suicide, while the officer who was involved in the shooting would eventually drink himself to death.

In 1988, the province of Manitoba had a population of about one million people. Two-thirds of these, or about 660 000, lived in Winnipeg, the provincial capital. An estimated 12 percent of the province's population was Native. The 1986 census indicated that Winnipeg had a Native population of about 28 000 (Sinclair, 1999: 7, 9, 11), a little more than 4 percent of the city's population. This number should be taken as being low, as a good number of urban Natives are itinerant, moving often from reserve to city. The 1991 Native population of Winnipeg was estimated as being between 40 000 and 50 000 (Frideres, 1998: 240–241). On the police force, which had 1140 members, there were only 9 Native constables, slightly less than 0.8 percent of the force.

While underrepresented on the police force, Aboriginals were (and are) grossly overrepresented in provincial and federal jails in Manitoba. In 1988, at least one-half of the inmates of Manitoba's jails were Native, while at the federal Stony Mountain Prison, north of Winnipeg, the number was even higher. A young Native lawyer, writing in the *Winnipeg Free Press,* suggested that as many as 80 percent of the people charged in Winnipeg courts were Native because they were "easy targets" for the police (Sinclair, 1999: 9). The shooting of J.J. Harper lends some credence to that claim.

At the time of his death, John Joseph Harper was 36 years old. A member of the Wasagamack Band of the Island Lake area of Manitoba, he was active in First Nations politics. When he died, he was executive director of the Island Lake Tribal Council. Harper was married and had three children.

On March 8, 1988, Harper had started a night of drinking at about 8 p.m. While at the St. Regis Hotel, he drank brandy and coffee with a number of friends. At 10:30 p.m., he left and went to the Westbrook Hotel and drank some more, having at least one beer. When the hotel bar closed, Harper and some friends went next door, to a lounge called DJ's. Harper spent about an hour there, talking, dancing, and consuming at least one more beer.

There is contradictory evidence concerning Harper's mood that night. Employees at DJ's would later testify that Harper had been acting aggressively and that he was "spoiling for a fight." Bill Pryor, a DJ's employee, testified that he had had to escort Harper out of the bar. Another worker, Sandra Harrop, said that she saw nothing unusual that night. Harper's friends said that he was not acting belligerently and left the bar of his own volition, without any assistance from Pryor. Tests would show that Harper's blood-alcohol level at the time of his death was .22, almost 3 times the legal limit to drive. Chief Medical Examiner Dr. Peter Markesteyn would later conclude that, given Harper's history of alcohol consumption, he could likely consume large amounts without appearing to be as impaired as someone who did not have a similar history (www.ajic.mb.ca).

When DJ's closed at 2 a.m., Harper started on his last walk home along Winnipeg's Elgin Avenue.

Like Harper, police officer Robert Andrew Cross was in his thirties. He was born in 1954, the son of a man who worked in an RCMP lab in Ottawa. He had joined the Winnipeg Police Department on March 26, 1984, when he was one month short of his thirtieth birthday. It was his second attempt at joining, having been turned down the first time. Among other reasons for wanting to be a police officer, Cross wrote in his application that "I have been told I always have an excellent way of dealing with people" (Sinclair, 1999: 47). That would be tested in the early hours of March 9, 1988.

Cross had been big as a child, and in junior high had developed a reputation for having an aggressive attitude and being a bit of a "tough guy." He got married in 1975 and again in 1987. He got along well with his policing colleagues. He was elected class president of his recruit class and was popular with his fellow officers.

On the night of March 8, 1988, Cross was working with Constable Kathy Hodgins, his partner of about three years. She was the more senior of the two, having nine years experience to Cross' four. They had started their shift at 10:00 p.m. and were scheduled to finish at 8 o'clock the next morning.

Melvin Pruden and his cousin Allan were young Saulteaux, 19 and 14 years old, respectively. At around midnight on March 8, Melvin saw a car, an Aries, with its motor running. He kicked the window in and the two of them drove away in it. The car was reported stolen almost immediately. The two would joyride for about two hours before the car was spotted by Constable Cross and his partner.

At about 2 a.m., Cross and Hodgins were patrolling the area around the Westbrook Hotel. Shortly after having issued a speeding ticket, they observed the stolen car, which had been reported earlier, drive past. They gave chase, with Cross at the wheel.

The roads were slippery, so the pursuit was not at high speeds. Pruden ran several stop signs and at least one red light in an attempt to elude the officers. While giving chase, Hodgins broadcast details of the vehicle, traffic violations made by the driver, and location and speed of the cars involved. Pruden hit a snow bank while attempting a turn, and both youths fled the scene on foot. Cross and Hodgins did not see the car as it came to an abrupt stop, but they did see the two suspects fleeing the scene. This enabled the officers to issue their first description of the two car thieves, saying that they were two males in dark clothing, one shorter than the other.

Cross drove the patrol car about two more blocks, jumped out and gave chase on foot. Meanwhile, Hodgins backed the car up, checked the stolen vehicle, and turned it off. Afterward, she returned to her own vehicle and waited for her partner to return. Cross was giving chase to Allan, the younger of the two youths. During the foot race, Allan would claim that he heard Cross yell "halt" or "stop" and saw him reaching to the back of his right hip for his revolver. Cross would later deny any such action. This would be the first of a number of allegations concerning Cross' use of his service revolver in the case (www.ajic.mb.ca).

Cross finally caught Allan, took him to the cruiser, sat him in the back and questioned him. Hodgins made notes on a scratch pad, rather than the more usual police notebook. At the Aboriginal Justice Inquiry, she would testify that she lost those notes. Hodgins then communicated some of the information related by Allan over the radio and through the car's computer system. She described the other suspect as "Native, black jacket, blue jeans, and approximately 22 years old." She claimed that she gave that age in order to get a "fixed figure for the description" (www.ajic.mb.ca). Allan would later state that he told the officer that his friend's age as being between 17 and 19 years. After questioning Allan, Cross and Hodgins waited and watched while listening to the police radio.

Two pairs of officers, Constables Isaac and Hampton and Constables Poneira and Eakin, then arrived. Constable Hampton encountered Pruden, and according to the young Native man, pointed a gun at him, telling him to stop or the officer would shoot. Hampton would deny speaking with the suspect. Pruden ran and Hampton radioed Poneira, who gave chase but was soon outdistanced by the suspect. Poneira radioed a description of the suspect as being a male Native, about feet nine inches tall, with a slim build and wearing a grey jacket and jeans. Like the other descriptions, it painted a picture quite unlike the stockier and much older J.J. Harper. Constable Isaac, who was in a patrol car, spotted the suspect, left his car and eventually apprehended Pruden in a backyard. Constables Poneira and Eakin arrived shortly thereafter.

How the arrest unfolded is in doubt. Pruden later testified that Constable Isaac slammed his head against the hood of the cruiser and called him a "fucking Indian." The officer denied doing and saying these things. What is certain is that they broadcast the arrest and felt that the pursuit was complete. They had apprehended the criminals and did not need to look for any other suspects.

At approximately the same time as this was occurring, Constables Danny Smyth and Douglas Hooper stopped to talk to Constable Hampton, heard gunshots, and within one minute heard Cross radio for assistance.

Cross had left the cruiser at 2:37 a.m. One minute later he heard that the second suspect had been arrested. He was heading in the direction of where Pruden had been apprehended when he encountered J.J. Harper walking home after his night out with his friends. What exactly happened when the two encountered each other is still a mystery.

Cross would state that he approached Harper and asked for identification. Harper said that he didn't have to show identification and continued walking. Cross claimed that he then reached out and placed his hand on Harper's arm and turned him around. Then Harper pushed the police officer, knocking him to the ground. Cross would testify that as he fell, he grabbed Harper, pulling him down on top of him. The two men struggled on the ground. Cross claimed that he felt tugging at his holster and thought that Harper was trying to get his gun. In the struggle, according to Cross' story, the revolver was removed from the holster with both men fighting for possession of the weapon. The gun discharged, hitting Harper in the chest. The Native man staggered back a few steps and then collapsed. It took Cross a while to regain his composure. He radioed for his partner and an ambulance at 2:40 a.m.

The seven other officers arrived on the scene shortly afterward. Smyth and Hooper testified to the Aboriginal Justice Inquiry that Cross told them that "He went for my gun and I shot him." Hodgins would say that Cross told her that "He jumped me Kath. I was on my back on the ground. He went for my gun." Eakin would say during the inquiry that Cross told him, "I approached him, asked him for I.D. and he hit me, knocked me down, and went for my gun, it came out and he got shot."

Smyth and Poneira attended to Harper, trying unsuccessfully to stop the bleeding. At one point, Harper was semi-conscious and thrashing about but not saying anything comprehensible. Smyth stayed with the wounded man, applying pressure to the wound from the time he returned with the first-aid kit until they arrived at the hospital.

As senior officer at the scene, Constable Hodgins should have secured the scene and overseen the collection of evidence. Hodgins did not secure the scene, she said, because of her concern for her partner. The process was begun by the acting sergeant that night, who arrived at 2:54 a.m. and who deferred a few minutes later to Inspector Eric Hrycyk, who was in charge of all officers and divisions in the city that night. Hrycyk instructed the other officers to secure and examine the scene and to canvass the area for potential witnesses. Acting Inspector Kenneth Dowson of the Crime Division was also called out. He went to the Health Sciences Centre. Upon learning of Harper's death at 3:23 a.m., he sent Hooper and Smyth to collect Harper's personal effects and to notify his family of his passing.

What followed created much controversy. Harper's family was not notified of his death until about six hours later. The shooting scene was cleaned up before the sun rose at 6:57 a.m. There had been two large pools of blood and one smaller one. In the early morning, a police detective watched and made sure that the firefighters sloshed water on the blood and then poured sand over it.

Should they not have waited and checked more carefully for evidence? The collection of evidence seems generally to have been quite sloppy. A reporter later found Harper's eyeglasses in the snow, completely missed by the police and firefighters. And what about Cross' service revolver? The city police hadn't dusted the gun or the holster at the time of shooting. In fact, the gun wasn't checked for fingerprints until one week later, when it was sent to the RCMP forensic lab. One thumbprint showed up, belonging to the RCMP technician. No witnesses had been found. Gordon Sinclair Jr., the reporter who later wrote the book *Cowboys and Indians: The Shooting of J.J. Harper*, which was quite critical of the investigation, questioned whether the police had even tried to find witnesses (Sinclair, 1999: 39).

On March 10, the Winnipeg Police Department's Firearms Board of Enquiry submitted a report to the Chief, clearing Cross of any wrongdoing. Police Chief Herb Stephen issued a news release that identified the deceased but not the officer involved in the shooting, and indicated that Harper's death was precipitated by the assault on Cross by the victim. On April 5, Judge Enns of the Provincial Court headed an inquest into the death. On May 26, he issued his written report. It was a curiously mixed statement. One the one hand, the judge expressed his belief that Cross' decision to question Harper "could easily be perceived as yet another instance of police harassment" (York, 1990: 151) by the Cree man. Judge Enns admitted that Winnipeg natives had an "utter distrust" of the police and felt that the Winnipeg police should "vigorously pursue a program of recruiting natives" to help alleviate the tension between the two groups. He also expressed his opinion that police harassment was merely a "perception" and that Cross should be completely exonerated of blame.

The judge's report did little to settle the issue. Important questions were left unanswered. More troubling questions were raised when Don Gillmor, a former friend of Cross', wrote an article that appeared in *Saturday Night* magazine. In it, an unidentified police officer (later revealed to be Cross) stated that Harper was "the author of his own demise" because "the natives drink and get into trouble. Blaming the police for their troubles is like an alcoholic blaming the liquor store for being open late" (www.maji.mb.ca). Cross also stated that officers at the shooting scene and shortly thereafter said, with reference to the dying Harper, "That's right. Bleed him dry" and "If you're lucky, that fucker dies." Another officer suggested that because a prominent Native activist had been killed, Cross had shot "the wrong Indian," implying that if the victim had not been somebody politically visible, the incident would not have become an issue.

The Manitoba Aboriginal Justice Inquiry

With the unsettled atmosphere brought on by the Helen Betty Osborne case and the J.J. Harper case, just to mention the two most salient cases, the Manitoba Aboriginal Justice Inquiry was set up in September 1988. It was led by two provincial judges. One, Murray Sinclair, was a Saulteaux. Its investigation of the Harper case was quite thorough. That it posed a real threat to the Winnipeg police department's official version of the story is seen in the tragic fact that the man in charge of the Harper investigation, Kenneth Dowson, then Acting Inspector of Crime Division, committed suicide with his service revolver on September 20, 1989, the day he was to appear before the Inquiry.

In their 1990 report, the judges noted that "the evidence is clear that racism exists within the Winnipeg Police Department" and stated that Cross "stopped the first Aboriginal person he saw, even though that person was a poor match for the suspect in other respects and a suspect had already been caught." Their harshest words seem to have been saved for the investigation of the shooting:

> It is our conclusion that the City of Winnipeg Police Department did not search actively or aggressively for the truth about the death of J.J. Harper. Their investigation was, at best, inadequate. At worst, its primary objective seems to have been to exonerate Const. Robert Cross and to vindicate the Police Department.
>
> We believe that evidence was mishandled and facts were obscured by police attempts to construct a version of events which would, in effect, blame J.J. Harper for his own death. Our review of the taking of Cross' statement leads us to conclude that he was assisted in its compilation rather than being questioned. We have found that at least one officer rewrote his record of events. (www.majic.mb.ca)

Ten years after the Harper shooting, the Winnipeg Police Department had 98 Native officers. There had been nine (out of a force of over 1000) when he was shot. The Inquiry had called for a total of 133 Aboriginal officers.

The next year, Robert Cross died of "acute alcoholism" (Sinclair, 1999: 391).

THE 911 CASE: FIRST ARRESTED, LAST ASSISTED?

Native people have some justification for believing that in policing matters, they are as quickly seen as perpetrators as they are slowly served as victims of criminal acts. The case referred to in the newspapers as the "911 case" would appear to support that belief. It raises the question of whether Native peoples are victims twice over: victims of criminals and victims of systemic racism.

Beginning around nine o'clock in the evening of Friday, February 15, 2000, Doreen Leclair and Corrine McKeown (or McKeowen), Métis sisters, aged 51 and 52 years, respectively, made five 911 calls to the Winnipeg police from their north end home. Eight hours later, the two sisters were found stabbed to death.

There are conflicting accounts of what exactly happened that night. What is clear is that the first 911 call was made around 9:00 p.m. According to one source, the women complained that a former boyfriend, William John Dunlop, aged 30 years, was outside the house and that the police did not respond until after the women were dead. In another account, it was stated that the police responded to the first call, visited Ms. McKeown, found nothing amiss, and left the home. Regardless of which account is true, nothing happened in response to the next four phone calls.

By the time the third call was made, the women were in serious difficulty. The tapes reveal that the women were telling the operator that a man violating a restraining order had stabbed Ms. McKeown. In response, the operator told the women that they were partially responsible for the situation in allowing the man into the house, and that they should resolve the situation themselves.

When the fourth call was made, the words of the women were virtually unintelligible, although one of them could be heard saying "Please help me" (*CBC News Online,* www.cbconline.org, consulted May 11, 2001). At this juncture, the operator promised to send a squad car to help the women, but no car was dispatched. A fifth call was made to 911, but the women's voices were drowned out by the barking of dogs. By this time, the operator was becoming concerned and hung up the phone and dialed the house. When a car was finally sent, it was too late.

Not surprisingly, this tragic case has raised interconnected questions of racism, sexism and class prejudice. Nahanni Fontaine, an Aboriginal women's advocate, said that cases such as this one were not going to go away until the police started looking at the underlying issue involved, which in her mind was racism (NatNews@one list.com, February 19, 2000). Others pointed to other contributing factors. Tracy Lloyd, of the Fort Garry Women's Resource Centre, had just completed a study of how the justice system handles domestic violence. She observed that many women had complained of the way police dealt with their calls for help, suggesting perhaps that the gender of the victims had as much to do with the case as did their race. Finally, Native groups suggested that if the calls had come from a wealthier part of town, the police would have arrived promptly, suggesting that notions of social class also determined response time and the way that the calls were handled. Thus race, gender, and social class all might have played a role in this tragedy.

In response, Winnipeg Police Chief Jack Ewatski initiated an investigation and suspended with pay four 911 operators and a duty inspector. The investigation involved four full-time investigators reviewing in excess of 1000 hours of taped telephone calls and formal interviews with forty-six people. A five-volume report was issued in May 2000. For Native people and their supporters, it left many questions unanswered.

One year later, in May 2001, Manitoba's Chief Medical Examiner, Doctor Thambirajah Balachandra, called for an inquest, stating that the two deaths might have been prevented if alternative procedures or preventative measures had been in place. The purpose of the inquest would be to examine police policy on domestic violence and assault, and to recommend ways to improve 911 procedures. The Police Association opposed the idea of an inquest, suggesting instead that the money might be better spent on bolstering police resources. Carl Shier, the police union president, claimed that the police have too many calls to handle and that an inquest would only demonstrate that there aren't enough officers patrolling the streets.

The first part of Shier's statement is probably true. Concerning the second point, it might be better to ask whether the problem is more that there aren't enough Native officers patrolling the streets.

William John Dunlop, aged 30, was sentenced to life in prison in April 2001. He will not be eligible for parole until he has served 17 years. Police Chief Jack Ewatski has admitted that there was a mishandling of the 911 case but denied that racism was a factor. Doreen Leclair and Corrine McKeowen remain dead.

NOTES

1. Pemmican is a Cree term for buffalo jerky made by pulverising thin strips of dried lean buffalo meat, then adding crushed, dried saskatoon berries and hot fat produced by boiling the marrow of buffalo bones.

REVIEW QUESTIONS

1. How did the policing of the bison hunt reflect the egalitarian nature of Métis culture?

2. What were the main criticisms of the Dakota Ojibway Police Service Commission? How were these weaknesses corrected?

3. Generally speaking, how was racism manifested in The Pas in 1971?

4. What role did racism play in the initial police investigation of the Helen Betty Osborne case?

5. In what ways did stereotyping of Native peoples play a part in the J.J. Harper and 911 cases?

chapter seven

Aboriginal Policing in Ontario

LEARNING OBJECTIVES

After completing this chapter, students should be able to:

1. Identify the factors that led to the killing of Dudley George.
2. Outline the development of Aboriginal policing at Sagamok.
3. Describe and identify the significance of the Great Law of Peace.
4. Contrast the peace and war strands of the Great Law of Peace.
5. Explain the division between elected band council and traditional government at Six Nations and Akwesasne.
6. Discuss the policing situation in Akwesasne up until 1990 from the points of view of the warrior and the peace factions.

The Native peoples of Ontario include both Algonquians and Iroquoians. The former include the Anishinabe or Ojibwa (including those people called Mississauga, Chippewa, Ottawa, and Potawatomi), the very closely related Algonquin, as well as the Cree and the Delaware. The Iroquoian peoples of Ontario include the Six Nations of the Iroquois (Mohawk, Oneida, Onondaga, Cayuga, Seneca, and Tuscarora), of which the Mohawk are predominant.

POLICING NATIVE PEOPLES IN ONTARIO

As reserves are under federal jurisdiction, the Royal Canadian Mounted Police (RCMP) were, until 1974, the policing agency for Native peoples in Ontario. In 1974, the Task Force Report on Policing in Ontario put forward the case that provincial jurisdiction ought to prevail over federal on reserves for Criminal Code offences not including federal statutes, which resulted in the withdrawal of the RCMP in favour of the Ontario Provincial Police (OPP).

In 1975, an Indian Special Constable Program was started subject to the selection, training, and authority of the OPP. The officers could enforce both the Criminal Code and band bylaws. They were selected and trained by the OPP and were under their authority rather than that of the band council. By the end of the 1980s, about 65 communities were served by 132 special constables (Forcese, 1992: 285).

During the late 1980s, the OPP offered a 35-week course in Moosonee (at the southern tip of James Bay) for Native people who wished to become special constables, accepting about 15 students per course. The graduates were to work as police on reserves or in correctional services (Forcese, 1992: 142).

In 1992, in a ground-breaking move toward Native self-government in Ontario, control for the development of Native officers was transferred from the OPP to Aboriginal agencies such as the Anishinabek Policing Services (see below).

THE ANISHINABE OR OJIBWA

The Anishinabe (this name is written several different ways) or Ojibwa are the largest Native group in Ontario and are among the leaders in Aboriginal policing initiatives in Canada. In Ontario, these initiatives include the Anishinabek Policing Services, the Wikwemikong Tribal Police Service, and the Nishinabe-Aski Police Service. See Box 7.1 for a discussion of another type of initiative taken by the Anishinabe.

Box 7.1	The Occupation of Anicinabe Park

On the weekend of July 20–21, 1974 a conference was held of Ojibwa who lived in the area of Kenora, a town then of about 10 000 people. It was held in Anicinabe Park, a small municipal park. According to one of the organizers of the conference, Louis Cameron, the conference was held for the following reasons:

> While we were planning the conference we started bringing out the issues. [This included] police harassment. They arrest about 5,000 native people in one year and they really brutalize the people. The town police and O.P.P. have been immune to

human ways. They've just mechanically operated their law and order on the people while the people don't even understand what the police were doing and especially throwing them in jails and beating them up or handcuffing them and parading them up and down the street in police cars. This is degradation of Indians by the police. (Cameron, quoted in Burke, 1976: 379–380)

The year before, members of the radical American Indian Movement (AIM) had occupied Wounded Knee in South Dakota, a place where the American army had gunned down innocent Sioux women, children, and Elders during the nineteenth century. So it is not surprising that some of the people in the park, mostly young men, suggested that they take up arms and occupy the park, which the federal government had bought for them in 1929 and then sold out from under them 30 years later.

A list of demands emerged, including the following justice issues:

1. the removal of a particular, anti-Native provincial judge;

2. the establishment of a police college equipped to train Native officers and to teach non-Native officers how to deal with Native people; and

3. the appointment of Native Justices of the Peace.

The occupation lasted for 39 tense days. A White vigilante group was highly vocal in advocating the removal of the Native people from the park by force. The occupation ended peacefully, with the people in the park laying down their arms and leaving the park once some agreement was arrived at with the government. But it wasn't an agreement with the government that was the main gain for the people. They gained a collective rather than personal sense of the negative circumstances of their lives. In Cameron's words,

> In laying down our arms and leaving the Anicinabe Park grounds, the terms were secondary. I think the absolute thing that happened was that native people for the first time since maybe a hundred years back had taken up armed struggle to liberate themselves and direct confrontation to solve their problems and to meet the situation head-on. (Cameron, quoted in Burke, 1976: 387)

Dudley George: "A Tragedy on Both Sides"

As we have seen in a number of cases, non-Native police can be put into "no-win" situations when they are pressured by governments to act in a more aggressive manner in Native protests than what the police themselves might think of as prudent. The politics of Native policing can in this way obstruct the practice of good policing. The Dudley George case is a perfect example of this situation.

Background: Expropriating Land

In 1928, Stoney Point band number 43 was pressed by the federal and provincial governments to sell 377 acres of its reserve in southwestern Ontario to "private interests." In 1936, without band permission, 108 of those acres were purchased for Ipperwash Park. In making the park in 1937, a cemetery was dug into and violated.

Then came World War II. Natives volunteered in high numbers. In May of 1942, the Ojibwa of Stoney Point were asked to make another sacrifice for their country. The Department of National Defence, invoking the *War Measures Act*, expropriated the remaining land of the Stoney Point band, even though 85 percent of the band members opposed the expropriation. They would receive $50 000 in compensation for 2211 acres of land (about $23 an acre), and were promised that "If, at the termination of the war, no further use of the area is required by the Department of National Defence, negotiations will be entered into with the Department of Indian Affairs to transfer the lands back to the Indians at a reasonable price determined by mutual agreement" (www.web.net/~acaa/info-leaflets/04.html, consulted September 9, 1999).

The Stoney Point people were forced to live in the less than prime territory of their Kettle Point neighbours and were not given the same number or quality of houses as those they had been compelled to give up.

On May 31, 1946, the Advanced Infantry Training Centre was closed, but negotiations did not follow. The armed forces made peacetime use of land expropriated for war. From 1960 on, it was used for a six-week cadet training camp and recreation facility.

Trying to Regain Lost Land

While the Stoney Point people never stopped trying to regain their land and their community, it wasn't until 1981 that they achieved a measure of success. The federal government agreed to pay $2.4 million in compensation for the nearly 40 years' use they had made of the land. But the return of the land was delayed pending an environmental assessment, especially necessary after the land had been used as a shooting range. This would put plans on long-term hold.

In 1985, a small step was made in that the members of the Kettle and Stoney Point band were permitted to hunt and fish on the land during provincially approved seasons. The Department of National Defence agreed to review the need for the camp for military purposes every four years—not much of a concession, as they would not voluntarily want to give up the land.

In March 1992, the Standing Committee on Aboriginal People tabled its report recommending that the federal government return the land to its former Aboriginal inhabitants and their descendants, saying that the government's reasons for continuing to occupy the land were "spurious and without substance." The Department of National Defence initially held its ground, literally, claiming that there was a continuing need for them to retain the Camp Ipperwash lands for military purposes. Eventually, the cadet camp was closed, but the Department continued to assert possession of the land, agreeing merely to "consult" with the Kettle and Stoney Point First Nation, a word that Native people have learned to distrust.

In 1993, the Stoney Pointers took more radical steps to regain their land. On May 6, they moved onto the old firing range, living in makeshift dwellings, small trailers, and tents. They would be opposed on two fronts: Native and Armed Forces. On the former front, Tom Bressette, Chief of the Kettle and Stoney Point First Nation, showed his opposition to the move by asking the premier of the province to demand that it stop issuing general welfare to the Stoney Point people occupying Camp Ipperwash.

On September 12, the Stoney Pointers occupying the base walked from Stoney Point, by the shores of Lake Huron, across the breadth of Southern Ontario to Ottawa, to press the federal government to recognize their rights. The trip took two and one-half weeks. Along the way, they stopped off at Peterborough, as the Trent University Native Studies Department had organized a rally for them. Mainstream media coverage was light; there were no blockades or confrontations with "warriors."

The relationship between the Armed Forces personnel and the Stoney Pointers deteriorated. On June 27, 1995, Glenn Morris George, angered by the fact that the army had placed iron "tire slashers" on the roadway leading to a burial ground, started to remove them. Captain Allan Howse saw this and got into a verbal fight with him. Out of the series of events that took place between George, Howse, and at least one other member of the Armed Forces, George would be charged with two counts of assault, one of mischief, and one of uttering a death threat. Howse would allege that George drove a tractor that bumped an Armed Forces truck, causing $900 damage.

On July 29, 1995, somewhere between 15 and 20 military personnel moved out, and around 100 Stoney Pointers moved in. Cleve Jackson would be charged later with reckless driving when it was alleged that he drove a bus through the drill hall that day. Stoney Pointers claimed that he was not the driver of the bus, that the only reason that he was charged was because the Military Police saw his picture on the cover of the *London Free Press* and then decided that he was the culprit. The following year, Judge Louise Eddy dismissed the charges.

The summer would end, unfortunately, with a passing written shot that would have repercussions later on. Kettle and Stoney Point Band Councillor Gerald George had a letter printed in the local *Forest Standard,* containing the following inflammatory remarks: "I am glad that these Army Camp Indians call themselves separate from my First Nation because I would not want any of my fellow band members to act like animals" (*Forest Standard,* August 30, 1995, www.web.net/~acaa/info-leaflets/04.html).

The Occupation of Ipperwash Park

On September 4, 1995, at least 24 Stoney Pointers occupied Ipperwash Park, which had closed for the winter season. They posed no physical threat to anyone. They expressed their concern about a sacred burial ground that was located in the Park. This burial ground had been well-documented in archaeological site reports on file at Queen's Park and in Ottawa, but both the provincial and federal governments would initially deny knowledge of these reports.

To understand what happened next in terms of the responsibility of policing services, we have to know what the role of the Ontario government was in giving direction to the OPP on September 5 and 6. Exact details are hard to come by, especially as the government has been less than open in its dealing with this matter. The standard OPP practice at that time was to avoid confrontation with protesters. That would be altered in this case. The evidence (Oziewicz, 2001; Mackie, 2001; Toronto Star editorial, 2001) seems to suggest that the newly-elected government wanted to prove that it didn't just talk tough, but acted likewise, indicating to senior OPP officials that it wanted aggressive action taken. Certainly the OPP was not given a mandate to negotiate, and was not told to respect the claims of the Stoney Pointers.

"Escalating Violence Against Police"

Prior to the confrontation in Ipperwash Park, the OPP underwent a thorough preparation for battle, requesting from the Armed Forces 50 gas masks, 50 pairs of night-vision goggles, equipment for intercepting cellular telephone calls, 100 bulletproof vests, 2 Huey helicopters, and two Bison personnel carriers. Two hundred and fifty OPP officers were mobilized from across Ontario. They would face about 30 people with no firearms.

At 7:55 p.m. on September 6, Stoney Pointer Stewart George got into an argument with Gerald George, the man who had referred to Stewart's group as "animals" in the *Forest Standard* letter. Stewart would take his anger with Gerald out on the latter's car. The next day, the OPP issued a news release stating that "A private citizen's vehicle was damaged by a number of First Nations people armed with baseball bats. As a result of this, the OPP Crowd Management Team was deployed." Stewart George would later plead guilty to one count of mischief (another charge would be dismissed) and would be fined $300.

At 8:19 p.m., Gerald George lodged a complaint with the OPP. At about 10:45 p.m., a team of 32 officers of the Crowd Management Unit, dressed in riot gear and equipped with shields, batons, and sidearms, advanced on about 30 unarmed Native men, women, and children. The officers would be protected by a more heavily armed eight-man Tactics and Rescue Unit, a SWAT team.

Cecil Bernard George, a Kettle and Stoney Point band councillor, walked into the middle of the oncoming confrontation in an attempt to defuse the potentially explosive situation, but he was too late. The OPP beat him with clubs and kicked him. He later filed a civil action suit, in which a doctor's report would reveal that he had injuries to 28 different places on his body.

The assault on Cecil George caused Warren George, 22, to drive slowly onto the scene, trying to put his car between his people and the police. An officer pointed a gun directly at Warren, who then swerved and braked, making contact with five officers, one of whom would suffer a sprained ankle. In February 1998, Warren would be found guilty of criminal negligence causing bodily harm and assault with a weapon (his car). A charge of dangerous driving was stayed. He was sentenced to six months and banned from driving for two years. He was prohibited from possessing firearms for 10 years. Judge Pockele, in pronouncing sentence, said that Warren lacked "remorse" for what he had done and had become part of the "escalating violence against police" in the situation.

At about the same time, a youth made a similar attempt to block the advance of the police. This time the vehicle used was a bus. Seven officers drew their weapons and fired, with a bullet striking the young man in his lower right back. The youth was acquitted of charges, Judge Graham stating that "It is reasonable for (the youth) to assume that a breach of the peace was occurring and that Bernard George was being assaulted."

The Killing of Dudley George

Thirty-eight year old Anthony O'Brien (Dudley) George had been involved in every aspect of Stoney Point resistance, the occupation of Camp Ipperwash, and the march to Ottawa. His face was familiar to the police. He looked the part of the militant Indian, long hair, short beard, and sunglasses. His familiarity and his "militant look" would make him an easy target for police anxiety. It is alleged that before the police advance, the OPP said to him, "Dudley, you are going to be first."

Acting Sergeant Kenneth Deane was second in command of the Tactics and Rescue Unit. He would testify later that he saw muzzle flashes coming from the bushes and that moments later Dudley stepped onto the road and scanned the police, pointing a rifle, which Deane would allege Dudley would throw away after being hit in the collarbone by Deane's shot. This was proven untrue in court. The Native people fired no shots, although the police are rumoured to have fired up to 1000 (perhaps Deane had mistaken one of those for unfriendly fire). Dudley was not carrying a gun.

Deane shot Dudley in the chest with a German-engineered Heckler and Koch submachine gun that fires hollowed-tipped, exploding bullets, but the Stoney Pointer did not die right away. Although police cars and ambulances were stationed in the area around the park, these were not deployed to try to save his life. Marcia Simon, a Stoney Pointer, tried to call an ambulance, but was grabbed and arrested while trying to do so. Dudley's brother Pierre, his sister Carolyn, and a youth, drove him in a 1977 Chevrolet Impala to the nearest hospital, some 50 kilometres away. When a tire blew in their car, they tried to call an ambulance from a farmhouse. No luck. They completed the trip to the hospital driving on the rim. When they got to the hospital, the OPP, who had been monitoring the progress of the car, took Pierre and Carolyn into custody, claiming that they would be charged with attempted murder. They were held overnight and then let go. Dudley died at 12:45 a.m. on September 7, 1995.

The Investigation

The Special Investigations Unit arrived within hours of the shooting, but were prevented by the OPP from entering the park until two weeks later. Although they are required to file a report within 90 days after a shooting incident takes place, their report wasn't released until July 23, 1996, more than 10 months later.

Deane was charged the next day with criminal negligence causing death, carrying a maximum penalty of life imprisonment. The trial began on April 1, 1997. On April 29, 1997, he was found guilty. Judge Fraser stated that Deane had "concocted a story ... in an ill-fated attempt to disguise the fact that an unarmed man was shot" (www.kafka.uvic.ca/~vipirg/SISIS/Ipperwash/tapr2997.html). The judge told Deane that "You were not honest in your statements to police investigators, to the SIU and to this court." Brian Adkin, President of the OPP Association, said outside the court that he felt that government inaction on the land claim had created a "tragedy on both sides, a tragedy for the George family and a tragedy for Sergeant Deane."

On July 4, sentence was passed down. Deane was given a conditional sentence of two years less a day to be served in the community, and told to do 180 hours of community work. Deane appealed the decision, and lost the appeal on February 18, 2000. By then, he had served his sentence, with no penitentiary time. He lost his appeal to the Supreme Court in January 2001. In May 2001, he was served with a letter from the OPP saying that they were seeking his dismissal as he had been convicted of a criminal offence. The OPP Police Association is funding his defence in this matter.

As a result of their activities during the summer and September of 1995, 62 charges were laid on the Stoney Pointers. Most were dropped. For example, 20 charges of forcible entry were dropped because the police were unable to establish how the people got into the park. More significantly, 23 charges of forcible detainer were dropped because "The accused have raised the defence of colour of right on the basis that there is a Chippewa burial ground within Ipperwash Provincial Park and that therefore they were justified in being in the Park during the time set out in the charges" (www.web.apc.org/~ara/spoint/sppr1.htm).

Case Study: The Sagamok Anishinawbek First Nation

Marcia Barron (1998) has examined justice reforms in the Sagamok Anishinawbek First Nation (formerly known as Spanish River) in northern Ontario. The community is located halfway between Sault Ste. Marie and Sudbury. An important component of her analysis was the changing face of policing. This study serves as a good example of the social and political movements at both the federal and community level that propel changes in First Nations communities.

Special Constables

In 1959, the first supernumerary special constable was appointed in the community. Reflective of the typically complicated bureaucracy imposed upon First Nations, the officer was appointed under warrant by the RCMP, paid by the Department of Indian Affairs (and ultimately responsible to them), and was required to work under the supervision of the OPP, who were doing most of the on-reserve policing at the time (Barron, 1998: 132–133).

Not only was he put in the unenviable position of policing his kin and neighbours, one of the officer's duties was to enter the homes of "intoxicated Indians" in order to arrest them for violation of the Indian Act proscription on liquor on reserves. Barron quotes a letter from the regional Director of Indian Affairs to the local superintendent explaining that their department paid for the special constable because "liquor appears to be the basis of the law enforcement problem in this case." Thus, the early constables, it would seem, were "there to enforce the *Indian Act* and exert control over the use of alcohol on reserve" (Barron, 1998: 133). In this particular community, the position of special constable was terminated as the band voted for liquor privileges in 1961. The position was left vacant for four years, when a special constable was again commissioned.

The decision to again appoint a special constable was brought about by a number of factors. In 1965, a local official from Indian Affairs advised his superior in North Bay that he had received a "continual stream of complaints" from "serious-minded citizens" on the reserve about the "lawlessness" and "drunkenness" in the community. As well, he voiced his concern that the OPP were allegedly not responding when they were called. Barron also notes that by appointing the special constable, Indian Affairs was also fulfilling its mandate to control liquor consumption on the reserve and was also appeasing the mayor of nearby Massey, who had complained about the lack of policing in Spanish River. She cites a memo from Indian Affairs that outlined the officer's role: "He would act as on-the-spot Peace Officer, interpreter and guide for the O.P.P. and ... would be available for truancy, trespass and other minor matters" (Barron, 1998: 134). The officer was encouraged not to use excessive force in making arrests, to call in the outside police as soon as he was able to, and to provide information to the "regular" police in preparation for court appearances (those appearances being not part of the constable's duties). The constable would have the powers of a peace officer and was charged with enforcing the "general law of the land." The superintendent advised his superior that he felt very few would be willing to do the job.

Eventually, not one, but two special constables were hired. They were trained by the OPP and reported to the force's detachment office in nearby Espanola. Because there were only two officers, they worked shifts alone, and only on weekdays and evenings. Overnight and on weekends they were merely "on call." Not surprisingly, residents complained that most disturbances occurred when there was no police presence. It was then necessary to call either the Sagamok police or the OPP. Response times were alleged to have been often unsatisfactory (Barron, 1998: 135).

The Anishinabek Police Service

In the 1990s, Native policing began to change dramatically at Sagamok. Among other changes, the communities of Sagamok, Garden River, Saugeen, and Curve Lake withdrew from using the OPP and formed the Anishinabek Police Service (APS). In March of 1992, they signed a five-year tripartite agreement. Then, in 1996, they signed a three-year agreement that also allowed them to include thirteen more First Nations (Steckley and Cummins, 2001: 223). As a result, Sagamok's complement of police officers increased to five, allowing for patrols overnight and on weekends, when people felt that they were the most needed.

Under this new agreement, the First Nations officers were called "Anishinabek Peace Keepers." Local policing committees comprise one elected councillor, and at least two other community members are included to maintain a measure of community control. The inclusion of non-elected members attempts to ensure political independence for the committee; thus, they must not be a part of any elected government. Selected members of these committees from each member First Nation sit on a Board of Directors of the overall Anishinabek Police Service.

Early Problems: Kinship, the Culture of Policing, and Interagency Cooperation

The early days of the APS in Sagamok have not been without difficulties that need to be overcome. Barron wrote that, "personal divisions and lack of leadership" in the policing committee have posed problems. For the APS Peace Keepers, there have been the difficulties involving kinship, also found elsewhere, of officers policing their home community. In Barron's words, they often find themselves caught "between their kin and their profession" (Barron, 1998: 136). There are perceptions by some members outside their kin who contend that the officers favour their relatives, while, on the other hand, extended family members are sometimes resentful when charges are laid on them by their own kin. At the time of Barron's research (1993), it was hoped that this situation might be improved by the addition of Native officers from outside the community (Barron, 1998: 136).

Also unresolved at that time was the issue of the culture of policing. The officers were trained by the OPP and operated according to the policing model set by mainstream culture. Some residents felt that the APS officers "should be different from White police" (Barron, 1998: 136). For some community members, that had been achieved to a certain extent. The most commonly expressed view of the APS at Sagamok recorded by Barron was that they "understood us better" because they were Anishinabe. They were perceived as taking a gentler, more helpful and more "studied" approach to incidents, as opposed to being "pushy." In contrast, some Sagamok members viewed OPP officers as holding stereotypes of Native people and as treating the people roughly. It was suggested by some that OPP officers should study Native culture because First Nations people react differently to different situations (Barron, 1998: 138).

Significantly, for some members of the community these same contrasts are seen as marks of APS inferiority. There is the general perception that the APS police are more lenient than the "outside police," despite the fact that they laid charges for the most common offences of assault and liquor act violations at roughly the same rate as local non-Native officers.[1]

According to Barron, while the APS police perceive their relationship with social services (e.g., crisis-intervention team and family violence–victim support service) to be "good" and "reciprocal," this is not necessarily a mutually held view. Social services preferred the Sagamok police to the outside force but generally felt that they were not well enough trained in family-crisis intervention. Barron concluded that in this area there was "clearly room for improvement in training and interagency communication" and that it appeared that the Sagamok police were "underutilized in proportion to the need for intervention" (Barron, 1998: 138).

At the beginning of 2000, there were 20 Ojibwa communities involved in the APS. Headquarters is located in the Garden River (near Sault Ste Marie), which is situated in the middle of the widespread participating communities that stretch from the northwest to central to southwestern Ontario. Currently working out of the headquarters is the police chief of the organization, an administrator, one staff sergeant for the north and one for the south, a court case manager, financial assistant, pay and benefits clerk, computer systems manager, and an office assistant.

Table 7.1 details the communities involved in the APS, their on-reserve population as of 1991, and the staff working out of each detachment. The communities of Henvey Inlet, Magnetawan, and Wahnapitae are also served by the Anishinabek Police Service.

TABLE 7.1	Ojibwa Communities Involved in the Anishinabek Police Service	
First Nation	On-Reserve Population (1991)	Detachment Staff
North		
Fort William	506	1 commander, 2 constables, 1 court officer/secretary
Garden River	901	1 commander, 4 constables, 1 court officer/secretary
Heron Bay	378	1 commander, 2 constables, 1 court officer/secretary
Long Lake #58	321	1 commander, 4 constables, 1 court officer/secretary
Long Lake #77	179	combined with Long Lake #58
Pic Mobert	292	1 constable
Rocky Bay	240	2 constables, 1 court officer/secretary
South		
Christian Island	554	1 commander 2 constables, 1 court officer/secretary
Curve Lake	751	1 commander, 3 constables, 1 court officer/secretary
Dokis	183	1 constable
Kettle Point	798	1 commander, 5 constables, 1 court officer, and 1 secretary
Nipissing	539	1 commander, 3 constables, 1 court officer/secretary
Sagamok	993	1 commander, 3 constables, 1 secretary/court officer
Saugeen	651	1 commander, 1 detective sergeant, 5 constables, 1 secretary, and 1 court officer
Shawanaga	89	1 commander, 1 constable, 1 secretary/court officer
Wasauksing	259	1 constable

The Cree

The Cree communities are for the most part served by the Nishnawbe-Aski Police Service in northwestern Ontario, which covers 46 communities, both Cree and Ojibwa. In the First Nations Chiefs of Police Association (FNCPA) study, the remoteness of these communities was pointed out as a problem in meeting the training needs of this police service. The study mentions that "for the Nishnawbe-Aski Police Service in Northern Ontario it actually costs them more to fly their officers out of the communities and get them to the training facility than it does for the cost of the training once the officers get there" (FNCPA, 2001: 9, "Training").

IROQUOIS POLICING

Background: The Great Law of Peace

You cannot truly understand any Iroquois justice issue without having some knowledge of the Gayanerengo:wa (Mohawk "it is a great good") or the **Great Law of Peace,** a centuries-long tradition.[2] The following is a very basic outline of the story.

A woman and her adult daughter went to live on their own.[3] They were worried about the warfare surrounding them. The daughter gave birth to the Peacemaker. As a child, he had a vision in which he saw a way to have peace. When he became a man, he decided to share his vision of peace with the warring five Iroquoian nations living to the south. He went first to a Mohawk community, where he was accepted by a peace chief, Hiawatha ("He makes wampum"). Hiawatha spoke for him and helped to bring about the acceptance of the Peacemaker's vision.

After the Mohawk accepted the vision, the two men then successfully convinced the neighbouring Oneida to follow suit. Their biggest obstacle was the war leader of the Onondaga, Thadodaho, so the Peacemaker arranged it so that the middle of the five nations would be the last visited. There, Thadodaho would be approached not only by the Peacemaker, but also by Hiawatha and the four other nations. The Cayuga were convinced, and then the Seneca, although the war leaders of the Seneca were still not sure.

At the meeting of the five nations, the Peacemaker spelled out how the people would be brought together in one confederacy. They were divided into two "moieties" or halves. One, referred to as the "fathers" (sometimes the older brothers) was made up of the Mohawk, Seneca, and Onondaga. The other, referred to as the "sons" (less often as the younger brothers), consisted of the Oneida and the Cayuga. The chiefs would sit in council with the "fathers" on one side of the fire, the "sons" on the other.

The council of the confederacy was made up of 50 chiefs or "**sachems**": the Onondaga with 14, the Cayuga with 10, the Mohawk and the Oneida with 9 each, and the Seneca 8. With no majority-rule vote, this is more an honouring distribution than one that gave power to the nations with the greatest numbers. The Onondaga were further honoured by being named the Firekeepers, or hosts of the meetings of the council. The Seneca war chiefs, who were finally convinced to accept the Peacemaker's vision, were honoured by being named the Doorkeepers, controlling access to the meetings of the council.

Issues would be resolved through consensus, as opposed to majority vote. When an issue was to be discussed, it was first presented to the Mohawk chiefs. They talked about it and arrived at some kind of consensus decision. The Mohawk would pass on their consensus decision to the Seneca, who would discuss the issue by themselves and try to arrive at a consensus, ideally one in support of what the Mohawk had decided on. The issue would then be passed through all of the peoples until it got back to the Mohawk, who took it to the Onondaga, who would ratify the agreement. If there was a split opinion, then the Onondaga were responsible for breaking the tie or for suggesting a new compromise that would be discussed by the others.

They did not call themselves Iroquois (a European name thought to come from the Basque verb "to kill"). Their own name, **"Haudenosaunee"** (Monture-Angus, 1995: 249), usually pronounced something like "hoh-deh-no-shoh-neh," means "they are of the extended house" or "they build a house," signifying that all the peoples are together under one roof. References to this form of government, or the teachings of the Peacemaker, often use the word **"Longhouse"** (e.g., Longhouse government, Longhouse religion), partially because of the people's name for themselves, and partially because the traditional homes (after which the council and religious buildings are modelled) of the Iroquois were long and narrow. Non-Native writers have variously referred to Iroquois government as the "Confederacy" or the "League."

Each nation also brought an arrow that would be part of a group bound together by sinew, to show that they were stronger together than they were apart. They became six nations when the Tuscarora, a related people driven off their land by White settlers, were invited to stay by the Oneida.

Two Strands of Interpretation of the Great Law

There are two basic strands of interpretation of the Great Law of Peace. They can somewhat simplistically be labelled a "peace or pacifist tradition" and a "warrior tradition." Journalists Geoffrey York and Loreen Pindera, in their excellent book on the conflict at Oka, liken the division to that between the pacifist Martin Luther King Jr. and the "warrior" Malcolm X in the 1960s fight for civil rights for African-Americans (York and Pindera, 1991: 268). As those two leaders fought in their own ways for justice for African-Americans, those adhering to both strands of the Great Law of Peace have fought for justice for their people in different ways. They both agree that the traditions of the people are the root of that justice, they just disagree as to the means that should be applied to achieve that end.

Near the end of the story of the Great Law it is told that a great white pine tree of peace was planted, with weapons used to fight each other thrown at the roots, symbolizing that the five nations would not fight each other. Those who interpret the Great Law of Peace along the warrior strand point out that this "pacifism" only applies within the longhouse, while those of the peace tradition interpret it as applying more generally. In the words of Jake Swamp, a Longhouse chief in the Mohawk community of Akwesasne for more than 20 years, his adoption of the peace strand came with the realization that: "I suddenly realized, hey, the weapons were done away with ... If anyone picks up a weapon, he's breaking the Great Law, because all the weapons were buried. If people truly believe in peace, they will never pick up weapons" (quoted in York and Pindera, 1991: 265).

In major conflicts like the "Battle for Akwesasne" and the standoff at Oka, these two strands would be seen in the positions people took concerning Mohawk warriors.

The Peace Strand

The peace strand in the interpretation of the Great Law is rooted in part in the teachings of Handsome Lake (1735–1815). The name "Handsome Lake" is a Seneca sachem name. In 1799, the man bearing that name had a series of three separate visions. During the last vision, he received instructions from the Creator. These involved maintaining traditional ceremonies and positive family values and opposing alcohol and witchcraft. They also counselled peace with non-Native people. During the remaining years of his life, Handsome Lake preached those instructions. When he died, his words were recounted and formed an oral tradition that came to be known in English as the **Code of Handsome Lake.**

That strand of the Great Law of Peace was first put into writing in 1912, when John A. Gibson, who bore the name Handsome Lake, dictated some 500 pages of oral text to the anthropologist Alexander A. Goldenweiser. It wasn't published until 1992 (Woodbury, Henry, and Webster). However, versions of that strand have been taught over the years by influential cultural/spiritual leaders such as Cayuga sachem Jacob Thomas, who maintain the oral tradition of the Great Law, as some feel that something would be lost if the Great Law were to be reduced to writing.

The Warrior Strand

The warrior strand interpretation has a written tradition, first published in 1916 by Arthur C. Parker (1881–1955), a Seneca anthropologist. His family was closely connected with Handsome Lake followers, and he published a version of the Code of Handsome Lake in 1913. However, his version of the Great Law of Peace has been used in the warrior strand. This is perhaps because in the 117 wampums or articles that are included in his version, very literally translated instructions to warriors as to how to act to defend the confederacy or league are prominently featured. Part of this written warrior tradition includes the *Warriors Handbook,* a collection of sometimes tongue-in-cheek and humourous, sometimes serious, and often outrageous statements by Kahnawake Mohawk Longhouse chief, artist (he created the Mohawk Warrior flag), and writer Louis Hall.

This strand of interpretation is more commonly found among traditionalist Mohawks than among traditionalists in other member nations of the Confederacy. In part, this is because neither Handsome Lake nor his early followers made substantial contact with the Mohawks, which means that his influence is least felt among those people of all the Six Nations. The nature of the conflicts that the Mohawk communities have had to face may be another factor in this as well.

Six Nations Policing

During the American Revolution, a Mohawk named Thayendanega ("He Sets Two Sticks Side By Side") or Joseph Brant, led most of the Iroquois to fight on the British side. The British government rewarded the loyalty that cost the people their homeland by purchasing land for them in southwestern Ontario from the Mississauga. In 1785, the mixed Six Nations community had a new home. From some of their original land the city of Brantford, named after Joseph Brant, was formed.[4]

In 1923, the Six Nations Iroquois still used the hereditary sachem government that had been set down through the Great Law of Peace. The federal government,[5] who wanted them to have an elected system, opposed this. The Six Nations decided to take their fight to the League of Nations (precursor of the United Nations), where they applied for sovereign nation status. They received the support of Estonia, Ireland, Panama, and Persia, but Britain intervened, and the proposal was dropped.

That same year Colonel C.E. Morgan, a former South African colonial administrator, was appointed as the Indian superintendent at Brantford. In the fall of 1924, Morgan arrived with 20 RCMP officers.

They interrupted a meeting of the sachems, declared their government abolished, broke open their safe, and seized their legal records. This included wampum belts, sacred symbols of Iroquois treaty-making and government. The police even went into people's homes to remove loose wampum (shell beads) that might be used to make new belts. An election was staged on October 21, 1924. The population of Six Nations had been recorded as 4615 in 1920. Only 52 people voted in the election. The community has been divided on the issue ever since.

The RCMP never quite won the trust of the Six Nations people. On March 5, 1959, about 1300 Six Nations people marched to the council house. They were led by a group calling itself the Mohawk Warriors. The elected council fled out the back door as the Mohawk Warriors were removing the locked front door from its hinges. A community meeting was held, which roughly 5000 people attended. They drafted a proclamation in which the elected council was abolished and the Longhouse council restored. They also appointed a 133-member police force to replace the unwelcome outside force, at that time the RCMP. The police force began patrolling the reserve, arresting motorists for traffic infractions.

The federal government moved quickly. First, they ordered the new police to stop making arrests. Then, one week after the takeover,

> [A]t three o'clock in the morning, sixty RCMP officers attacked the council house, where about 130 people had gathered to resist the expected raid. A riot quickly developed, led by the Iroquois women, who tried to push the police out. As television cameras recorded the scene, the police clubbed the Iroquois and dragged them out of the council house (York and Pindera, 1991: 165).

The successors of the RCMP in this role, the OPP, would fare little better in earning the trust of the people. Sergeant Rob Davis, a six-year veteran of the Six Nations Police Service, states that "I can remember seeing two OPP officers trying to cover the whole reserve when I was a kid ... There was a lack of respect for them because they were seen as outsiders. A lot of people wouldn't even talk to them if they witnessed a crime."

The Six Nations Police Service

In 1985, the Six Nations Police Service (SNPS) was formed, taking over from the OPP. The formation was led by Police Chief Keith Lickers, then a seven-year member of the RCMP. Speaking to a reporter recently of the challenge of creating a police force for the community of some 11 000, he said, "There was only myself and one other officer who had any experience or history in policing when we started here ... We had to start from scratch and train new recruits. This meant almost our entire service was comprised of young, inexperienced officers."

From the beginning, the officers were from the Six Nations community. Lickers looks positively upon some of the unique policing challenges of Native people policing their own community. He feels that the officers have a vested interest in improving a community in which they and their family have been raised, and that, unlike in more urban policing settings, the officers can actually see the positive effect they are having. He sees a role-model effect of young people seeing community members forming their own police service. He also believes that when the people see that officers are known community members rather than anonymous officials, they trust them more, as they know that the officers understand what life is like in the community. Lickers puts a positive accountability spin on the fact that the service came into existence by virtue of a band-council resolution, and could be taken out of existence by another such resolution:

> If band council has to do something as drastic as disband us, they would only do so if there was a lot of pressure from the community to do that. The only time you would see that pressure is if we weren't doing our jobs. Therefore the fact that we still exist at all is an endorsement of our efforts.

The SNPS deals with the thorny issue of an officer having to arrest a relative by assigning unrelated officers to particular cases. The SNPS can do this as they are a relatively large service, having 20 members.

Critiquing the Six Nations Police Force

As with all police services, the SNPS is not without its critics. One is Mohawk writer/broadcaster Brian Maracle, who wrote a book, *Back on the Rez: Finding the Way Back Home*, describing his first year back (1993–1994) in the Six Nations community of his childhood. His critique of the SNPS has a twofold nature. He feels that the police commission and the police service are too close, so that the former is not sufficiently tough on the latter. This point is made in a chapter tellingly entitled "Don't Do It Again or We'll Have to Get Tough, Sir," referring to an alcohol-related conviction in which he feels the commission was too lenient on the police chief.

The second critique concerns what Maracle feels is "the colour of the law," that the SNPS reproduces what he believes are the inequities of mainstream policing services, without putting a more egalitarian Native influence on the policing. He sums up his argument with the following:

> So, given that we'll probably have to put up with a white-oriented police force for some time to come, I think it should be subject to the same kind of discipline as other police forces. The problem is that the local police commission has undermined the concept of discipline and public accountability. As a result, the Six Nations police are becoming more and more like the other parts of the Eurojustice system—a system that is arbitrary and discriminatory, a system that punishes the poor and the meek while protecting the wealthy and powerful. (Maracle, 1996: 158)

Akwesasne and Policing

Akwesasne ("Where the Partridge Drums") is a community near Cornwall that is divided along several critical faultlines: Canada/United States; Christian/Longhouse; warrior faction/ peace faction; elected council/traditional government; cigarette/anti-cigarette; and gambling/

anti-gambling. Fierce factionalism, such as that which has developed at Akwesasne, has its own dirty logic. It can take originally fair and reasonable ideals such as unity, sovereignty, and peace and taint them so they become, at times, not a lot more than the colours of a biker gang. Noble causes become temporarily forgotten in the amnesia of personal and family vendettas. Power and wealth, originally pursued to further worthy causes, can become more purely personal goals. It should be noted that in Murphy and Clairmont's study of Aboriginal policing in 1996, of the officers surveyed, 51 percent said that community factionalism or in-fighting was "Somewhat a Problem" and 20 percent said that it was a "Big Problem" (Murphy and Clairmont, 1996).

Outside-run police forces are left with hard choices. They can easily become players in the factionalism game if they are not careful, furthering the agenda of one side against another (see Box 7.2 for an example of how the media can play into this). The people want and need a unified police force that all can respect, but this can only be established with great difficulty.

Box 7.2	**Taking Sides**

Writers can easily be drawn into the factionalism game, assigning "good guy" and "bad guy" roles to one faction or another. New York journalist Rick Hornung, in his sensationalist work *One Nation Under the Gun: Inside the Mohawk Civil War* shows preference for the pro-gambling Mohawk Warrior faction in the clash of the late 1980s to 1990. He portrays the casino owners as more innocent "entrepreneurs" than they were, failing to adequately make note of their criminal connections and activities (e.g., concerning the smuggling of hard drugs and guns). Likewise, he seemed overly dazzled by the rhetoric of the Mohawk Warriors (his main informants for the book), while ignoring the "man with a gun" bullying that did take place.

The authors themselves hold to a position that is more sympathetic to one faction over the other. We have sympathy for the peace/anti-gambling group, a sympathy that could well show up in the writing of this chapter.

Blame is easily attached to individuals, but it is a long historical process and unique set of circumstances that brought factionalism to the community. It began with the imposition of elected democracy.

The First Division: The Imposition of Elected Democracy

Imagine this scenario. Police entice the leaders of a people to meet with them under the false pretence of a business deal that will financially benefit the people. The police then gun down the foremost leader in the midst of arresting the others. That happened in the Mohawk community of Akwesasne.

The Great Law of Peace had established that the Mohawk had nine sachems or chiefs, three from each of their three clans. One would be considered the head chief and the others would be sub-chiefs. Each clan also had three clan mothers. This had been the system used by the people of Akwesasne since the community was established during the mid-1700s.

With the *Indian Act* of 1876 and the *Indian Advancement Act* of 1884, the federal government of Canada officially gave itself power to impose its version of "democracy" upon the Mohawk of Akwesasne in their community government. The federal Indian agent could disallow the election of any given person should he deem the person unsuitable.

In 1891, in the first election at Akwesasne, the five chiefs who won were all found guilty of following the non-Native practice (illegal but not uncommon) of dispensing alcohol to gain votes. Problems also occurred with chiefs elected the next year. The people wanted to return to less disruptive traditional practices. A petition signed by over 1000 Akwesasne, Kanesatake, and Kahnawake Mohawk stated that

> The *Indian Act* breeds only sorrow, contention, hatred, disrespect of family ties, spite against one another, and absence of unity among us Indians. It also creates two distinct parties at the elections ... There is only one way to recover brotherly feelings, that of substituting the seven lords appointed by each of the seven totems according to the ancient customs which we know gave us peace, prosperity, friendship and brotherly feelings in every cause, either for personal good, or to the benefit of the whole community" (Mitchell, 1989: 116–117).

In 1898, the Indian agent, with police backup, failed to enforce the European-style election process at Akwesasne. Nine months later, Indian Agent George Long brought two police officers with him to the schoolhouse where a federal government-imposed election was supposed to occur. In the words of the *Montreal Star:*

> They found [the schoolhouse] surrounded by about 200 aborigines ... They were refused admittance and a general riot took place. The police were badly assaulted and Indian Agent Long was seized and locked up in the school house. A guard was placed over him, and the Dominion Police were driven away. At six o'clock at night, Mr. Long was still caged up (York and Pindera, 1991: 160).

A few weeks later, on May 1, the federal government tried a different tactic. A contingent of RCMP officers pretending to represent a construction company sent a message to the leaders or chiefs of Akwesasne, claiming that they might want to purchase some stone from the community for the repair of the bridge that crossed the St. Lawrence (and the Akwesasne reserve). When the chiefs entered the Indian agent's office, they were seized and handcuffed. One, the brother of the head chief, was hurled to the floor. A woman notified the head chief, variously referred to as Jack Fire or Jack Ice, of what was happening to his brother. When he tried to free his brother, he was shot twice and killed. Over the following few weeks, 15 Mohawk were arrested and jailed. Five of the chiefs were imprisoned for almost a year. After a trial in the spring of 1900, they were released with a strong warning.

Shortly after the arrests, the police[6] took some 15 Mohawk to nearby Cornwall to hold an "election" of councillors. There are allegations that they supplied these people with alcohol. In subsequent years, the "elected representatives" of a community of thousands were put into office by as few as 20 voters. In 1986, May 1 was declared a "national holiday" in Akwesasne in recognition of the above incident.

The development of a Mohawk Warrior Society in Akwesasne has its roots in a confrontation between an elected council and its supporters, and the Longhouse and its supporters. In the spring of 1979, Loran Thompson, a Longhouse sub-chief in his thirties, saw some workers cutting down trees near his home on Raquette Point, on the American side of Akwesasne. They were following orders of the New York elected council who wanted to build a fence around the reserve. The Longhouse opposed that fence as potentially reducing chances to regain more of their traditional territory, so Thompson confronted the workers and confiscated their chainsaws. He was arrested by Akwesasne Police officers working with state troopers. The Akwesasne Police had been created by and answered to the elected council. Their relationship to the community at the time was not the best, as there were reported beatings of community members (Garte, 1981, citing Longhouse Chief Jake Swamp). Longhouse followers staged a protest, disarmed the Akwesasne Police, and briefly took over the building that held the police station and the elected council's headquarters.

Over the months that followed, Thompson's home became the refuge for those Longhouse supporters fearing arrest after this event. The state troopers arrived with a SWAT team and blockaded the roads leading to Raquette Point. The Mohawk at Thompson's place established bunkers but nothing much happened, although tension was high. When the troopers left, Christian Mohawk vigilantes who supported the elected council built their own barricades and threatened to storm the house and take the wanted men into custody. The troopers returned, but despite the great potential for violence, nothing serious happened.

Longhouse Chief Tom Porter said the following in an interview in November 1980:

> Either we do the slow, assimilated death or we do one that's going to be just shot, point blank by an M-16, by either the vigilantes or the state police ... But at least they're going to know if that doesn't happen ... that they're not going to change us and they're not going to get their way. They're not going to change these instructions which we call the Creator's instructions (Garte, 1981).

In 1980 and 1981, two of the three band council members were defeated in elections and were replaced by people more willing to cooperate with the traditionalists. They disbanded the Akwesasne Police force. In 1981, a judge dismissed the indictments against Thompson.

The Second Division: Customs and Cigarettes

Akwesasne is a community divided by jurisdiction, national and provincial. Slightly less than two-thirds of the community is in New York. The rest is found in Ontario and Quebec. The international border is on Kawehnoke ("island in water") or Cornwall Island, with an 8- to 10-foot tall chain-link fence topped with razor wire physically carving up the community. Complicating this matter is the **Jay Treaty** of Amity and Commerce, enacted in 1794 to deal with several border issues between the United States and Britain. Both governments were concerned that trading posts on the American side of the border would lose business if the Natives were not allowed to move freely across the border to bring furs for trade. So the Jay Treaty allowed them to cross the border with their personal "goods and effects" without having to pay customs duties.

Lieutenant-Governor John Graves Simcoe, speaking to the Six Nations representatives at Fort Erie on August 28, 1795, worded this agreement as follows: "[Y]ou have a right to go to the British Settlements, or to those of the U. States, as shall suit your convenience, nor shall your passing or repassing with your own proper goods and effects of whatever nature, pay for the same any impost whatever" (Mitchell, 1989: 113).

The legal status of the Jay Treaty is controversial. The United States has officially put it into law (see Kahnawake section in the chapter on Quebec), while Canada has not. Yet there have been unofficial understandings that have allowed the border-dwelling Mohawk the right to cross without a customs check. Six Nations or Mohawk passports have been recognized. There have been confrontations concerning customs. In 1968, when the federal government decided to levy customs on Mohawk crossing the border, the people seized the Seaway International Bridge. This resulted in the OPP and RCMP arresting 48 people.

This treaty, combined with the location of Akwesasne, brings into play an important aspect of policing Akwesasne: the cigarette trade.[7] First Nations people can purchase for personal use an unlimited amount of tax-free cigarettes in the United States. There are high taxes put on cigarettes in Canada. Cigarette manufacturers in Canada make the same profit per package regardless of taxes paid by the consumer. These manufacturers ship a great number of cigarettes to the United States, not unaware[8] that when taxes are high many of those cigarettes will make their way back to Canada through Akwesasne, by boat, or when the St. Lawrence is frozen, by truck or snowmobile (see Box 7.3).

Box 7.3	How Much Money Can You Make in the Cigarette Trade?

Akwesasne Chief Mike Mitchell, as quoted in a CBC interview in the early 1990s, described the profit margin for cigarettes at that time as follows:

> The money—it's unbelievable the money you can make and it's so easy ... You can buy a pack of cigarettes on the American side of the reservation for

$1.58 and you go across here in Cornwall and you have to buy it for close to $7.00 a pack, same pack, within a short distance of each other, so no one is surprised that all this is happening. (Kendall, Linden, and Murray, 2000: 203, citing a study by sociologist Margaret Beare, 1996: 272)

A stereotyping attitude toward Akwesasne exists that suggests all Mohawk smuggle cigarettes (not to mention drugs, alcohol, and guns). However, there is not a uniform feeling toward the cigarette trade in Akwesasne itself. Some feel it is a matter of rights. Some are forced to turn to it when times are hard and cigarette taxes (and therefore profit margin) are especially high. Some are completely opposed to the trade. Very few want the notoriety that the trade has brought to the community, nor the connections to organized crime and the smuggling of drugs and weapons.

Attempting a Unified Police Force

During the latter half of the 1980s, there was an attempt by people at Akwesasne to develop a unified council with a unified peacekeeping force. The council existed from 1986 to 1988, but was voted out when more divisive interests, including those involved with gambling in New York and hard-core smuggling, returned the people to a more divided system.

In 1986, what is referred to as the Tri-Council appointed conservation officers as constables to enforce their conservation bylaws. The bylaw establishing the authority of these officers was disallowed by the Department of Indian Affairs, which has the power to disallow any bylaw passed by a band council. The council tried to have their conservation officers trained by the Ontario Ministry of Natural Resources but the ministry refused, so the council went to New York to have their officers trained by the New York State Police and the

US Conservation Authority. The OPP charged one of the officers with unauthorized possession of a restricted weapon when they caught the officer carrying his service revolver. The council had tried to register the weapon but the RCMP had refused to do so because it did not consider the Akwesasne Police Force a law-enforcement agency, even though the officers held a measure of police authority from both Ontario and Quebec provincial governments. The charge was initially dismissed, appealed, and then dismissed again.

In 1989, Grand Chief Mike Mitchell described with great frustration what his council was going through:

> Our bylaw creating and empowering our police force in 1986 was disallowed because it was felt it was outside the authority of a band council. But what else would the Indian Act mean when it authorizes bylaws for "law and order"? And why have similar bylaws in other communities been enacted without being disallowed?
>
> As can be seen, many of these bylaws dealt in one way or another with the problems of peace and order. In that category we have had eleven bylaws disallowed, having to do with nuisance, trespass, residency, explosives, weapons, and so on. We are convinced that, if these bylaws had been in force, we would not have experienced the problems we have had recently in connection with the smuggling of cigarettes, guns, liquor, and drugs. (Mitchell, 1989: 128)

On October 13, 1988, 250 officers from the RCMP, the OPP, the Cornwall City Police, and the New York State Police and Border Patrol conducted a raid on Akwesasne, sealing off Cornwall Island for four hours. They were looking for cigarettes, illegal drugs, and weapons. They had not consulted the Akwesasne council or their partially recognized police service before this raid. In the words of Chief Mitchell, "Unfortunately, because of the massive abuse of police power represented by the October 13 raid, we cannot see ourselves trusting these outside agencies again. They have alienated the people of Akwesasne ... By this raid the Canadian authorities sent us a message: they do not trust us, nor do they want our co-operation. Our governing council and our police force were both kept ignorant of the planned raid, apparently because we were also suspects" (Mitchell, 1989: 131, 132).

The people's desperate need for this unified police force would be seen shortly after Mitchell wrote the article quoted above.

The Third Division: Gambling

Beginning in the early 1970s, gambling would come to the New York side of Akwesasne. Bingos and casinos were allowed in New York State. Slot machines weren't, but they arose in American Akwesasne anyway. Gambling became an issue over which the Longhouse supporters would be divided. In 1986, Longhouse Sub-Chief Loran Thompson proposed a contract to be financed by a private investor to operate a bingo. The Longhouse would get 51 percent of the profits and Thompson would get 19 percent from the private investor's profits. He claimed to have the signatures of three clan mothers in support of this venture. Longhouse Chiefs Tom Porter and Jake Swamp and many others in the Longhouse opposed the idea of connecting tradition with gambling. Thompson was removed as Sub-Chief and the deal fell through.

In 1987, the Tri-Council held a referendum on gambling, and the majority voted against it. This was ignored. It could not be enforced. New York State Police slot machine raids, encouraged by the anti-gambling elected council, became a common event in Akwesasne. On December 16, 1987, more than 200 officers came in and removed 293 machines.

In 1988, the office of the well-known and successful Native journal/newspaper *Akwesasne Notes* was destroyed by arson. The editor, Longhouse supporter Doug George, had been writing editorials opposing illegal gambling, drug and gun running, and the crime network that he felt was being established in the community by the Mohawk Warrior Society. George, who had supported Thompson in the Raquette Point matter, was now his bitter enemy, as well as a highly critical opponent of the Mohawk Warrior Society. In speeches and newspaper articles he was recorded as saying "As far as every legitimate Iroquois government is concerned, there can be no such thing as the Warrior Society ... This organization operates outside Iroquois law, without the sanction of Iroquois government. It is, by its essence, illicit" (quoted in York and Pindera, 1991: 264).

The opinion of the Mohawk Warrior Society was different. They felt that they were defending sovereignty by establishing an independent economy for the people. They deeply resented that the anti-gambling people, such as Doug George, Grand Chief Mike Mitchell, and the Tri-Council, resorted to bringing in outsider police to fight gambling. In the words of Mohawk Warrior Art Montour or Kakwirakeron ("Many Branches Lying About On The Ground"):

> Are we a nation? If we are a nation, do we rule ourselves? Are we sovereign? This is the real issue behind gambling. When one group of Mohawks began to express a desire for sovereignty and nationhood by establishing an economy, another group of Mohawks asked the police to come in. It is the trooper's job to exploit the division among us. The police are not the source of the problem. It is how we work among ourselves. The casinos are only the surface—look beyond them and see what we are as a community. (Hornung, 1991: 16)

On July 20, 1989, more than 400 FBI agents and New York State Police officers stormed the community, arresting 11 people on gambling charges. This was followed by 11 days of police blockades in the community. Later than summer, about 100 of the Mohawk Warriors met to determine how to prevent this happening again. They decided to establish the Mohawk Sovereign Security Force (MSSF). Eight patrol vehicles were painted white and bore the insignia of the MSSF. The officers' pay ($300 a week) was supplied by regular donations from the owners of the casinos and from cigarette retailers. Seen from one view, it was a private police force, and that was the way it sometimes acted, as little more than security guards for casinos. And sometimes some of their number would act like hired guns and criminals. But that is not how they thought of themselves. There was also another side to the MSSF, one that can be seen in the following quotations from John Boots and Art Montour, respectively:

> We are peacekeepers, whose only purpose is to protect ourselves from outsiders and traitors. We have no intent to provoke violence, nor do we want to hurt any one of our brothers and sisters in the Mohawk Nation.
> We will patrol our own land as the Mohawk Sovereign Security Patrol, and we will persist like the people of Vietnam and Afghanistan until the outside intervention is stopped. Just as Afghanistan was to the Soviet Union and Vietnam to the United States, Akwesasne will be to New York State and the United States. (Hornung, 1991: 28–29)

The police force that was recognized by the council at that time also had two sides, private and public. On the night of August 26–27, 1989, anti-gambling protesters marched on the Mohawk Warriors Society headquarters and set a newly built casino, the Lucky Knight, on fire. Among those alleged to have been at the scene at the time were Grand Chief Mike Mitchell, one of the leaders of the anti-gambling faction, as well as several off-duty members of the St. Regis Akwesasne Mohawk Police. On a number of occasions, the MSSF claimed that the St. Regis Akwesasne Mohawk Police had attempted to provoke them so that the MSSF would look bad.

The two forces competed for legitimacy as *the* official policing agency at Akwesasne. In December, 1989, Major Leu, the New York State Police Commander of the unit assigned to Akwesasne, met with the elected council to discuss making the MSSF the official policing authority on the American side of Akwesasne. The elected council refused this and asked to have Leu removed from his position.

Violence was escalating in the community. On January 20, 1990, St. Regis Akwesasne Mohawk Police Chief Ernie King is quoted in the *Toronto Star* as saying, "We are beyond saying that someone is going to get hurt. We now know someone is going to get killed."

From March 23 to May 1, 1990, there ensued what has been referred to as the "Battle for Akwesasne." It had impact not only in that community, but would help set the stage for the conflict at Oka, as some of the Mohawk Warriors who fought there would begin their fighting at Akwesasne.

The combatants took different positions on several issues, primarily that of gambling. On March 23, the anti-gambling faction, a loose alliance of "peace" faction Longhouse members, Christians, and supporters of the elected council, took the dramatic step of setting up barricades that blocked access to a strip of eight casinos on the American side of Akwesasne. They were led by Doug George.

George stated that they set up the barricades because they were "determined to hold out until the three councils could assure the people there would be an overall disarmament and ongoing negotiations to resolve the anarchy which was consuming Akwesasne" (George, 2000). In the telling words of that same writer, "In the end, the absence of a peacekeeping force to keep the sides apart meant a final clash was inevitable."

With the erection of the barricades, battle lines were formally and physically drawn. Sporadic battle ensued, with verbal abuse, fist fights, physical assault, and the firing of guns. Schools would be closed, and an estimated 2000 people temporarily left the community in fear of their lives. The Travelling College (well-known for its work in teaching Native culture and history) on Cornwall Island became a refugee camp and communications centre. On April 23 and 24, the MSSF and their supporters raided the roadblocks. Twenty-four cars were destroyed by fire and bulldozer. The barricades were torn down by April 25. There was a bombing at the tribal police station. A home of the George family became a defensive fortress for the anti-gambling side. Two Mohawk would be killed in gunfights. Doug George would be charged with murder but would be freed after a six-day preliminary hearing. The fighting ended on May 1, 1990, when provincial and state police sealed off the community. New York State declared the American part of the community under martial law.

Mohawk Warriors from Akwesasne, Loran and Larry ("Wizard") Thompson, Francis Boots, and Gordon "Noriega" Lazore, would become leading figures in the confrontation at Oka. They began their fighting in their home community.

Akwesasne Policing Agreement

The *Akwesasne Policing Agreement* (APA) was signed in 1990 and initially lasted until 1993 (subsequently renewed). It created the Akwesasne Mohawk Police, with jurisdiction over the Canadian part of the community. The American section is served by the St. Regis

Mohawk Tribal Police, who so far have a relatively unstable relationship as deputies of the local county sheriff's office. In 2000, they lost that status as a result of their denying entry into the community trucks hired by companies owing the elected council leasing fees.

The APA is unique in involving both the Ontario and Quebec governments, the OPP, and the Sûreté du Québec (SQ). The cost-sharing is Canada 52 percent and the two provinces 24 percent each. It also contains the following passage, unique in Ontario agreements:

> the parties share the objective that the Mohawk people of Akwesasne shall have autonomous and independent policing services and that such services shall be provided by the Akwesasne Mohawk Police under the control of the people of Akwesasne. (quoted in Stenning, 1996: 69)

The Akwesasne Mohawk Police faced a major challenge in the 1990s, in that outside policing agencies staged a series of police raids and sting operations in their community, arresting Mohawks for smuggling semi-automatic and automatic weapons, cigarettes, alcohol, and drugs.

They appear to have successfully met this challenge. For example, on April 28, 1997, following one year of undercover investigation, a dawn raid at Akwesasne was staged netting a sizable amount of alcohol and tobacco. This time, unlike the situation in 1988, along with the RCMP, the US Border Patrol, New York State Police, and the US Customs Service, the Akwesasne Mohawk Police were involved.

NOTES

1. This erroneous perception may be rooted in the low number of charges laid by the APS officers for impaired driving, the offence rated as constituting the biggest problem for Sagamok residents (Barron, 1998: 137).

2. While it is hard to put a precise date on the formation of the *Great Law of Peace*, most writers estimate the origin as either 1451 or 1536, two years when there was an eclipse of the sun, as related in the story.

3. They are usually said to have been living somewhere around the Bay of Quinte, toward the eastern end of Lake Ontario. Along with this interpretation is the belief that they were Wendat (Huron), the people who lived in the area at that time.

4. At the same time, another group of Mohawk, following John Deserontyon, founded a community at the eastern end of Lake Ontario. It is known as Tyendinaga, after Joseph Brant's Mohawk name.

5. This opposition was in part a lack of understanding of how Iroquois democracy worked and in part an attempt to get rid of the troublesome hereditary chiefs, who had often resisted federal government control.

6. On the American side of Akwesasne, police were also used to impose an elected council. In 1948, the people of that part of the community had voted to abolish the elected system and return to traditional governance. The next year, police guard was required to re-establish the foreign system.

7. For an insightful and often humourous look at the cigarette trade in the Six Nations community, read Mohawk writer Brian Maracle's *Back on the Rez,* especially the chapters entitled "If We Don't Sell Them, Someone Else Will," "The Big Smoke," and "Roasting the Media."

8. Allegations have been made that implicate officials of the major tobacco companies in transporting to the United States huge amounts of cigarettes, particularly of brands popular only in Canada. The allegation is they know that these cigarettes will eventually be sold in Canada.

KEY TERMS

Code of Handsome Lake
   (p. 98)

Great Law of Peace (p. 96)

Jay Treaty (p. 103)

Haudenosaunee (p. 97)

Longhouse (p. 97)

sachem (p. 96)

REVIEW QUESTIONS

1. What was the fundamental issue in the protest that led to the shooting of Dudley George?
2. Outline the development of Aboriginal policing at Sagamok.
3. How do Sagamok residents perceive Native officers differently from non-Native officers?
4. Why did the RCMP not earn the trust of the Six Nations people?
5. What two opposing interpretations of the Mohawk Sovereign Security Force can be made?

chapter eight

Aboriginal Policing
in Quebec

LEARNING OBJECTIVES

After completing this chapter, students should be able to:

1. Outline the historical relationship between the outsider police forces (e.g., the RCMP and the Sûreté du Québec) and the Mohawk of Kahnawake.

2. Describe the development of the Kahnawake Mohawk Warriors Society as an alternative police force.

3. Discuss the role of the Sulpicians in the Kanehsatake Mohawks' lack of rights relative to other Native and non-Native communities.

4. Critically analyze the role of the Sûreté du Québec in the Oka confrontation.

5. Identify the keys to the success of the Kitigan Zibi Anishinabeg Police Department.

6. Outline the development of policing among the James Bay Cree.

In Quebec, there are eight different Native groups: Mohawk, Algonquin, Abenaki, Huron, Cree, Attikamek, Inuit, and Innu (Montagnais and Naskapi). The Amerindian Police Service was first developed in 1978, originally to provide policing in 23 First Nations in Quebec. The Mohawk of Kahnawake dropped out of the service in 1979. In early 1995, nine communities withdrew from the force, leaving thirteen communities under its jurisdiction: six Montagnais, three Algonquin, two Attikamek, one Abenaki, and one Mi'kmaq. The service seems to have suffered in the early years from lack of definition of the roles of those who should be guiding it (e.g., the director-general of the police service, the police council, the board of directors, and the local public security committees); in one early review, it was considered to be "autocratic, centralizing, and rejecting almost any consultation or discussion" (Woods Gordon, 1982, cited in Stenning, 1996: 154). This characteristic, plus tension between the governing authorities and the Director-General, were probably due in large part to the fact that too much direction came from the provincial government and the Sûreté du Québec (SQ; the first director-general was a non-Native former SQ officer). Also, the Native communities and peoples themselves were permitted too little input because they were Aboriginal.

Today, Aboriginal policing is somewhat different in Quebec than in the rest of Canada. There is a greater number of smaller First Nations policing services serving only one community than is found in other provinces. Perhaps this is one reason why officers are so poorly paid relative to their First Nations policing services colleagues in other parts of the country, as was revealed in the First Nations Chiefs of Police Association (FNCPA) study conducted in 2000. Police chiefs, deputy chiefs, second class and fourth class constables, and recruits all have lower salaries than anywhere else in Canada, and for almost all other ranks the salary is lower than the national average for First Nations policing services (FNCPA 2001, 8.1, "Financial Compensation"). Murphy and Clairmont's survey published in 1996 revealed that the 27 officers studied who, in their terms, had been "SQ Coached," had the least amount of education and experience, were the least likely to receive upgrading training once they were hired, and had (along with band constables) the lowest level of satisfaction with the training they received (Murphy and Clairmont, 1996).

KAHNAWAKE MOHAWK POLICING: TWO SOLITUDES IN QUEBEC

There are few positive connections between the Kahnawake Mohawk, whose territory is near Montreal, and the French-speaking majority in Quebec. There is a long history of conflict between the French and Mohawk that began in 1609 when the "Father of New France," Samuel de Champlain, decided to strengthen the French connection with their new allies, the Montagnais, Algonquin, and Huron, by joining in a raid on the Mohawk in which 50 Mohawk warriors were killed and 10 to 12 taken prisoner. French-Canadian historians have in the past considered the Mohawk (and other Iroquois) as "des loups alteres du sang" [bloodthirsty wolves] (Smith, 1974: 28),[1] and there is still conflict between the two peoples. Most Mohawk do not speak French. Many Quebecois consider the Kahnawake Mohawk to be Anglos, or at least allied to the English-speaking minority in opposition to French sovereignty. Few firm institutional links exist, particularly, as we will see, in the area of policing. In the words of Mohawk educator and writer Gerald (or Taiaiake) Alfred,

> Quebec poses a clear and present threat to the Mohawks' efforts to develop autonomous institutions in such areas as policing and education. Kahnawake Mohawks have rejected the legitimacy of Quebec institutions within their community and responded to the perceived danger of an imposed Quebec sovereignty in their community by developing "alterNative" institutions. (Alfred, 1995: 17)

Birth of a Community

You could say that Kahnawake was a community born out of violence. In 1666, Alexandre de Prouville de Tracy led a 1000-plus invasion force into the heart of Mohawk country. Luckily, when the French army approached, the 300 to 400 Mohawk warriors, along with the more numerous women and children, easily eluded their less woods-wise antagonists. Unfortunately, the French torched the Mohawk villages, fields, and much of their crucial winter supplies of food, mostly corn.

In 1667, Jesuit Father Pierre Raffeix, feeling that de Tracy had pacified the Mohawk, encouraged half a dozen Oneida who had been visiting the Montreal area to winter on the south shore of the St. Lawrence. The mission, named St. François-Xavier, would become a success, at the population cost of the Mohawk communities in what is now New York State. In 1677, the village moved up the river to the Lachine Rapids and became known as Kahnawake ("At the Rapids"), named both after the location and the name of the eventually abandoned Mohawk community in more traditional territory from which it drew most of its population.

There has been a long history of conflict between the Mohawk of Kahnawake and outsider police agencies. For the most part, this stems from three factors: expropriation of land, the cigarette trade, and differing notions of how Kahnawake should be governed. The reserve, close to Montreal, has long been a particular target of expropriation, shrinking the original 17 800-hectare reserve to less than one-third its size (5260 hectares). Railways, highways, bridges, and the St. Lawrence Seaway have all been put through the reserve in this way. In 1922, two Kahnawake Mohawk chiefs were shot by Royal Canadian Mounted Police (RCMP) officers during protests against a federal construction project restricting Kahnawake access to the St. Lawrence.

In 1926, an important strategic event occurred. Paul Diabo, a Kahnawake Mohawk, was arrested in Philadelphia as an illegal alien. His defence was the Jay Treaty, and it was upheld. The right of the Iroquois people to free passage across the Canada-US border was reaffirmed by a federal judge. Another important consequence came of that case. The Mohawk of Kahnawake had been politically separated from the other Rotinohshonni (to write the word in Mohawk) or Iroquois for some 250 years. The Grand Councils, both at Onondaga, New York, and at Six Nations in Ontario, rallied to support the Kahnawake Mohawk in this case. The Longhouse had returned.

The Community Divides

In the 1940s and 1950s, a sharp division in the community emerged. On the one hand, there was the group that referred to itself as the "Intelligent Party." These people were educated, Catholic, spent a lot of time off-reserve, and wanted greater integration into Canadian society. The other side was a somewhat loose alliance of the growing number of traditional Longhouse people, and, somewhat unusual, the elected council (which in other Mohawk communities usually opposes the Longhouse). These allies wanted a more traditional style of government and wished for greater structural independence from the Kahnawakero:non or "people who live by the rapids." The latter group would gain in power in the 1950s with the development of the Seaway.

The St. Lawrence Seaway

The development of the **St. Lawrence Seaway** in the mid-1950s meant that land had to be expropriated along the river. In part because the Kahnawake reserve was already considered to be "federal land" and would be somewhat easier legally to obtain than privately owned land, Mohawk land was expropriated. This hit the Kahnawake people hard. It cost them a lot of land, 526 hectares. It separated them from the river that had been part of their lives for at least hundreds of years before European contact. The band council fought the expropriation every peaceful way it could, including petitioning Britain and the United Nations. Some people found it harder to resist and took cash settlements; resentment against them continues to this day. The RCMP enforced the expropriation, which reinforced their status as an "outsider agency."

The experience radicalized the community along traditional lines. In the words of Alfred,

> If the Seaway is viewed as the catalyst for the community's rejection of the Canadian government's legitimacy, then ... the Seaway is responsible for activating the traditionalist movement in Kahnawake. The legacy of the Seaway betrayal in Kahnawake thus contributes to the high intensity of the Mohawk assertion of independence. (Alfred, 1995: 162)

A Police Force of Their Own

Confrontations concerning the Seaway were only one instance of the RCMP being seen as acting against the people rather than for them. During World War II, although the Kahnawake Mohawk volunteered for battle in high numbers, others resisted conscription, feeling that it violated their sovereignty. Fights ensued between the Mohawk and RCMP. Longhouse meetings were raided by the RCMP. Drinking was a contentious issue. The Mohawk could not in the 1940s legally drink anywhere, so the RCMP raided restaurants and weddings where Mohawk were suspected of drinking. In one storied incident in 1948, a group of Mohawk men ganged up on an RCMP officer, beating him up as he was trying to make arrests in a restaurant. There were for a while special constables (Big Six Jocks, Tom Lahache, and Frank Lahache), sworn in under the RCMP Act, but their positive effect was limited by the inferiority of their position relative to "real" constables.

But as much as the RCMP were outsiders, this was even more the case with the SQ, the provincial police.[2] In 1969, the federal government was trying to transfer some of its responsibilities for Aboriginals to the provinces, including policing. The Kahnawake Mohawk quickly responded by creating their own police force, the Kahnawake Peacekeepers, the first Native-controlled police force in the country. The federal and provincial governments and their respective police forces did not initially receive this well. An elected councillor and chief of the Kahnawake Mohawk of the time, interviewed in the 1990s, described this resistance and how they overcame it. The Mohawk leaders were asked to go to the local RCMP headquarters. They entered a room where the RCMP stood on one side, the SQ on the other, feeling like they were running the gauntlet. They were told that their police force was illegal, merely a group of "vigilantes":

> But we had done our homework by contacting several judges on the Superior Court and got them on our side. They were looking for a solution to the problems here too, and we told the police brass that we would stop it on the condition that we work toward establishing an Indian Police Force in Kahnawake. And they said, "all right." So we called a big meeting with all the people, the police brass and the judges. We had the Attorney General on our side too. And then the government had to agree to establish the Indian Police here. (Alfred, 1995: 112)

A Divided Longhouse

The first real test of the Kahnawake Peacekeepers would reveal a major division in the community, a division within the Longhouse. As the Longhouse grew in support during the 1950s with the construction of the Seaway, as with Mohawk and Iroquois communities elsewhere, more than one tradition of interpreting the *Great Law of Peace* emerged.

In the interpretation of Mohawk writer Gerald Alfred, to which the following description owes much (see Alfred, 1995: 66, 82–87), the Longhouse situation in Kahnawake can be described as follows:

> There has been no unified movement toward or interpretation of Iroquois tradition in Kahnawake. Beyond the consensus that the *Indian Act* and Western political values are inappropriate, there has been no singularly acceptable framework established within which a standard interpretation of the Kanienerekowa's principles could be achieved. This lack of consensus has manifested itself in mainly negative ways and has led to serious confrontations within the community. (Alfred, 1995: 83)

The Longhouse would divide in three. One of the divisions is the Warrior Longhouse, from which the Mohawk Warrior Society would develop in Kahnawake in the early 1970s. The person most often connected with this Longhouse and with the Mohawk Warrior Society is Longhouse chief Louis Hall (see the chapter on Ontario), although his influence is typically over-estimated by outsider journalists. There is also the Mohawk Trail Longhouse, which is strongly influenced by the Code of Handsome Lake and by its connections with the longhouses of the Iroquois Confederacy outside the Mohawk nation. Its message is primarily one of peace. Finally, there is the Five Nations Longhouse, which could in a sense be called the "fundamentalist" branch of the Longhouse, following as close as possible to the letter of the *Great Law of Peace*. According to Alfred, it focuses on injustices perpetrated by non-Native society and is against any form of cooperation with non-Native authorities and institutions.

The Evictions of 1973 and Policing

In August and September 1973 there was a showdown between different factions. It had to do with evicting band members from the territory, non-Native people who had married into the community. According to Alfred, the confrontation was not over whether or not the people should be evicted; they were considered "non-desirable elements." The battle was over who had the authority to kick them out.

The Longhouse and its newly formed Mohawk Warrior Society made the first move in the evictions. The band council opposed this taking of authority, and the opposition became violent. The Warrior Society attacked the band council building, and the chaos escalated. Legionnaires armed themselves to protect the local legion. The 10 members of the Mohawk Peacekeepers, lacking support from the RCMP or the SQ, resigned. The chief and council, much against their wishes, sent out a formal request that the SQ enter Mohawk territory. This didn't resolve the issue; it just created deeper trenches of separation among Kahnawake factions. The chief later resigned, as he was tainted for bringing the SQ into Mohawk territory.

The Confrontation of 1979

In 1978, Kahnawake joined the Amerindian Police Service in its inaugural year. This would not last. As stated on the Kahnawake Mohawk Peacekeepers Web site, "our force was accountable to the Quebec government. This was unacceptable, and in 1979 the Mohawk contingent withdrew from the Amerindian Police and formed an independent law enforcement body" (www.Kahnawake.com/peacekeepers/past.htm, consulted October 2001).

In 1979, a tragic event distanced the Kahnawake Mohawks even further than they had been from the SQ. An SQ officer, Constable Robert Lessard, tried to stop a vehicle for speeding. The driver did not stop. A chase ensued, leading onto Mohawk territory. One man, the driver as it turned out, ran into his house, leaving the passenger in the car. The officer arrested the passenger, Matthew Cross, and put him in the back seat of his vehicle. The driver, David Cross, Matthew's brother, came out of the house carrying a pool cue. He proceeded to try to rescue his brother. In the course of that attempt, he smashed in the windshield of the police car, and he was shot two or three times in the upper chest by the officer and killed.

A coroner's inquest was held. The coroner ruled that Constable Lessard was criminally responsible for the death of David Cross, that the shooting was an "abusive use of force" and that his handling of his weapon was "negligent, unskillful and acting without thinking." He was charged with manslaughter in 1980 but was acquitted by Quebec Superior Court. The Kahnawake community was furious, none more so than David Cross' cousin Ron, later to become known at Oka as the Mohawk Warrior "Lasagna."

The Mohawk Warriors of Kahnawake Gain Power

One effect of the shooting was bridge-building between factions at Kahnawake. Although they would still disagree on some issues, a summer meeting of people from all sides resolved (and this resolution was made official by the elected council) that they should move toward a more traditional form of government.

In 1981, a clash between the SQ and another Native group, the Mi'kmaq of Restigouche (on the Quebec/New Brunswick border) furthered Kahnawake concern about how dangerous to their community the provincial police force might be. Some 400 heavily armed officers twice raided the community to enforce provincial fishing regulations on salmon. Helicopters, bulldozers, tear gas, and clubs were used to confiscate fish and nets and to quell protests against the raids. A number of Mi'kmaq men, women, and children were hurt in the police raid.

The shooting of David Cross and the police invasion of Restigouche caused the people to begin to think of arming themselves against the outsider police. The elected council and the Warrior Longhouse (often referred to by writers and community members as "the Longhouse") spent about $10 000 to purchase about a dozen rifles and semi-automatic weapons that would be put in the hands of trusted community members (some of them Mohawk Warriors) in the event of a police "attack." When the cigarette trade came to Kahnawake (with cigarettes supplied largely through Akwesasne) in 1985, it supported the development of the Mohawk Warriors as a "policing alternative." In 1985–1986, cigarette retailers supplied the Warriors with a reputed $350 000 (their share of the 70 cents per carton that "the Longhouse" received from the retailers).

It is important to note that the advent of the cigarette trade and eventually gambling (super-bingo) was not dividing Kahnawake at the time as it was Akwesasne. Their recent histories had taken different paths. Furthermore, the people of Kahnawake did not have the jurisdictions and laws of two countries to contend with, and their gambling was limited to super-bingo and not the more volatile casinos and slot machines. In this way, the Warriors of Kahnawake would eventually develop into an institution that could present itself as having the support of the majority of the community, not merely representing a more isolated faction, which was the case with their fellow Warriors from Akwesasne.

By 1987, the Kahnawake Warriors had developed a formal code, which forbade the consumption of alcohol or drugs and which strictly controlled the use of firearms. Their discipline and organization would be tested the following year.

On June 1, 1988, roughly 200 RCMP officers, complete with helicopters, semi-automatic weapons, and bullet-proof vests staged a massive raid on six cigarette stores in Kahnawake. They arrested 17 people and seized some $450 000 worth of cigarettes. Within one hour of that attack the Warriors seized the Mercier Bridge, which had its southern point in Kahnawake. They were well-armed and kept the bridge closed for about 29 hours. They lifted their blockade only when the province and the federal government promised to negotiate on the cigarette issue.

This gave the Warriors more support than they had ever had before, even from those who opposed the "buttleg" cigarette industry. Since they had acted decisively, and the Mohawk Peacekeepers had looked ineffective in the police raid, the Warriors were appearing to many as the most respect-worthy "alternative" police force in Kahnawake.

The cigarette industry continued to grow, and with it the influence of the Mohawk Warriors. Cigarettes paid for a force of 30 warriors (twice that of the Mohawk Peacekeepers), who were paid $335 per week for four shifts of 12 hours. They patrolled the territory in 10 vehicles, establishing checkpoints and watching for further outsider police raids. Also, wearing masks to preserve their anonymity, they intimidated people suspected of being drug pushers or other forms of social predator.

The Mohawk Peacekeepers

The relationship between the Mohawk Peacekeepers and the Mohawk Warriors was that of an uneasy truce. They would communicate with each other regarding people they both considered as criminal. Following orders from the elected council, the Peacekeepers did not act upon the arrest warrants for Kahnawake people involved with the cigarette trade or with the barricades on the Mercier Bridge. The relationship between the Mohawk Peacekeepers and outsider police agencies during the 1980s leading up to 1990 was that of mutual respect for territory but no real connection. Ronald Cross (a.k.a. "Lasagna") described that relationship as follows:

> For a lot of years up till 1990 the Peacekeepers were pretty well respected by the RCMP and the SQ. They kind of worked together hand in hand. I mean, they weren't allowed to come here, the SQ and the RCMP, so if a car was chased onto the Territory they would be in touch with the Peacekeepers here in Kahnawake and the Peacekeepers would take over from there because they knew if they did try to come into Kahnawake here would be people who would have stopped them and who knows what would have happened. So they would go up to the borderlines of Kahnawake, and there the Kahnawake Peacekeepers would take over. (Cross and Sévigny, 1994: 48)

During the Oka Crisis, however, the outsider police agencies treated the Peacekeepers more as "Mohawk therefore suspect" than as fellow police officers. In Cross' words,

> In 1990, during the crisis, the SQ pulled over the Peacekeepers and had them kneeling on the ground and took their guns and arrested them and charged them with weapons charges. These guys were Peacekeepers here in Kahnawake, and this is what the SQ did. It was on the front pages of the papers. But they recognized them from the time the SQ left here in the late 1970s until the crisis in 1990. They were even recognized in their courts when they took our people out of their courts and brought them over here. They were recognized. And all of a sudden now the governments don't recognize them—because of all the stuff that went on in '90. (Cross and Sévigny, 1994: 49)

The Second Taking of the Mercier Bridge

Shortly after the SQ raid on the barricades, a dozen Mohawk militants from Kahnawake, some of whom had been in the US army in Vietnam, seized the Mercier Bridge. It was an impulsive act that took the community by surprise. They hadn't informed either the Kahnawake Warriors Society or the band council of what they were going to do. In the words of Kahnawake Warriors Society spokesman Kenneth Deer,

> The seizure of the Mercier Bridge happened so fast ... There was no plan, no coordination. We were thinking of ways to help the Mohawks at Kanehsatake, and all of a sudden we hear that members of our community are on the bridge with guns. We had to stand behind them, but we didn't have any idea what it would mean. (Hornung, 1991: 205)

The Warriors rushed to the bridge to establish a show of solidarity and to try to set up some form of leadership alliance with the militants. Not all the community supported the bridge takeover. Joe Norton, Chief of the elected band council, initially was opposed to the move, but gradually he changed his mind, perhaps in the interests of demonstrating community unity in the face of outsider opposition.

The opposition would grow quickly as commuters living on the South Shore faced a three-hour commute in order to bypass the bridge. Crowds of as many as 4000 demonstrated their anger against the blocking of the bridge, some yelling obscene and racist remarks. As the summer progressed into August, the protesters grew violent, attacking and injuring SQ officers. At nightly demonstrations, effigies of Mohawk were burned. United Nations observers were blocked from going to Kahnawake, and journalists were threatened with violence. One night, 200 demonstrators protesting the arrest of one of their leaders went to the police station where he was held and broke windows and destroyed two squad cars. On August 13, more than 400 pelted the police with rock and metal objects, and had tear gas canisters lobbed at them.

On August 28, a convoy of 75 vehicles evacuating Mohawk children, women, and Elders who feared racial violence left Kahnawake. A local French radio station alerted local residents to this fact so they were available in force (about 500) to impede the progress of the convoy. A group of some 20 young men threw rocks at the cars, injuring at least six Mohawk. No one was charged. Ojibwa journalist Richard Wagamese, in one of his thought-provoking articles on the subject of Oka, felt, "The biggest criminals walked away" (Wagamese, 1996: 76).

The night of August 28, the community voted on whether or not to abandon the bridge barricade. About 80 percent were in favour, and the barricades came down.

The Peacekeepers after Kahnawake

The next few years were tense for policing in Kahnawake. The checkpoints at the entrance to the community persisted. Finally, on September 11, 1995, after about a year of some-times difficult negotiations, the federal government, the province of Quebec, and the elected council of Kahnawake signed a five-year tripartite agreement concerning policing. The agreement included statements that there would be cooperation between the Peacekeepers, the RCMP, and the SQ, but time will tell whether this is possible beyond a minimum degree.

The Kahnawake Mohawk Peacekeepers identify themselves by the Mohawk word "Rontenatanónha," meaning "they who mind or take care of the community." As of 2001, the force had sixteen Peacekeepers (constables), five Auxiliary Peacekeepers, five corpo-rals, two investigators, a Chief of Peacekeepers and an Assistant Chief. The current Chief, relatively recently hired for the position, began his policing career in 1986 with the Peacekeepers, managed the ambulance program from 1987 to 1990, returned as an auxil-iary officer in the fall of that year, was elevated to full-time Peacekeeper in 1991, and was promoted to Corporal in 1995.

KANEHSATAKE MOHAWK POLICING: THE EARLY STORY

During the early 1700s, there were Mohawk living in the Montreal area but not in Kahnawake. Along with some Algonquin and Nipissing, they were being asked to leave the island of Montreal, which was then being developed as a French trade centre, and live in one community a short distance away to the northwest: Lac des Deux Montagnes (Lake of Two Mountains). The people asking them to leave were the Sulpicians, a Catholic religious order with powerful connections in France. They had been granted a seigneury in 1717 by Louis XV, with the idea that the seigneury would be a mission community. By 1721, nearly 900 Native people had moved into the mission; by 1735 a second grant of land had been added.

The Sulpicians enticed the Mohawk, Algonquin, and Nipissing with verbal promises of collective, safe land ownership. In the words of an eighteenth century Mohawk chief, Aughneeta, speaking to a government official in order to get their rights to the land recognized,

> [O]ur priests ... told us ... that if we should consent to go and settle at the Lake of Two Mountains we should have a large tract of land for which we should have a Deed from the King of France as our property to be vested in us and our heirs for ever, and that we should not be molested again in our habitations. (York and Pindera, 1991: 86)

These promises were not in writing, and that would severely hamper Native claims to the land for more than 250 years. The Sulpicians, although they would allow families to settle land and build homes, would keep control of how the resources were used. Their per-mission was required to use land, sell crops, and, in an issue that would be a major source of conflict between the priests and the Native people, to cut wood.

The First Armed Conflict

Over the years, the people of the community called "Oka" by the Algonquin ("walleye or pickerel") and Kanehsatake (probably meaning "there is plenty of sand") by the Mohawk, would see other Mohawk mission communities, Kahnawake and Akwesasne, gain reserve status while they still remained under the control of the Sulpicians. Time after time they would petition for recognition of their rights, only to be turned down.

In 1868, the people felt they had a good chance of gaining reserve status, as the new Superintendent General of Indian Affairs sounded sympathetic. But the Sulpicians used their connections to have that year's attempt at a land claim fail, which brought about a major turning point in the community. The next year, the Algonquin left for land elsewhere in Quebec to develop a community known now as the Kitigan Zibi Anishinabeg First Nation (see pp. 123–125). The Mohawk reacted differently. First, in February 1869 Chief Joseph Onasakenrat ("White Feathers") or "Swan," accompanied by forty armed Mohawk, warned the Sulpicians that they had eight days to leave. The police arrived a few days later, in the early hours of the morning, and arrested four of the Mohawk. They were released but told that their cause could only be served through legal channels and by obeying the Sulpicians.

The next move of the Mohawks was religious and political. The Sulpicians had made effective political use of excommunication to keep the Mohawk in line. Most of the community then decided to convert to Methodism, a move that would divide the Protestant majority from a minority who remained Catholic and wanted to maintain a good relationship with the Sulpicians. When the Mohawk went to build a church, they were arrested for cutting the wood to build it. They hadn't asked permission (nor that they would have received it).

In 1872, the church was built. The Sulpicians had been able to "legally" have people's homes torn down if they had not asked permission to cut the wood, so it is not surprising that by December 1875, they successfully obtained a court order to have the Methodist church torn down.

In 1877, the conflict between Mohawk and Sulpicians escalated. The Mohawk had fenced in a pasture on common lands they had been using for over a century. They chopped down some trees to obtain building materials for the fence. The Sulpicians moved next. In the words of journalists York and Pindera,

> It was three o'clock in the morning when the Quebec provincial police arrived in Oka, armed with warrants for the arrest of forty-eight Indians. They burst into homes and dragged the sleeping men from their beds, firing off pistols in their ears. Eight suspects were rounded up altogether and hauled off to jail. (York and Pindera, 1991: 82)

The Mohawk gathered together and armed themselves. Chief Joseph Onasakenrat counselled resistance: "If the police come to take you without warrant, fire at them" (York and Pindera, 1991: 83). The next morning the Catholic church was burned down. Fifteen Mohawk were arrested for arson. After five unsuccessful trials, an English jury acquitted them. Box 8.1 relates a similar story.

Breaking Up the Land

While these events were going on, the Sulpicians were selling the land the Algonquin had owned to White settlers, who formed the town of Oka. In 1912, the Mohawk saw a land claim make it all the way to the Privy Council in Britain, only to fail yet again. In 1936, the Sulpicians sold their land to a wealthy Belgian baron. In 1945, the federal government bought 32 separate lots of land scattered through the area. The land amounted to about one

Box 8.1	Kennatosse: Fugitive from "Justice"

In 1902, Chief Kennatosse Gabriel, a Kanehsatake leader, was a fugitive from the law. Thousands of dollars were posted as reward for his capture. Police staged stakeouts and boarded ships, all in attempts to catch this "dangerous criminal." The local newspapers headlined rumours of his appearances, or of his buying arms and threatening bloodshed. His crime was "stealing" wood in the seigneury of Kanehsatake.

In a secret interview with a reporter from the *Montreal Daily Star,* published on May 27, 1902, Kennatosse said the following about his family's "criminal" past:

> I remember how my father was sent to gaol for three months for cutting three small logs in the woods to repair his house. I remember how others of my relations ... when they went out in the winter time to cut wood to keep their wives and children warm, were arrested in the bush and carried off to gaol, while their shivering wives and children, not knowing what caused the prolonged absence of their husbands and fathers, vainly waited for the fuel to warm their half-frozen bodies. (York and Pindera, 1991: 100)

That same year, Kennatosse went to Britain to bring his people's legal problems to the King. He was refused access. He was on the run for 15 years. Eventually, the charges against him were dropped. He died in poverty, his life's cause unresolved.

percent of the original seigneury. They did not consult the Mohawk about this, nor did they create a reserve from this land. The land would remain as Crown land with individual Mohawk being issued "certificates of possession." In 1947, the government of Quebec authorized an expropriation of the some of the baron's land, including the area known as "The Pines." In 1961, after the town of Oka began clearing trees to make room for a nine-hole golf course, a joint Senate-Commons Committee on Indian Affairs met and recommended that the Kanehsatake land issue be settled quickly. That recommendation was ignored. In 1975 and 1986, two land claims cases were launched by the Kanehsatake Mohawks but were rejected by the federal government.

Competing Political Systems

As with other Mohawk communities, division is part of the story of Kanehsatake. As mentioned earlier, there was a division between the Catholic-speaking minority and the Protestant majority, exacerbated by the fact that the former were more likely to be French-speaking than English-speaking. The Longhouse existed at Kanehsatake too, early as a small group, misunderstood and even ostracized by the Christians. Both groups, however, lobbied for more traditional government during the late 1960s. In the fall of 1969, a meeting of fewer than 100 people approved the adoption of a hereditary system, with three chiefs and three clan mothers from each of the three clans (i.e., Turtle, Wolf, and Bear). The people were divided on their acceptance of this new system. Longhouse people did not like that it was officially connected with the *Indian Act* and Indian Affairs. Opposition came as well from those who favoured an elected band council; they formed the Kanehsatakeron

League for Democracy. By 1977, further complications were added. The clan mothers deposed a set of traditional chiefs, who refused to step down, creating two sets of chiefs and clan mothers for a while. During the last years of the 1980s, chiefs were appointed and deposed several times.

Gambling

In September 1989, a bingo hall was opened at Kanehsatake. There was opposition in the community. The elected council was opposed to the introduction of gambling. Then, six days after the opening there was an SQ raid, and several Mohawk homes were searched.

Confrontation at Kanehsatake

In the fall of 1989, the Kanehsatake band council announced its objections to the proposed expansion of a private (not-for-profit) golf course that would extend into land that the people claimed as theirs and that would uproot their cemetery. Discussions began involving the Mohawk, Oka Mayor Jean Ouellette, representatives of the Oka Golf Club, and provincial and federal officials.

The unity of the people of Kanehsatake suffered when, on January 23, the clan mothers ousted Clarence Simon as Grand Chief and replaced him with George Martin. The band council office would be the scene of protest in January and of an occupation in April.

On March 10 and 11, a small group of Kanehsatake Mohawk women, children, and men protested the expansion of the golf course by mounting a barricade on a dirt path or side road that connected Route 344, a highway, with the cemetery and a lacrosse/baseball field. The protest was low key. Traditional ceremonies were performed, and there were no weapons.

As the negotiations dragged on, with an injunction against the protest applied, removed, and then applied again and the SQ presence in the background increased, the protesters began to worry that their cause would be lost. In May, they contacted the Akwesasne Mohawk Warrior Society, who had been in communication with them before. This contact was not well received by Grand Chief George Martin and members of the band council, who saw it as bringing in outside agitators. In the words of deposed (but still influential) former Grand Chief Clarence Simon,

> The Warriors just came here and took it upon themselves to put the barricades up ... At the beginning, we had some people who practiced our traditional religion who wanted to protest by putting up a little barricade on a dirt path. And it stayed that way until the town got the injunction. Then the Warriors came and cut down some trees and moved some stones. The next thing we knew, they brought guns. We didn't see that until it was too late. (Hornung, 1991: 226)

On July 11, the situation exploded. One hundred SQ officers, armed with tear gas, concussion grenades, and SWAT gear approached the barricade early in the morning. As they were asking Kanehsatake Longhouse members Ellen Gabriel and Denise Tolley who the leaders of the protest were, tear gas, and grenades were set off. The confrontation had begun.

Officially there is no recognition of who gave the order for the SQ to initiate the use of these weapons. No one in the upper echelon of the SQ formally authorized the assault or submitted any tactical plan for the move. The head of the union of SQ officers would say that the union did not know. In the words of an aide to Quebec Premier Robert Bourassa,

"The whole operation broke almost every rule in our book ... what a mess! More than a hundred policemen were told to attack, and no one knew who gave the order, when they gave the order, and what the attack plan was" (Hornung, 1991: 206).

In an exchange of gunfire, an SQ officer, Corporal Marcel Lemay, was shot and killed. It has never been proven whether the gun that killed him was fired by a Mohawk or an SQ officer. The SQ beat a sloppy retreat. The Mohawk captured police vehicles and moved the blockade to Route 344.

The situation escalated from there. More than 1500 SQ and 500 RCMP officers would become involved, eventually to be replaced by 4400 Armed Forces troops, both at Kanehsatake and in the conflict at Kahnawake that would follow (see below).

A few points need to be made. One is that throughout the standoff, the contingent of Mohawk and their Native supporters behind the barricades was made up of a significant number of women and children, as well as the more prominently media-featured Warriors. In the words of Ellen Gabriel, a Kanehsatake Longhouse leader who was at the confrontation at the beginning and would become one of the main negotiators, "We have women and children here, and we are not armed. What can we do against an army? There are not just Warriors here. A lot of you don't realize that there are not just Warriors here" (Hornung, 1991: 251).

Another important point is that there was not unity at Kanehsatake concerning the presence and actions of the Warriors. Grand Chief George Martin publicly protested against the fact that band council members were not in the Mohawk negotiating committee that included representatives from his community, Kahnawake, and Akwesasne. After he issued a statement referring to the committee members from Akwesasne and Kahnawake with the words "This is not their territory, not their reserve ... they should get the hell out" (Hornung. 1991: 230), six Warriors beat him up and fired guns at his house. Ronald Cross, in a book written a few years after the confrontation stated that "A lot of us got fed up with the people from Kanehsatake because they weren't there to help us. They had asked us to help them, and as soon as the shit hit the fan they hid or they ran away" (Cross and Sévigny, 1994: 94). While the confrontation was going on, Cross and another Warrior slipped away briefly on September 1 to beat up Kanehsatake band councillor Francis Jacobs, who had threatened to give the SQ the names of several masked Mohawks who had burgled a nearby home, and his son.

The confrontation ended on September 26, when after dumping and burning their weapons, the Mohawk Warriors and the women and children who were with them, left the treatment centre that had become their base and faced the angry soldiers and SQ officers who would take them prisoner. The Warriors would be singled out for beatings by SQ officers who believed that the Mohawk had killed Lemay and had generally made them look bad. On October 19, 1999, in response to an official complaint lodged by Ronald Cross, three SQ officers were suspended without pay, two for thirty days and the third for sixty days, for manhandling Cross when he was handcuffed. In the words of the Turtle Island Native Network, posted on their Web site the next day, "The officers are no longer with the provincial force so the ruling carries no monetary penalty but it does go into their service record" (www.turtleisland.org).

Kanehsatake since the Confrontation

In late July 1995, the chief of Kanehsatake, Jerry Peltier, ordered the burning of marijuana fields rumoured to contain $10 million worth of the illegal substance. The story was that it was intended for sale to one or more of Quebec's notorious biker gangs. Peltier had rejected an SQ offer for a joint (pun not intended) operation between Native officers and the SQ. Lacking a police force of their own at that time, the Kanehsatake chief had to ask in officers from Akwesasne and Kahnawake. Peltier intended the burning to be a symbolic gesture. In Peltier's words, "This is a demonstration that the Mohawk people can be allowed to run their own affairs."

On December 19, 1996 an interim tripartite agreement on police services was signed with the community to eventually give the Peacekeepers of Kanehsatake full policing authority. Almost one year later, their police station was inaugurated.

But simply having a police force has not overcome some of the most important obstacles to policing with which the community is confronted; it could not escape its recent history. Kanehsatake gunrunners were arrested by the RCMP in 1998 (not in Kanehsatake territory). Again, connections were made to biker gangs.

Further, a series of events taking place late in September 2001, 11 years after the major conflict, has demonstrated the shaky ground upon which the force stands. On Wednesday, September 26, the police raided a house looking for drugs. A man was arrested, but released that same day. It seems that no drugs were found. This led to threats the next day, with men on Harley-Davidson motorcycles and four-by-four vehicles circling the Kanehsatake Mohawk Police station, and to shots being fired at the station that Friday, narrowly missing several officers. The Kanehsatake Mohawk Police withdrew to the Oka SQ station, waiting for backup from other reserves. It arrived from Akwesasne, Kahnawake, and the Mi'kmaq reserve of Restigouche.

That Friday night, a delegation of the arrested man and members of his family went to the band council meeting and demanded that Larry Ross, who had been acting chief of police for one year, be dismissed. Threats were made concerning what would happen if this didn't happen. In the words of Grand Chief James Gabriel, the man's relatives said that "there was going to be war if he (Ross) stays there, and people are going to get hurt, so council felt it preferable to terminate the employment" (Grant, 2001: A2). Ross was dismissed. In an interview that appeared in an article in the *Montreal Gazette* on September 30, he said, "I'm still extremely nervous for my officers ... I'm concerned about the ones who wanted to make a positive difference. I'm concerned about the officers who wanted to do their job" (Grant, 2001: A1).

The band councillor responsible for policing and justice felt that Ross's words were just irresponsible fear-mongering. It will remain to be seen whose words speak the greater truth. Chief Gabriel's statement concerning the damage done to the institution of the police service is valid: "It's a major setback for the credibility of law enforcement in our territory and we have a hell of a lot of work to do in reinstalling confidence in people, in re-establishing the credibility of the KMP" (Grant, 2001: A2).

ALGONQUIN POLICING: THE KITIGAN ZIBI ANISHINABEG FIRST NATION

Kitigan Zibi ("Garden River") is the largest of the nine communities that make up the Algonquin Nation in Quebec, with an estimated band population of 2350 people. It is located about 130 kilometres north of Ottawa. The people had lived in Kanehsatake (Oka in Algonquin) up until the mid-1800s, when they left to form a community that used to be called Maniwaki ("Mary's country") because the people were Catholic.

The community first had its own policing services when they worked through the Amerindian Police Service in 1981. In the words of the Assembly of First Nations study of Aboriginal policing, "Despair was felt in the early days of Amerindian policing when officers were identified as 'Special Constables'" (FNCPA, 2001). Four years later, they moved to greater independence by transferring their policing to their own force, referred to variously in the literature as the River Desert Police Department and the Maniwaki Peacekeepers. The stated objectives of that initiative were:

1. to preserve the community's First Nation identity;
2. to have less non-Indian involvement and representation at administrative levels;
3. to have more control over the community's destiny; and
4. to establish a police administration office within the community.

(FNCPA, 2001; www.fncpa.ca/hrdc/mod4-5/appendixd.htm)

Following the introduction of the federal First Nation Policing Policy, in April 1992, the community entered into a three-year tripartite agreement, allowing the Kitigan Zibi Anishinabeg Police Department (KZAPD) to become a fully functional force, the equivalent of any in Canada. This agreement was renegotiated in March, 1995.

Today the KZAPD has a chief of police, five full-time officers, and one part-time officer; it has a high satisfaction rate from its community. In a recent survey, 91 percent of the members of the community surveyed felt that the KZAPD was the best policing organization to meet the needs of the community for peace, order, and security. This compares favourably to the 55 percent of community stakeholders in the First Nations Chiefs of Police Association (FNCPA) survey of First Nations Self-Administered Police Services who felt that the policing service in their community was effective. In this study, posted on the Web in 2001, the KZAPD was one of two Native-run police services chosen for best practices examples.

There are several keys to the success of this police service, only some of which can be exported to other Native communities, in Quebec or elsewhere. One is that there is, in the words of the FNCPA study, "a very stable political environment" in the Kitigan Zibi Anishinabeg First Nation. The chief councillor has been consistently elected to his position for 23 years, and there have been few other changes in the makeup of the band council. There are no readily apparent factions in the community. Also important is that there have been no major clashes between the Quebec provincial government and Kitigan Zibi Anishinabeg First Nation, something that puts it in the minority in Quebec. Largely because of this lack of conflict, the relationship that the KZAPD has with the SQ seems positive. Of course, the Mohawk, Mi'kmaq, and James Bay Cree communities are not in that position. Neither is the Algonquin community of Lac Barriere, which has had a long series of conflicts concerning logging and land claims and other Aboriginal rights issues concerning a local provincial park.

One particularly strong aspect of policing at the Kitigan Zibi Anishinabeg First Nation is the relationship between the police and the youth of the community. In 1995, the KZAPD was one of four forces, and the only Native-run force (the others were in Toronto, Windsor, and Ottawa) to be engaged in a pilot project mentoring Native youth. Aboriginal youths from 12 to 24 were paired with police officers, riding in cruisers, observing police duties first-hand, visiting the mentors' homes, and travelling together for outings. One officer said, "I took great pride in seeing the barriers fall and the sense of openness that developed in our communication." (*First Nations Policing Update,* July 1995, no. 3). In a 1996 interview with a reporter working for the federal Aboriginal Policing Directorate, the chief of police, Gordon MacGregor, one of two officers then coaching the community's baseball team, stressed "The importance of being among the people, being visible and approachable especially to the youth and young children ... people see you as being human and as a father, not just as a police figure" (Stewart, 1996).

Dedication to training also seems to be an important aspect of the success of the KZAPD. One of the conditions of the signing of the first tripartite agreement in 1992 was for the constables already in the force's employ to earn the basic training equivalency diploma as evaluated by the Institut de la Police du Québec. The officers would then have powers equivalent to those of any other officer in the province.

All the officers successfully completed the training, enabling them to conduct investigations throughout the province. The chief of police went beyond the qualifications required in the agreement, taking managerial courses for senior officers, followed by additional courses offered at the Police College in Ottawa. When, as the result of the Poitras Commission, the *Québec Police Act* was amended to include more training for SQ officers, with Native police having a five-year delay, the chief of police of the KZAPD prepared a five-year forecast of the training needs of his force to bring them up to speed.

CREE POLICING

The Cree have lived in the James Bay region for approximately 5000 to 6000 years. While we can never be sure of their population at the time of contact with Europeans, it is estimated to be at least 20 000 people. However, it was not until 1971 that the Cree in present-day Quebec ever came together for a common cause. Until that time, the Cree of Quebec had been living in fewer than a dozen villages in an essentially traditional way, hunting and trapping for food and income. They would spread out over the land for the winter months, exploiting territories that had been in families for generations. The care of the land was vested in a series of older men, whose job it was to maintain and perpetuate it.

When northern Quebec was handed over to the province by the federal government in 1898 and 1912, it was under the strict stipulation that the Cree (along with the Inuit and the Innu) have their rights dealt with through some sort of treaty. No Quebec provincial government had done anything to fulfill these requirements prior to 1971.

In April 1971, the premier of Quebec, Robert Bourassa, announced that the province was going to initiate a huge hydro-electric development project that would involve harnessing the rivers of the James Bay watershed. The government seemed oblivious to the fact that these rivers ran through the Cree hunting territories and were, in fact, essential to the Cree way of life. The government's position was that the project would be constructed on provincial lands and would be beneficial to everybody, including First Nations people.

The Cree leaders, representing about 6000 people and eight bands, met in Mistassini on June 29, 1971, two months after Bourassa's announcement. During the three-day meeting, the Cree leaders decided that they would fight with all of their ability to protest and derail the government's plans. They would not tolerate the flooding of the area. Through a petition, they requested that the Minister of Indian affairs intervene on their behalf.

The Native battle over the James Bay Project would go on for nearly five years and would involve the province of Quebec, the federal government, the Cree, and the Inuit. The culmination would be the first major settlement of a Native land claim in recent years. The

James Bay and Northern Quebec Agreement (JBNQA) has generated dispute and debate since it was signed in 1975. Initially, it was believed that it would pave the way for all subsequent land-claims settlements, but since its signing it has come to be reassessed and reconsidered. The Agreement was signed by the government of Quebec, three Quebec Crown corporations, the Grand Council of the Crees of Quebec, the Northern Quebec Inuit Association, and the Government of Canada. It involved 6650 Cree from eight communities and 4386 Inuit from fifteen communities.

Pursuant to the JBNQA and its successor, the *Northeastern Quebec Agreement* (1978), the Quebec Aboriginal Police Force was formed in 1978 to provide service to a number of Cree, Innu (Naskapi), and Inuit communities in northern Quebec. Later, Montagnais (Innu) communities were included. Officers were initially appointed as special constables under the Quebec Police Act, and were under the supervision of the SQ, with one special constable for every five hundred Cree in each community.

Given the political objectives of the JBNQA, policing was envisioned as undergoing a three-stage evolution. In the first stage, the administration of the program was to be undertaken by the SQ in consultation with the Native community advisory committees. In the second, perceived as a transitional stage, separate police forces would be established through resolution of First Nations governments under Section 81 of the *Indian Act*. Administrative service agreements would be signed between the individual bands and the SQ, under which the latter would continue operational supervision of the officers while administrative control would be gradually assumed by First Nations governments. In the third stage, First Nations government would have full responsibility for the Native police forces in their communities. In that regard, the Grand Council of the Crees of Quebec has been striving for a Cree regional police force and a Cree regional police commission.

However, the program has not evolved as initially planned, in part because of the antagonistic relationship between the Quebec government and the Cree over the separation referendum, and, more recently, over logging practices and deals encouraged by the Quebec government. As Stenning (1996: 130) suggests, in the mid-1990s most communities were still in the second or transitional stage. He further argues that the Quebec Aboriginal Police Force was at that time in a state of limbo, with the SQ reducing its supervision over Cree special constables and the individual communities not showing particular enthusiasm about assuming control. In Stenning's words, "The constables are described as being without adequate support or direction, either from the communities or the SQ" (1996: 131). No agreements or initiatives have been developed since that time to the present (2001) to substantially change that state.

NOTES

1. These are the words of French historian François Garneau, whose works were first published in 1845, and were republished as late as 1969–1971.

2. In 1968, the Caughnawaga Iroquois Police was formed, a policing body that was accountable to the Quebec government and was sworn in under the *Québec Police Act*. Not surprisingly, it lasted for only a short time.

KEY TERMS

James Bay and Northern
  Quebec Agreement (p. 126)

St. Lawrence Seaway
  (p. 113)

REVIEW QUESTIONS

1. Outline the series of clashes that the Mohawk of Kahnawake have had with the outsider police services (e.g., the RCMP and the SQ).

2. Compare the development and operation of the Mohawk Warriors and the Peacekeepers of Kahnawake with their counterparts in Akwesasne.

3. Discuss the role of the Sulpicians in the Kanehsatake Mohawk's lack of rights relative to other Native and non-Native communities.

4. Compare the conflicts between the Sulpicians and the Mohawk in the nineteenth century with the confrontation at Oka in 1990.

5. Identify the keys to success of the Kitigan Zibi Anishinabeg Police Department.

chapter nine

Aboriginal Policing in Atlantic Canada

LEARNING OBJECTIVES

After completing this chapter, students should be able to:

1. Describe the practice of traditional policing among the Innu and the Mi'kmaq.

2. Outline the series of events that led to the development of a police force among the Innu of Davis Inlet.

3. Discuss the role of institutional racism in the Nova Scotia justice system in the Donald Marshall case.

4. Outline the history of the Unama'ki Tribal Police Force.

5. Critically analyze the Burnt Church confrontation as a policing issue.

In Atlantic Canada, there are four Native groups: the Innu (Montagnais/Naskapi), Mi'kmaq, Malecite, and Inuit. Native policing in the four Atlantic provinces is primarily the responsibility of the Royal Canadian Mounted Police (RCMP), secondarily the various municipal policing services.

ABORIGINAL POLICING IN NEWFOUNDLAND

There are three Native groups in Newfoundland: the Innu and Inuit in Labrador and the Mi'kmaq on the island. The RCMP do not seem to have been well-received initially by members of the isolated communities in Labrador. The following is a comment from an Innu from Sheshatshit:

> I remember when the RCMP first came to Sheshatshit around 1950, by boat from Goose Bay as there was no road at that time. People were really scared of them. We thought they controlled everything, they were telling us what we should do. When they came we were still living in tents ... As people thought the RCMP could do anything, they were even afraid to hunt (Harrison, Meric, and Dixon 1995).

According to C. Lambert, writing in 1978, many of the Inuit of the community of Nain often looked upon the RCMP as being much more intrusive in their lives than traditional means of social control:

> Many people in Nain feel that the community was "more peaceful" when the elders were handling social and marital problems more actively. They resent the introduction of foreign institutions such as the RCMP ... they take great offence at the policing coming to their homes, searching for home brew, sometimes without a warrant or an interpreter and for often "picking up drunks on the way home from the bar." (Lambert, 1978: 64–65)

Recognition of their legal status has been difficult for First Nations in Newfoundland to achieve. When Newfoundland joined Canada in 1949, the Native people in what became the tenth province did not automatically gain legal status as "Indians" or "Eskimos." Native communities in that province have had to fight for forms of recognition that Native groups in the rest of Canada more or less take for granted. In Newfoundland, all First Nations policing is undertaken by the Mounties, either through the force's regular officers or by supernumerary First Nations constables under the supervision of the RCMP.

The first to take up the latter option was the Mi'kmaq community of Conne River, who did so in 1988. Their constables have powers to enforce band bylaws through the Federal *Indian Act*, and to enforce provincial laws and the *Criminal Code* through their affiliation with the RCMP.

Traditional Policing among the Innu

Like all First Nations, the Innu had traditional means of maintaining peace and social solidarity, as well as having ways of dealing with people who violated social norms and mores. The maintenance of social harmony was essential and a variety of methods were used to perpetuate peace within the group.

For the Innu of northern Quebec and Labrador, public opinion was traditionally a powerful force in bringing about compliance, principally in preventing infractions from occurring. In a society in which individuals are dependent upon other community members when ill or injured, or having bad luck hunting, the favourable perception of others, and public goodwill generally, are important. Favourable public opinion brought about cooperation and assistance among band members, and bad public opinion rendered assistance and working together less likely. As Julius Lips observed, public opinion could enforce law by *active* or *passive* means.

The Innu recognized a number of offences against both individuals and the group as a whole. People who repeatedly trespassed (e.g., on the hunting or trapping territory of a family or group) would eventually be made aware of the fact that they were doing so and would be asked to stop. Such a confrontation would usually bring about a cessation. If not, public awareness of the transgression, and subsequent public opinion and gossip, would result in the trespasser either ceasing his trespassing or being driven out of the band. The latter punishment was a serious one, exercised only in extreme circumstances. As Lips observed, writing in the 1930s, "It is not the occasional trap thief, trespasser, or tent burner, but the habitual peace breaker, the constant trouble maker, who is punished with expulsion. But once the community acts, he is outlawed and abandoned to starvation" (Lips, 1937: 223).

Theft and arson were two of the more common offences. In the case of arson, restitution had to be made to the aggrieved party by the person who started the fire. If the offender continued in his actions or failed to make compensation, the victim would try to mobilize public opinion in his favour. The arsonist could then be exiled from the band.

In the case of murder, manslaughter, or accidental killings, the aggrieved family would seek redress. Typically, the task fell to the sons, brothers, or grandsons of the victim. Revenge was seen as essential, and it was just the murderer, not the murderer's relatives, who had to pay the penalty. If the victim did not have kin available to do the deed, band members would sometimes take it upon themselves to do so. The execution of a murderer would usually be by shooting or by drowning.

Davis Inlet

In January 1993, Canadian television screens bore shocked witness to the stark truths of life in the Innu community of Utshimassit, more commonly known as Davis Inlet. Six children were shown who had been sniffing gas fumes and who had nearly succeeded in committing suicide. The community had been forcibly moved twice, once in 1948, and again in 1967. They had walked back home the first time after 70 people had died over a 2-year period. In the words of Olive Dickason,

> Once more, it was a move that made it impossible for them to continue their traditional caribou-hunting way of life. The government's expressed reason: the new location was better suited for building housing and sewage systems. For the Innu, the sense of powerlessness at being once more involuntarily cut off from their customary pursuits led to a spiral of welfare dependency, alcoholism, gasoline sniffing, and suicide. (Dickason 1997: 398)

The community would feature in the national news again near the end of 1993. On December 16, about 30 Innu entered the courtroom in Davis Inlet, where Provincial Court Judge Robert Hyslop was presiding. Chief Katie Rich passed a note to the judge, telling him he was no longer welcome in the community and was to leave Davis Inlet immediately. In a later interview, Chief Rich would say that she and the others felt that Judge Hyslop would not listen to community suggestions, had been too quick to incarcerate, and was known to rush through the passage of a case if the weather was bad. According to her, he did that so he could leave and stay in another community for the night. Chief Rich believed strongly that as the people had effective traditions in dealing with offenders, they should have significant input into how criminal actions were handled. In a later interview, she would say,

I'm sure that most of the elders knew how to deal with a person who did something wrong. For example if a husband abused his wife in the old days a whole bunch of women would come together and confront the man. These sort[s] of things, interventions, had an important role in how to deal with men who abused their wives and children. There were some cases where the children would be taken away from a family where they were being abused. A lot of the skills that our people had, to deal with things like abuse, have a role to play in the court system. There are cases that we think should go to court, as long as we have a say. That's the main thing. (Harrison, Meric, and Dixon, 1995)

Throwing out Judge Hyslop also entailed kicking out his RCMP escort, leaving the community with no officially recognized police. In January 1994, the Innu Nation, a political organization representing the approximately 1700 people of Davis Inlet and the more southerly community of Sheshatshit,[1] invited an international team of observers in, Peace Brigades International (PBI) "because of fear that the RCMP would return without the community's agreement and a violent confrontation would occur" (Harrison, Meric, and Dixon, 1995).

The province and the community entered into negotiations to try to resolve the issue. The talks broke down on September 2, 1994, when Newfoundland Justice Minister Edward Roberts objected to the participation of Rich in the discussions between the province and the Innu. She had been charged, and would eventually be convicted of contempt of court. Roberts then ordered the RCMP to prepare to force their way into the community, saying, "The court will sit in Davis Inlet and the rule of law will prevail." The Innu asked the PBI observers to return. They took the further precaution, on September 6, of blockading the lone airstrip into the community with dozens of oil drums, making it too dangerous to land a plane.

In April 1995, a third PBI team would arrive for the trial of Rich and two other women (one a tribal police officer), and would interview her on May 11, 1995. The results of their interview with her were posted on the Web twice that year (see Harrison, Meric, and Dixon, 1995 and PBI, 1995). Asked how the community had fared when the RCMP were kicked out, Chief Rich said that

It was difficult at one point when we didn't see the RCMP, but we tried to explain to the people that anyone could call the RCMP at any time. I did in fact call them in, on New Year's Day I think, and I felt that was a way to show the people that they could call the RCMP at any time. But they had to ask the permission of the community to come in. They couldn't just come in at any time. By doing that I think I showed the people that they could call and the RCMP could come as long as they were invited. There were times when our tribal police couldn't handle things and they called them, and that's the way it should be. If our tribal police need support from the RCMP, they should be able to call them. (PBI, 1995)

Also interviewed at that time was Simeon Tshakapesh. Along with John Tshakapesh, he had received some police training and was a member of the tribal police force that was not officially recognized by the federal or provincial governments. According to Rich, the community had approached the government for the two men to do a six-week on-the-job training stint with the RCMP, but were turned down. Rich claims there was talk of the men being charged with impersonating officers. When Simeon Tshakapesh was asked how it has been since the RCMP left, he said that the people were engaged in trying to restore their own laws. When pressed by the interviewer as to what that meant, he said,

Looking after people the way they should be. For example, in an assault we deal with the offender, and they might get sent to treatment. Sometimes they come back and don't re-offend. We are involved in an ongoing process of healing rather than punishment. If we do see a repeat of the offence, then the RCMP is sometimes called in if the person is not willing to work on their problems. (PBI, 1995)

On January 11, 1996, the Innu Peacekeepers were sworn in as supernumerary constables of the RCMP. Katie Rich feels that this agreement would not have been signed if they hadn't taken the aggressive actions they did. There is reason for optimism concerning this agreement, as the views of at least some of the RCMP officers seem in line with those of the community. RCMP Officer Gary Jay was quoted as saying,

Our policy towards Innu, Aboriginal people is to believe in their uniqueness. The closeness of the community allows us to take this holistic approach. We recognize and accept this community approach. We recognize Aboriginals have rights which have existed previous to settlement, and continue to exist. The exact nature of those rights are being interpreted by the court. Those rights are above the law.

The Innu community appears to have taken more ownership over justice issues. They haven't completely eliminated the Canadian justice system, but it isn't appropriate for them in some circumstances (Harrison, Meric, and Dixon, 1995, and PBI, 1995).

ABORIGINAL POLICING IN NOVA SCOTIA

Traditional Policing among the Mi'kmaq

In Nova Scotia, there are 13 Native communities, all of them Mi'kmaq. While essentially egalitarian, the Mi'kmaq had a more formal socio-political structure than did the Innu. As discussed in Chapter 2, a key component of Mi'kmaq leadership was (and to a lesser degree still is) the **saqmaw,** which was a patrilineal position, that is, one followed from father to son (usually the eldest son). Saqmaw leadership existed at a number of different levels, from small autumn and winter groups, to larger summer populations, to the district level (there are seven Mi'kmaq districts), and finally to the nation level with the Kji'saqmaw or "great leader." In the matter of offences, the saqmaw acted as a mediator, overseeing wrestling matches that were used to resolve relatively minor offences, and consulted concerning compensation in serious matters such as murder or wife stealing (Bock, 1978: 116).

The Donald Marshall Case: Racism and the Justice System

There is a long history of Euro-Canadian law not serving the Mi'kmaq of Nova Scotia well. In the mid-1700s, during a conflict between the two peoples brought on by the sudden movement of about 2400 White settlers, uninvited and unexpected into what is now Halifax and what was then the heart of Mi'kmaq territory, a bounty was put on Mi'kmaq heads, dead or alive. Despite the fact that peace was brought about by a treaty of 1752, the bounty was not removed from the law books. In 2000, the Mi'kmaq were still fighting to have it removed from the laws of Nova Scotia. When Andrew Meuse, chief of the Bear River band, promoted a petition in 1828 that called for the end of the sale of alcohol to his people by unscrupulous traders, a law was put in place that left the decision up to the discretion of local magistrates. None of them acted to stop the trade. But the most famous instance of the Mi'kmaq suffering from Euro-Canadian law is the Donald Marshall case.

On May 28, 1971, 17-year-old Donald Marshall Jr., a Mi'kmaq (and son of a chief), along with a friend of his, Sandy Seale, were walking through a park in Sydney, Nova Scotia. They spotted two White men in the park and decided to ask them for some money. This led to a scuffle in which Seale was stabbed to death by one of the men, Roy Ebsary, who had been carrying a large knife. There were no witnesses to the murder other than the three who had been directly involved.

Marshall quickly became the prime suspect. Three teenagers who had been in the area, but had not witnessed the stabbing, gave their testimony to the police concerning what they knew, which was little. Gradually, they were coerced by Detective Sergeant John MacIntyre into implicating Marshall with stories that became the same tall tale. One of the teenagers, a 14 year old, would eventually testify that he had been threatened with a jail sentence if he did not tell the story MacIntyre wanted to hear. In the trial that followed that November, the prosecutor, violating the ethics but not letter of the law of his profession, refused to let the defence see the original versions of the teenagers' testimony. Marshall was convicted of murder by a jury of 12 white men. The judge sentenced him to life. MacIntyre would become chief of police in the Sydney police force in 1976.

Ten days later, Jimmy MacNeill, who had been Ebsary's companion on the night of the stabbing, went to the Sydney police to tell them that Ebsary had committed the act. His description of the killer matched that which Marshall had given during the trial. The police questioned Ebsary (who had been charged less than a year before with the possession of an offensive weapon—a knife), but accepted his denials as truth.

Eleven years later a man came forward to say that when he had lived in Ebsary's house, he had heard the man brag of killing someone in 1971. He knew Marshall, so he visited him in prison. They contacted Marshall's lawyer and the RCMP reopened the case in 1982, assigning Harry Wheaton, the plainclothes coordinator of the RCMP in Sydney, to the investigation. Wheaton and his investigative partner, Corporal Jim Carroll, had to be especially diligent in pursuing this case, as the file that the Sydney police gave them did not initially contain all the items it should have had (i.e., Jimmy MacNeill's statement of Ebsary's guilt). Their diligence was rewarded, as they would eventually speak with the three key witnesses, who would admit that they had lied in their coached official statements to the Sydney police.

The case went to the Nova Scotia Court of Appeal in the spring of 1982. While the Crown prosecutor acknowledged that the Mi'kmaq man should be acquitted, he also asked the five judges involved to exonerate the criminal justice system of any blame on the grounds that its reputation must be upheld, that "It seems reasonable to assume that the public will suspect that there is something wrong with the system if a man can be convicted of a murder he did not commit" (York, 1990: 161–162). The judges accepted this position, and despite the fact that they acquitted Marshall in 1983, they blamed him more than the system for the lack of justice he received. They felt that he had initiated the series of actions that had led to his conviction and that in the trial he had been "evasive" in his answers. A later report (the Hickman Report, see p. 134) would condemn the actions and words of the Nova Scotia Court of Appeal as amounting to "a defence of the criminal justice system at Marshall's expense, notwithstanding overwhelming evidence to the contrary" (quoted in Harris, 1990: 408–409).

The RCMP investigator, Harry Wheaton, was appalled by the cavalier attitude of senior officials of the Nova Scotia justice system during and immediately after the successful appeal, as can be seen in his reaction to a speech at the time by the most senior such official:

> The Attorney General of Nova Scotia came to our annual officers' mess dinner and said that he didn't understand why the press was making all the fuss over the Marshall case. I had to be restrained from leaving the room in the middle of his speech. The man simply didn't realize the suffering and heartache involved in this thing, nor the immense social issues that are still at play. I just couldn't stomach the trivializing of a case that changed so many people's lives and my whole outlook as a policeman. (Harris, 1990: 402–403)

Fortunately, the matter did not end with the appeal. A two-year Royal Commission (the Hickman Commission) was to follow that would reveal the anti-Mi'kmaq prejudice that was deeply embedded in every aspect of the justice system. It was learned that Sydney police officers often referred to Mi'kmaq as "broken arrows" and "wagon burners." No Mi'kmaq to that point had ever been a police officer, or even a member of a jury in Sydney. In the words of the three non-Nova Scotian (one from Quebec, one from Ontario and one from Newfoundland) senior justice officials who released their seven-volume **Hickman Report** on January 26, 1990:

> The criminal justice system failed Donald Marshall Jr. at virtually every turn from his arrest and wrongful conviction for murder in 1971 up to, and even beyond, his acquittal by the Court of Appeal in 1983. The tragedy of the failure is compounded by evidence that this miscarriage of justice could—and should—have been prevented, or at least corrected quickly, if those involved in the system had carried out their duties in a professional and/or competent manner. That they did not is due, in part, to the fact that Donald Marshall Jr. is a Native. (quoted in Harris, 1990: 407)

Shortly after the release of the Hickman Report, Nova Scotia's Attorney General apologized to Marshall and his family, saying "The justice system failed Donald Marshall Jr. and I accept that one of the reasons he was wrongfully convicted and imprisoned was that he is a Native" (Harris, 1990: 410).

One of the recommendations that came out of the Donald Marshall Inquiry (as the Hickman Commission is also called) was that a Tripartite Forum be established "to mediate and resolve outstanding issues between the Mi'kmaq and Government" (www.unsi.ns.ca/tripartite.html). Policing was one of those issues.

Unama'ki Police Force

On July 12, 1994, in part because of issues raised by the Donald Marshall Inquiry and the discussions around the Tripartite Forum, the Unama'ki (sometimes spelled as Una'maki) Tribal Police Force became the first independent or stand-alone First Nations police service in Atlantic Canada. During its first two years of service, two RCMP officers were seconded to the force. In 1995, nine First Nations recruits graduated with 16 non-native RCMP recruits from the RCMP academy in Regina, and after taking recruit training under RCMP supervision in Nova Scotia, became the central core of the Unama'ki Tribal Police Force.

When in full service, the force provided police service to five Mi'kmaq communities in Cape Breton: Eskasoni, Chapel Island, Membertou, Waycobahá (or Whycocomagh), and Wagmatcook. The police service's board of directors consisted of band chiefs and one other member from four of the communities. Eskasoni, located 40 kilometres from

Sydney, had the most personnel, not surprising as it is the largest Native community in Atlantic Canada, with a population of 2959. Among others, there were the chief of police, a sergeant, a corporal, a school liaison constable, a court liaison constable, three other constables, a chief dispatcher and four other dispatchers, a secretary, and, for the local jail, two matrons, five jail guards, and a supervisor for the guards. Chapel Island, with a population of less than 500, had a corporal and a constable. A substation was built for Membertou that had a corporal and two constables. Waycobah had a police station, a corporal, and a constable who served as a public-relations officer.

In the last few years, the Unama'ki Tribal Police Force has suffered some setbacks. In 1997, John Toney retired. He was a Mi'kmaq who had been a leading figure in policing Eskasoni since 1971 (see Box 9.1). In 2000, one of the nine graduates who had been working for the UTPF at the rank of corporal was hired by the Cape Breton Regional Police Service, taking away one of the better officers.

In March, 2001 it was announced that, after seven years of service, the force was being phased out because of financial constraints. The province had audited the force over the winter and had noted several financial difficulties. The province decided that changes were needed before it would consider more funding for the force. While it would not state clearly in any public media what those changes were, it did say that the communities had made the decision to disband the force. At that time, the communities were involved with negotiations with regional police forces and the RCMP to take over patrols. If this is followed through, it will represent a major setback to Aboriginal self-policing initiatives.

The situation today in Nova Scotia generally gives one pause. In 1991, there were an estimated 10 000 Native people living in the Halifax area, yet there were not any readily apparent Native-focused policing initiatives in the area. In 2000, it was noted that there were only 16 Aboriginal police officers in Nova Scotia and that, of these, 13 worked for the Unama'ki Police Force. On the 2001 Web site for the Halifax Regional Police Service (www.police.Halifax.ns.ca, consulted October 2001), there were no references in any of the many aspects of the site to Native peoples or Aboriginal policing.

Box 9.1	**John Leonard Toney: An Aboriginal Policeman's Exemplary Career**

John Leonard Toney was born in the Mi'kmaq community of Whycacomagh, in Cape Breton, and moved at an early age to the larger community of Eskasoni. He began his career, as a number of Native police officers have, in the military. He served in the American army in Iraq, Iran, Turkey, and Vietnam before returning to Eskasoni. In 1971, he started his policing work as a supernu-merary constable with the RCMP, and he became the Eskasoni Police Force of one. He worked with the force as it grew, becoming the chief of police, a position he held until 1997. Toney was an exemplary figure in that he successfully made policing part of the culture he was very proud of and added his culture's touch to police work in his community.

ABORIGINAL POLICING IN NEW BRUNSWICK

There are two different First Nations in New Brunswick, the two closely related peoples of the Mi'kmaq and Malecite. With the exception of the St. Mary's First Nation, which is situated within the city limits of the provincial capital of Fredericton and is therefore policed by the city's municipal force, all Native policing in New Brunswick is conducted by the RCMP. Until recently, the only Native input was through Circular 55 special constables.

On September 5, 1997, tripartite agreements were signed with two New Brunswick Native communities, both Mi'kmaq: Buctouche First Nation and Indian Island First Nation, interestingly two of the smallest bands in the province. Under the agreement, the Buctouche First Nation is served by an Aboriginal member of the RCMP-First Nation Community Policing Service, and the community provides an office. In addition, they have established a community consultative group whose function is to set policing priorities for the community.

The Second Donald Marshall Jr. Case

Traditionally, the Mi'kmaq derived as much as 90 percent of their food from the sea (Miller, 1995: 349), a pattern of resource dependence that doubtless must have lasted for centuries. We should assume, then, that the Mi'kmaq had developed a relationship with this resource base that would have allowed them to sustain its long-term use, rather than squander it for short-term gain. In short, they should have had and should still have a good sense of what is required to conserve the marine resources upon which they have depended for so long.

In August 1993, Donald Marshall Jr. was arrested and charged with three violations of the Fisheries Act: fishing without a licence, fishing out of season with illegal nets, and selling eels without benefit of a licence. He admitted that he had caught 463 pounds of eels during the closed season and then sold them for $787.10. However, he claimed rights under a treaty signed in 1760 between the British Crown and the Mi'kmaq and Maliseet in Nova Scotia and New Brunswick, and the culturally related Passamaquoddy of Maine.

Marshall was convicted on all three charges, and these convictions were upheld in the Nova Scotia Court of Appeal. He took the case to the Supreme Court of Canada (SCC), where the convictions were overturned because the SCC recognized that the treaty had granted the Mi'kmaq the right to fish and to trade products from hunting, fishing and trapping for "necessaries." On September 17, 1999, the Supreme Court of Canada stated that Marshall

> caught and sold the eels to support himself and his wife. Accordingly, the closed season and the imposition of a discretionary licensing system would, if enforced, interfere with the appellant's treaty right to fish for trading purposes, and the ban on sales would, if enforced, infringe his right to trade for sustenance.

The SCC declared that the treaty right

> is not a right to trade generally for economic gain, but rather a right to trade for necessaries. Catch limits that could reasonably be expected to produce a moderate livelihood for individual Micmac families at present day standards can be established by regulation. (Editorial, *Toronto Star,* September 29, 1999)

The fallout from the decision was immediate and affected 34 Native communities in the Maritimes and in eastern Quebec. Not surprisingly, these First Nations felt that the SCC's wording gave them the right to a self-regulated fishery, including the highly lucrative lobster fishery (i.e., earning tens of thousands of dollars a year); (Rick MacLean, *CBC News Online,* www.cbconline.org, consulted October 2001). Their non-Native colleagues in the lobster fishery reacted immediately, demanding that the federal government stop the Native entry into the industry, fearing that otherwise the lobster stock would be overfished and ultimately lost. They called for Federal Fisheries Minister Herb Dhaliwal to intervene. On October 1, 1999, he issued a statement that he was not going to disallow a right that had been denied Native peoples for centuries, and asked for calm while he worked for a long-term solution to the problem.

It would soon get ugly. In the early hours of October 3, 1999, about 150 boats headed out into Miramichi Bay in protest. They cut lobster traplines and destroyed $210 000 worth of traps belonging to the Mi'kmaq of Esgenoopetitj or Burnt Church, New Brunswick. Shouting matches and threats ensued. Angry mobs later trashed three fish plants and vandalized fishing equipment. Threats, assaults, and the carrying of weapons increased. At least one Mi'kmaq was injured.

What had been needed before this happened were clear, coordinated directives given to policing agencies as to how they should operate in what would soon become a highly volatile situation. Two federal agencies concerned with policing were involved: the RCMP and the Department of Fisheries and Oceans (DFO). There needed to be a distinct Native face on the policing as well. The Unama'ki Tribal Police Force or even Native policing services from other jurisdictions should have been brought in to work alongside the federal agencies. But no directives coordinating federal agencies and Native agencies were issued. It was another story of outsiders imposing and enforcing their rules on a Native community. The policing that resulted was not satisfying to any of the players in this tense game.

The Native players felt particularly vulnerable. It is not surprising, then, that when the conflict received its greatest amount of television coverage, viewers saw what looked like the familiar images from Oka: Native men wearing army fatigues and headbands. What they were seeing were members of the Mi'kmaq Warrior Society, a group which probably owed its origin primarily to the confrontation in 1981 at the Mi'kmaq reserve of Restigouche in Quebec (see the chapter on Quebec). They represent an attempt to fill the vacuum of a Native component to the policing of the politically disturbed waters surrounding Burnt Church.

The Mi'kmaq Warrior Society has operated in a way that is different from its Mohawk counterpart. It has functioned more as a diplomatic police force than anything else. Members are chosen because they can handle themselves coolly under trying situations. During the tense times at Burnt Church in 1999, they were unarmed. They were asked in to keep the peace, to make sure that boats and equipment were not vandalized by outsiders, and that the situation did not get out of hand. While their presence wasn't as visible in the on-again/off-again media show of the confrontation at Burnt Church over the two years that followed, their existence demonstrates the need in Burnt Church for a Native component in the policing of the area.

The Christian Peacemaker Teams (CPT), a violence-reduction initiative of the Mennonite and Brethren Churches and Quakers/Friends Meetings, are also there in a quasi-policing capacity, as neutral observers. They are there to observe what goes on as a kind of non-partisan conscience and to try to promote a Christian spirit of peace in potentially violent situations. It could be argued that if peacekeeping were properly exercised at

Burnt Church, there would be no need for such groups. John Finlay is a writer and a reserve corps member of the CPT. One day, he and others went to hold a short Christian worship service on the wharf where the DFO kept its boats. As they drove up, Finlay noticed an RCMP officer apparently recording the licence plate numbers of the cars they drove. During the service, he noted the following:

> At one point a person whom I suppose to be a local walked past our group and appeared to be agitated. He heard some of the Bible reading and said, "Don't say that to me," as if he felt the reader was speaking directly to him rather than reading. As the reading continued uninterrupted he stopped, turned, and then took a step toward us. The fury in his eyes was as intense as I have ever seen. One of the team just explained that we were Christian Peacemakers and having a worship service. At the same time one his friends whom he was originally walking toward called on him to continue on his way. He did so with the loud suggestion, "You fucking peacemakers get out of here! Go back to Burnt Church and do your fucking peace work with the fucking Indians." (*CBC News Online,* www.cbconline.org, consulted October 2001)

Burnt Church became a particular focus of tension, as 32 of the 34 communities involved in the dispute had agreed to a government-directed "voluntary," self-imposed moratorium on fishing. Burnt Church and Indian Brook (in Nova Scotia) were holdouts.

From early in 2000, the federal government set out to resolve the situation more permanently. They bought up licences from non-Native people for use by Native people and tried to get all the Native communities to sign or agree in principle to sign Interim Agreements that would bring them into the fishery and solidify the DFO's regulatory power in terms of catch limits and enforcement. By August 27, 27 bands had signed on. Again, Burnt Church was not among the converted. On August 9, they rejected an offer that included a new two-million dollar wharf and five well-equipped boats, but which came at a cost of a forty-traps-per-fisher limit to the community of about twelve hundred people.

What the Burnt Church people wanted was self-regulating authority to police themselves in this matter. They set up their own management scheme, issuing permits and treaty tags to any community member who wanted them and establishing a fall and spring fishery. A limit of 15 000 traps was set for the autumn fishery and 5000 for the spring season. Under their management program, the total increase in lobster fishing pressure in Miramichi Bay would be 5000 traps (www.rism.org).

Not surprisingly, the DFO did not recognize the Burnt Church management plan, nor the non-DFO tags. In mid-August 2000, DFO officers conducted a late-night raid on lobster traps in the bay. A boat and over 700 traps were seized and four people were arrested. The Mi'kmaq of Burnt Church were enraged. They mounted a blockade of Highway 11, a major commercial corridor in the province. Allegations and counterclaims were hurled back and forth. The Mi'kmaq claimed that DFO officers pointed guns at them, while the DFO responded that only pepper spray had been used, and that only one police baton had been pulled out.

Fisheries Minister Dhaliwal backed the DFO officers, saying that they would continue to seize lobster traps and make arrests. The people of Burnt Church continued to exercise what they perceived to be their treaty rights by setting more lobster traps. Equally determined, DFO officers seized traps and increased the physical intensity of their enforcement. From August 13 to September 22, the DFO estimated that it pulled 3616 traps. Officers harassed, beat, and arrested Native fishers, even ramming boats belonging to Burnt Church members (see Box 9.2). The Mi'kmaq responded to this increased aggression by throwing rocks at the DFO vessels. Band members and a DFO officer were injured. Threats were uttered and shots were fired. The situation only calmed down when the time for lobster fishing ended.

In 2001, the federal government tried to avoid the violence that had marred the previous two years. The government initially issued the Burnt Church Mi'kmaq a temporary licence for a one-week season that lasted from August 20 to 27, 2001. Its objective was to allow Native fishing to proceed while a long-term agreement was negotiated. The Burnt Church community was not happy with the limitations that accompanied the licence: they could not sell their catch (it was confined to food and ceremonial purposes), and DFO tags had to be on anything that was harvested.

The government then proposed allowing the people to use small boats to set 900 traps for two months every fall. The community responded by blocking all entrances to the reserve and escorting the media out of the area while they continued setting their traps. The RCMP sent in extra officers. Non-Native fishers again called on the government to bring their Native colleagues into line with them. As the deadline for an agreement passed without resolution, Ottawa issued a new licence allowing the Burnt Church Mi'kmaq to fish for food and ceremonial purposes until October 20, 2001. Nothing was resolved.

How can this be resolved? While the economic and biological aspects of the issue are beyond the scope of this book, the policing aspects are not. As long as the situation remains involving non-Native DFO officers combating Native fishers, enforcing rules set by non-Native people (with non-Native RCMP officers "picking up the pieces"), the situation will not be resolved peacefully. Clearly, more Native input is required, both in establishing the limits and in enforcing them.

Box 9.2	**Burnt Church Diary**

Fenton Somerville is a Mi'kmaq and a resident of Esgenoopetitj. He maintained a diary of events that transpired in his community in 2000. On August 30, a DFO boat rammed a Native fishing boat. Somerville comments on the event and on the media handling of the incident:

> I looked up at the screen just in time to see three Natives jumping off their rammed boat. A friend of mine was being clubbed by the officers as he was trying to rescue the guys in the water. He was saved from being hauled onto the DFO boat by other Natives throwing stones. The officers had to let him go to shield themselves from the rocks.
>
> It was satisfying to finally see a national network actually video a DFO boat ramming a Native boat. It's been a tactic used by the DFO before, but of all the media that gathered during these past weeks, none had managed to get it on camera.

On Sunday, September 3, 2000, a confrontation between Native and non-Native fishers occurred on Miramichi Bay. Thirty large commercial fishing boats, accompanied by an RCMP ship and a Coast Guard helicopter, powered their way to confront the Mi'kmaq in their dories (small fishing boats). Here are Somerville's comments on the events:

> A person who was ... the first one to the scene said the police only put their hands up in a gesture of helplessness. As if there was nothing they could do. He said they taped the whole thing from the high deck of their ship. There were shouting matches between the Natives and non-Natives. He said he got the feeling that the RCMP were waiting for the Natives to make the first move. (*CBC News Online*, www.cbconline.org, consulted October 2001)

ABORIGINAL POLICING IN PRINCE EDWARD ISLAND

Prince Edward Island has no First Nations-governed policing operations. As of 1996, there was, in fact, only one Native special constable who, under the supervision of the RCMP, assisted in policing the one Native community of Lennox Island.

NOTES

1. For the Innu Nation's confrontation with the justice system, see Steckley and Cummins, 2001: Chapter 15, "Fighting for Recognition: The Sheshatshit Innu and the Megaprojects," 150–158.

KEY TERMS

Hickman Report (p. 134)   saqmaw (p. 132)

REVIEW QUESTIONS

1. Outline the series of events that led to the development of a police force among the Innu of Davis Inlet.
2. What role did the institutional racism of the Nova Scotia justice system play in the Donald Marshall case?
3. Outline the history of the Unama'ki Tribal Police Force.
4. How did the Supreme Court of Canada interpret the treaty of 1760?
5. Critically analyze the Burnt Church confrontation as a policing issue.

chapter ten

Aboriginal Policing in the Territories

LEARNING OBJECTIVES

After completing this chapter, students should be able to:

1. Outline the principles and measures employed in Kaska customary law and Netsilik traditional justice.
2. Contrast how mainstream Canadians and Native peoples might perceive legendary RCMP officer Sam Steele.
3. Set into a cultural and historical context the reason why Sinnisiak and Uluksuk killed Father Guillaume Le Roux and Father Jean-Baptiste Rouviere.
4. Identify the unique challenges of policing in Nunavut.

There are two distinct groups of people living in the Territories of Canada: the Dene or Athabaskan-speaking people, and the Inuit. The Dene live in the western part of the Territories, in Yukon Territory, and the Northwest Territories. They include the Chipewyan, Yellowknife, Dogrib, Hare, Slavey, Sahtu, Gwich'in, Hän, Upper Tanana, Tutchone, Tahltan, Tagish, Kaska, Beaver, and Sekani peoples. The Inuit are found across the Arctic.

TRADITIONAL NOTIONS OF LAW, ORDER, AND JUSTICE IN THE TERRITORIES

First Nations in today's Territories had their traditional concepts of right and wrong, as well as customary means of dealing with offences. Anthropologists refer to these concepts and practices as **"customary laws."** While there was no formal court system or full-time police officers, compliance with social norms and behaviour was expected. If these norms were violated, punishment was dealt out.

Kaska Customary Law

The Kaska are a Dene people who live in northern British Columbia and southern Yukon, and have lived in the area for thousands of years. They are a hunting people who have had contact with non-Native people for only about 200 years. Sustained contact did not exist until the middle of the nineteenth century.

John Honigmann conducted extensive research among the Kaska in the 1940s. He documented their culture as it existed at that time and, through interviewing Elders and consulting historical records, how their culture was prior to and during early contact. He paid considerable attention to social control and conflict resolution. He noted that the Kaska had to deal with a set of offences not unlike those found in non-Native Canada. He noted that the primary aim in dealing with the offences was to rebuild harmony and stability within the community.

The Kaska made a clear distinction between wounds inflicted intentionally and those that occurred accidentally. In terms of wounds inflicted by assault, a payment was made to the victim. No such payment was made if somebody suffered an accidental injury at the hands of another person. Similarly, there was a distinction made by the Kaska between manslaughter and murder. In cases of murder, settlement might be made through a large payment, made over a year or more, or by blood revenge. Anthropologists talk about **"weregild,"** payment made by the responsible person (and that person's family) to compensate an injured person or the relatives of a slain person. John Honigmann states that in cases of compensation among the Kaska, "Weregild required the cooperation of all the members of the murderer's family" (Honigmann, 1964: 90), undoubtedly a means of preventing any such action from becoming a full-scale feud. When vengeance took place, it was up to the victim's brother or uncle to undertake the task of exacting vengeance. This retaliatory action was always directed at the actual killer and not against members of the killer's family. In the case of manslaughter, no vengeance followed, but a payment was expected, albeit much smaller than in the case of murder.

Payment and retaliation were not the only means of dealing with a murder, however. In some cases, especially when the victim and murderer were young people of approximately the same age, the family of the slain person might seek the adoption of the murderer in place of the victim. In some cases, this would take place with manslaughter as well. The victim's family would seek such redress through a kindly disposed headman (community leader). In such instances, the murderer's family would typically try to coerce the murderer to accede to such demands. The person would then grow up as a member of the adoptive family. Finally, if the murderer escaped from the area, at least a temporary halt to any proceedings designed to bring about compensation would occur.

The penalty for mistreatment or killing a child was severe, but again, it depended upon the circumstances. If a woman were suspected of neglecting her child to the point of starvation, she would be banished and driven from the community. "Let her starve," people would say, in the hope that other people would learn the importance of treating each other kindly (Honigmann, 1964: 90). Infanticide, typically occurring when a baby was born out of incest, merited public condemnation. Incest itself brought considerable shame, and public opinion judged it harshly. Magical retaliation might ensue. Men, in particular, were made to feel the shame of being caught in incestuous relationships, and were sometimes known to go to such extreme forms of self-punishment as leaping into a fire or cutting off their penis.

It is important to note that law, social control, and conflict resolution among the Kaska were, for the most part, community based. Honigmann suggests:

> [S]ocially approved punishment in pre-contact Kaska life consisted chiefly of unfavourable pub-lic opinion, fines, exile, and blood revenge ... Nobody explicitly enjoyed the power to impose punishment on behalf of the total community. Hence, most social pressure was informal or indi-vidualized. It should be clear that negative pressures did not exhaust the techniques for main-taining equilibrium ... Potlatching, affinal ties, games, and minor rituals undoubtedly played their parts in preserving harmonious social relations. (Honigmann, 1964: 92)

When the Kaska became subjected to mainstream Canadian laws and justice, there was still a strong inclination to adhere to their traditional system. During the 1940s, Honigmann observed that there was a tendency for the Kaska to "remain as much as possi-ble aloof from White man's law or system of justice" and that interpersonal grievances within the Native community were seldom brought to the adjudication of White courts (Honigmann, 1949: 149). As a consequence, all cases had as their complainants the police, the Indian Agent, or other White men. Thus, in the 1940s, the Kaska still relied on tradi-tional means to bring about resolutions to aberrant behaviour and to maintain social con-trol and order.

In 1998, the Kaska of the Liard First Nation were the first Aboriginal people to sign a tri-partite agreement on policing with Yukon Territory and federal government. Because of this agreement, this community of 800 some people would get four Aboriginal police officers sta-tioned at the local RCMP detachment. As part of this agreement, the community formed a committee that influenced decisions on such key justice issues as restorative justice issues involving pre-charge diversion, bail, and sentencing. This may not seem significant to non-Native people with no understanding of the problems of First Nations justice. The importance of this agreement, however, was underlined by Chief Ann Bayne: "This agreement is a signif-icant step for our First Nation towards self-government ... It will recognize and respect our laws and traditions and ensure our community attains and maintains control of our destiny and that of future generations" (www.sgc.gc.ca/Releases/e19980709.htm, consulted May 10, 1999).

Netsilik Traditional Justice

The Inuit ("men, people"), like other Native peoples, had customary ways of maintaining social harmony and for dealing with those people who threatened the stability of the com-munity. The Netsilik or Netsilingmiut ("People of the Seal") are part of a culturally linked grouping that anthropologists refer to as the Central Inuit. The Netsilik homeland stretches from 88 degrees west to 100 degrees west longitude (pretty much directly north of Manitoba) and from 68 degrees north to 73 degrees north latitude, on the coast of the

Arctic Ocean and on some large islands. This is certainly one of the harshest environments on earth. Primarily seal hunters, as their name suggests, the Netsilik also hunted caribou, musk oxen, and polar bear. To cope with their environment, they had an elaborate technology well-suited to their needs.

As was the case with other Aboriginal peoples in Canada, the Netsilik had a variety of means for dealing with the resolution of conflict. It is important to note that any antagonism or interpersonal animosity that was left unchecked in an Inuit band could result in disaster for the entire community. Asen Balikci made the following observations regarding this essential point:

> In dealing with aggression in the Netsilik community, the whole field of social control was characterized by flexibility ... Netsilik society did have behavioral norms, mostly concerned with the broad interests of the community as a whole. There were definite obligations with regard to food procurement and food sharing. Freedom of access to important natural resources was also essential. When camp stability was endangered by individuals who disregarded these community interests, or upset the social balance by disruptive aggressive activity or by evil sorcery or insanity, the community did take action—even to the extreme of execution, if it was needed. (Balikci, 1970: 193)

What is of essential importance here is that the welfare of the community or group took priority over the demands of the individual. Furthermore, it was the group that exacted retribution and brought about social harmony, not another individual. Thus, the collective took precedence over the individual.

What were considered deviant actions among the Netsilik? As indicated above by Balikci, the hoarding or denial of food was a major offence, as was denying somebody access to all-important resources. Many other conflicts had to do with access to women. Failure to give a girl who had been promised in marriage, wife stealing, and jealousies implicit in wife-exchange partnerships were all potential areas of conflict. Resentment concerning superior skill or laziness in hunting could cause conflict as well.

A number of means were used to maintain social harmony and to regain stability if this harmony were lost. Mockery and derision were behaviours that served as forms of social control. Nobody wanted to be laughed at or insulted (Balikci, 1970: 174). Similarly, gossip was used to check deviant behaviour, albeit, like the other forms of control, it could anger someone as well.

Withdrawal was another means of maintaining peace. If somebody did not like another person in the band, or a group of people, they simply moved to a more distant location. Balikci noted, as well, that even in more recent times people who do not like each other have the openings of their dwellings facing away from each other's house. Conversely, people who do get along have the doors facing each other.

More formal methods of conflict resolution existed. These included fist fights, drum or song duels and approved executions, all designed to bring disputes into a public forum to be resolved conclusively. It was recognized that any man could challenge another to a fist fight for any reason. Stripped to the waist, the challenger received the first blow. These were delivered, one at a time, to the shoulder or temple until one man gave in. Once completed, the quarrel was acknowledged as being over and done with.

Song or drum duels involved extensive preparation and public display. Songs were prepared privately in advance, with the wives of the two opponents (Balikci's research spoke only of male combatants) learning the words of the songs. They were presented in public, with the wives singing while the husbands drummed. The singer hurled every conceivable kind of insult and accusation at his opponent, while the audience revelled in the performance. Each wife sang her husband's song in turn, with the duellists giving free rein and expression to their hostility. While public, and undoubtedly a mode for the cathartic release of emotions, song or drum duels were not always conclusive. In such cases, the duellists sometimes resorted to fist fights, which inevitably brought disputes to a decision (Balikci, 1970: 185–189).

Executions were used for people who were considered too violent or out of control. Such people might be considered to be insane, or sorcerers, or simply dangerous individuals. In these cases, for the preservation of the group, drastic measures had to be taken. Again, it was a public decision involving the group. The decision was made informally by relatives within a camp. Non-relatives were said not to be involved. The executioner was typically a close relative, and performing the act was considered a duty. Furthermore, by having the deed done by a close kinsman, it precluded the possibility of revenge.

THE RCMP AND THE TERRITORIES

"... when we first had the RCMP come around. We were so scared of them. They were so big, they looked like moose and musk ox to us" (Nora Ruben, quoted in Brody, 1987: 214).

Three of the most recognizable images of Canada—the Royal Canadian Mounted Police (RCMP, or "Mounties"), the high north country, and the northern Aboriginal (Inuit or Dene)—are tightly interwoven. Although the Mounties began in 1873 as the "North-West Mounted Police" (NWMP) and first earned their reputation by moving First Nations peoples onto reserves in the West, being actively involved in the second Riel Resistance in 1885, and in some high-profile cases in the prairies (e.g., meeting Sitting Bull—see the section below on Sam Steele—and killing Almighty Voice—see the chapter on Saskatchewan), the near-mythical image of the Mountie was primarily shaped by their early years in the North. The indefatigable police officer, driving his dog team across tundra and through boreal forest, has been seared in the world consciousness as few Canadian images have. Dozens of early Hollywood movies, as well as novels, comic books, cartoons ("Dudley Do-right"), early television's "Sergeant Preston of the Yukon" with his trusty dog, Yukon King, and more recently Constable Benton Fraser of the television series *Due South*, have all kept the Northern image of the Mountie alive.

This image-making began in the mid-1890s with the NWMP policing the Klondike Gold Rush. By 1895, there were 20 officers in Yukon Territory. Three years later, there were 250. At the same time, the NWMP began establishing posts and patrols throughout the North, reaching the coast of the Arctic Ocean by 1904.

Superintendent Sam Steele

No one man did more to contribute to the image of the Mountie than the aptly named Samuel Steele, called variously the "Lion of the Frontier" and the "Lion of the North," and eventually rewarded for his work for the British Empire by being knighted. Born in the colony of Upper Canada in 1849 and raised as a farm boy, Steele's military and policing career spanned more than 40 years. His initial training for the job was at the Royal Military School of Toronto. From there, he joined the Canadian militia at the age of 16 years. When the NWMP was formed in 1873, Steele enlisted as a Sergeant Major, and was subsequently involved in various pivotal events on the Canadian prairies. He hounded Métis leader Louis Riel and eventually forced his surrender and arrested him. When Sitting Bull sought refuge in Canada following the defeat of Custer at Little Big Horn, it was Steele who was given the task of meeting him (as can be seen in a television "Heritage Moment") and eventually sending the great Sioux leader back across the border.

In Yukon Territory during the Klondike Gold Rush, Superintendent Samuel Benfield Steele was omnipresent. In addition to being the Commanding Officer of the NWMP from July 1898 to September 1899, he was also appointed a member of the first council of the new territory, established and chaired the first board of health, chaired a board of licence commissioners, and supervised the winter mail services. It was in his capacity as the Commanding Officer of the NWMP, however, that he received the greatest acclaim and recognition. Even though the Gold Rush brought to Yukon Territory "toughs, gamblers, fast women, and criminals of every type," Steele successfully brought justice to the wild frontier of Canada.

Rarely is Samuel Steele's image investigated in anything more than a superficial way when it comes to how he might have been seen by First Nations people. It is usually stated that the Native people respected his honesty, morality, and courage, which no doubt has a certain ring of truth about it. But he was active in imposing laws on Aboriginals that in retrospect can be seen as being ethnocentric at best, racist at their worst. In his book about the famed Blood warrior Charcoal (Si'k-okskitsis, "Black Wood Ashes"), in whose man-hunt Steele was involved, Hugh Dempsey wrote: "Steele's goals were simple. With the co-operation of the Indian agent and with or without the help of the chiefs, he would stamp out the Sun Dance, prohibit the Indians from owning guns, and severely restrict their movements off the reserve" (Dempsey, 1979: 94).

Acting to eradicate the Sundance, the single most important ceremony of the Prairie First Nations, shows that Steele did not believe in freedom of religion for Natives. In restricting where they could go, he acted to deprive them of their basic right of freedom of movement. He would not be the same hero to Native peoples of the North that he would be to mainstream Canada. The image of the Mountie likewise differed.

The Trials of Sinnisiak and Uluksuk: Inuit Men, White Men's Justice

Sinnisiak (sometimes written as Sinnisak) and Uluksuk (sometimes written as Uluksak) were Copper Inuit from the Coppermine region of the Northwest Territories. They found their way into Canadian history as being the first Inuit tried for murder under Canadian law. Their case is important not only for this reason but also because it brought into sharp focus the different perceptions of justice as they are held by the Inuit and by Euro-Canadians.

The Copper Inuit live west of the Netsilik people and just as far north. Generally speaking, they relied on some but not all of the same means of social control and conflict resolution as did the Netsilik. Song duels existed, but fist fights were not all that common. Execution killings agreed upon by the victim's relatives and blood-vengeance killings were both prac-tised. Like the Netsilik and all other Inuit groups in Canada, they believed strongly that a person must maintain a balanced sense of self-control. Too little self control, or too much, focusing too intently on an issue, were distrusted as traits that could be dangerous.

In 1911, when this story begins, the region the Copper Inuit called home was still relatively unknown to non-Native people. Canada's legal status in the territory was based more on assumption than on concrete substance. The federal government did not assume legal responsibility for the welfare of Inuit in the Arctic (as they did for "Indians," and, in fact other Canadians) until compelled to do so by a 1939 decision of the Supreme Court. One small example of this lack of responsibility was the fact that although the Old Age Pension Act was passed in 1927, it wasn't until April 1, 1949 that an Inuk (singular form of the plural "Inuit") first received a pension cheque (Tester and Kulchyski, 1994: 94). As we will see from this case, they would be much more ready to assume judicial and policing authority over the Inuit than they were to assume responsibility for their general welfare.

In the early years of the twentieth century, missionaries were still actively competing for northern Aboriginal souls to convert to Christianity. In July 1911, a French missionary named Father Jean-Baptiste Rouvière arrived at Fort Norman in the Northwest Territories. He was a member of the Oblates, a Roman Catholic order renowned throughout the North for its zeal and dedication to missionization. Father Rouvière had been doing his work at Fort Good Hope since 1907, converting mainly Dogrib and Hare, two Dene peoples. Fort Norman, at the junction of the Bear and Mackenzie Rivers, was the leaping off point to the barren lands of the extreme North where, it was then said, there were Inuit people still to be converted. Also, the Anglican missionaries were closing in from the east. That is why, after four years working with the Dene, Father Rouvière looked north. As Robin put it, Father Rouvière and his superiors wanted to save the Copper Inuit from "the twin clutches of Anglicanism and barbarism" (Robin, 1976: 152).

With his superiors' blessing, and the assistance of some Dene, Father Rouvière set out with the deep sense of purpose that typifies the Oblates in their Native missionary work in Canada. They travelled northeast, looking for the Copper Inuit. Near summer's end, 1911, Father Rouvière and a trader named John Hornby set up a makeshift trading post/mission at a small lake called Imaerinik, at the edge of the barren grounds. The missionary shortly thereafter met his first Inuit. His impressions of them were most favourable. Throughout the fall, they met regularly. Still he wanted to do more, and was not happy when the Inuit left the area with the October snow while he remained behind at Lake Imaerinik.

In March 1912, Father Rouvière was more determined than ever to journey north to be with the Inuit. He first went back to Fort Norman to replenish his supplies and to make contact with Father Guillaume Le Roux, another missionary who was to assist him. Like Rouvière, Father Le Roux was a native of France, and dedicated to his faith and calling. Unlike Rouvière, who was 12 years his senior, Father Le Roux appears to have lacked patience and self-control, not making him a good person to work with the Inuit. He was said to be aggressive, overbearing, and prone to fits of rage (Robin, 1976: 159). In terms of Inuit psychology, this made him a dangerous man.

In mid-July, the two men set out, taking the same route that the older man had taken the year before. When they reached Lake Imaerinik, the summer was nearly spent, so they began preparing for winter, at the same time meeting with a group of about 60 Inuit who were camped near the lake. Rouvière did the bulk of the heavy work, while Le Roux met with the Inuit. He made nearly two dozen such visits before the Inuit left for the winter sea ice in early November. The priests were pleased that the Inuit seemed to show interest in their work, and several could be induced to make the sign of the cross. It is not known what the Inuit thought of the two men early on. In the brief and fleeting contacts they had had, true understanding between the Inuit and missionaries would not have been possible. It is not known whether the Inuit were clear on how the missionaries might differ from the other White men, the traders, who visited them. Rouviere and Le Roux wanted to bring an Inuit family back to Fort Norman with them in order to train them as interpreters, guides, and language instructors. That does not seem to have been seen as a practical option by the Inuit. Despite promises of material goods for those who returned with the missionaries to Fort Norman, no one took up their offer (Robin, 1976: 159–160).

During the winter of 1912–1913, the missionaries heard, via the Dene, that the Anglicans were planning to do their own missionizing among the Copper Inuit. That summer the two men intensified their efforts at conversion, with Le Roux even travelling as far as the Coppermine River. The Inuit gave the two priests names, "Ilogoak" for Le Roux and "Kuleavik" for Rouviere. Conversion, though, was slow. One reason may have been the company that Le Roux and Rouviere kept. They appeared to be quite close to the Dene, the traditional enemies of the Inuit. As well, the trader Hornby, with whom they shared a small post, was not well liked by the people.

As the missionaries moved farther north, and away from the traditional territory of the Dene whom they had earlier relied on, they began to depend more heavily on the Inuit. The two men lacked the skills and knowledge to function effectively in the Arctic; they needed to be taken care of. One man, Kormik, hunted for Le Roux, while Uluksuk's wife made the priests' winter clothes. To try to ensure cooperation, the missionaries distributed typical trade items such as needles, nets, and traps to the Inuit. Rifles were promised but were not forthcoming. Kormik allegedly expected to be given a rifle by the missionaries (Robin, 1976: 161).

The Oblates received word that an Anglican missionary named Fry was planning to rendezvous with 400 to 500 Copper Inuit at Coronation Gulf. This prompted the Catholic missionaries to even greater feelings of urgency. As the brief Arctic autumn waned and the Inuit began to move out in small groups to their winter hunting grounds, the two White men decided to go with them.

The missionaries left with Kormik and a number of others, travelling with seven or eight sleds. Among the other people in the group were two young hunters named Sinnisiak and Uluksuk. They all headed north toward the mouth of the Coppermine River (that gave this group of Inuit their English name). All was not well. Some of the Inuit were growing disenchanted with the priests, who were something of a burden as they did not cope well with the hard travel. Furthermore, the missionaries were sharing a tent with Kormik, who still felt that they owed him a rifle (and some traps) for the work he had done for them. With his wife's help, when the priests were not looking, the Inuk took a gun and some food from the priests. Le Roux and Rouviere demanded the return of the weapon. When Kormik refused, Le Roux loaded another rifle and threatened the Inuk with it.

At this point, later testimony from other Inuit suggests that the Inuk was considering killing both of the missionaries because of the perceived dangerous nature of their behaviour. From the Inuit perspective, they were hoarding goods and not engaging in what they perceived to be "normal" sharing. The White strangers did not seem to be able to hunt and were not seen to be reciprocating adequately for the favours bestowed upon them by the Inuit (e.g., hunting for them, helping them travel, sharing their tent and food, sewing their clothes). In addition, Le Roux was bellicose and belligerent. From an Inuit perspective, these men could be seen as threatening the security of the group. Kormik's mother, acting on the advice of some band members who feared being killed by the missionaries, returned the gun. The damage, though, was done.

The priests were unsure at this point as to what they should do. Should they continue to travel with the band, or should they return home, to come back later? Finally, within a few days of their arrival at the winter camp, they made the decision to return home.

The priests faced great difficulties as they travelled alone. They were inexperienced in facing the Arctic winter without Native assistance. They were tired from all the travelling they had been doing. Their dogs were tired. They had little food. It might be legitimate to say that without help from the Inuit whom they had just abandoned, they would die on the trail.

On their second day out, after a horrendous first day and night alone, the two missionaries spotted two Inuit who were unarmed and accompanied by a dog. They were Sinnisiak and Uluksuk, who were returning to the winter camp after having gone to help some families make the trip north. The priests convinced the two men to help them, telling them they would be paid with traps. Sinnisiak and Uluksuk joined the dogs in harness, pulling the heavy sled until nightfall, whereupon they built an igloo for the night. The next morning, figuring that they had helped enough, and fearing that they might get lost or go too far out of their way if they journeyed any further, the two Inuit prepared to leave. This angered the priests, who were dependent upon their assistance and who had assumed that they would continue to pull in harness with the dogs. Regardless, the Inuit set out by themselves, only to get lost in a storm. Then, their dog alerted them to a cache of food that the priests had left earlier. They had barely approached the cache when the priests materialized, led by Le Roux brandishing a rifle.

Communication as usual between the two groups was bad. The Inuit would later testify that at this point they asked Le Roux whether he would kill them if they didn't help, and the White man had answered in the affirmative. The Inuit were put back in the harness with the dogs, and they set out in the middle of a blizzard. According to the Inuit, when they attempted to speak to the White men the missionaries would cover their mouths, and every time they slowed down or stopped, they were pushed or threatened with the rifle.

Eventually, Sinnisiak conveyed to Uluksuk that he intended to kill their captors before the White men killed them. On the pretence of needing to relieve himself, Sinnisiak slipped out of his harness. When Le Roux relented and turned his back, Sinnisiak pounced on the man and stabbed him with a knife. The priest made a dash for the rifle on the sled, while Sinnisiak held Rouviere at bay with the bloody knife. Uluksuk and Le Roux fought for the rifle until the latter, stabbed several times, finally fell down dead. Rouviere ran for his life, until he was brought down by a shot from Sinnisiak. They finished him off with knives and an ax. Believing that the men, or their spirits, might attempt vengeance, they then ate part of their victims' livers. They then took the rifles and ammunition, covered the bodies with snow, and returned to their winter camp. The next day, other members of the band went to the spot and retrieved items from the sled and from the bodies that would aid in their survival.

It took a while before the killing became known to the outside world. By the spring and summer of 1914, rumours were circulating. Inuit were seen dressed in the priests' clothes and carrying items such as binoculars and rifles that had belonged to the two missionaries. It wasn't until the spring of 1915 that the North-West Mounted Police were brought in, and an expedition was formed to find the missing men.

The Mounties Get their Men

In 1908, the North-West Mounted Police had conducted an Arctic expedition known as the Hudson's Bay Patrol. The officer who led the expedition, which extended from Great Slave Lake to Hudson Bay, concluded that there was virtually no need to have a significant police presence in the Arctic, as the Inuit were so peaceful. This fit in comfortably with a stereotype that many non-Native people had of the Inuit being a cheerful, smiling, childlike group of people (unlike the stereotype of the "war-like Indians"), so the Mounties did not have a station in Copper Inuit territory when they were called upon to look for murderers in the high North.

Charles Deering (sometimes spelled Dearing) La Nauze, a 27-year-old officer with a decade of experience, much of it in the North, left Regina in early May of 1915. With him were two colleagues, Constables D. Withers and J.E.F. Wight. They first journeyed to Edmonton, the jumping-off point for the North. While there, they stockpiled goods for a three-year trip. They knew that finding the killers in the Arctic could be a long-term project.

They stopped over at Fort Norman, and in August, after having sent their supplies ahead with nine Aboriginals, the three officers headed off to the barrens. They took with them Darcy Arden, an Inuk interpreter, and a guide named Ilavinik, his wife Mamayuk, and his daughter Nagosak. It was not until one month later that they reached the vicinity of the priests' house. From there, they made short forays toward the lands of the Copper Inuit.

Meanwhile, a second patrol was organized, led by Corporal H.V. Bruce. Bruce held high opinions of the Inuit but became suspicious when certain possessions of the two priests turned up in the hands of a number of Inuit, including Uluksuk and Kormik. These suspicions were confirmed when La Nauze and Bruce got together and Ilavinik had a conversation with two brothers, Nachim and Ekkeshvina, who revealed the names of the killers. This was corroborated shortly thereafter by a number of Inuit, primarily Koeha, a respected Elder, who related the entire sequence of events. The Inuit expressed their regret over what had happened. They said that they had not told any of the White traders in the area because they were afraid of the vengeance that would be visited upon them. The trader Hornby had once told them that if they ever killed a White person, they would be killed in return.

Shortly afterward, the Mounties found Sinnisak on the sea ice, arrested him and brought him to Bernard Harbour, where he was charged with the two murders. He came peacefully. Undoubtedly, he understood very little of the legal implications and ramifications of what the police were saying to him. Regardless, he gave a full statement of the killings of the priests, despite the fear he felt of reprisals. Sinnisiak at first tried to go without sleeping, as he feared the White men would stab him in his sleep. Eventually, of course, he collapsed from sheer weariness.

With Sinnisiak in jail, guarded by Corporal Bruce, La Nauze set out by dog sled to find Uluksuk. Within one week, he found a small band travelling on about six sleds. The officer and his party were welcomed warmly by the people, except for one man who held back: Uluksuk. When confronted by the police, he acknowledged that he knew why they were there. He went peacefully with the officers, and, at his preliminary hearing, gave virtually word for word the same account as Sinnisiak (Robin, 1976: 178; See Box 10.1 for the media version of the capture of Sinnisiak and Uluksuk.)

In the summer of 1916, the group travelled to the NWMP regional headquarters of Herschel Island. There they spent the winter, Sinnisiak and Uluksuk doing odd jobs for the Mounties, and presumably being very homesick while anticipating an unknown fate in an unknown land.

In May 1917, they left for Edmonton, where the trial would take place. Included in their number were Koeha, who would act as a translator and witness, and the interpreter Ilavinik. The trial in Edmonton dealt only with Sinnisiak. The Crown prosecutor, Charles Couisolles McCaul, wanted to make the case an exemplar: the White man's justice had been brought to all the other First Nations, it remained only to be brought to the Inuit; they must be taught to respect the White man's law. The defence attorney, J.E. Wallbridge, argued that the Inuit were in fear of their lives, and acted out of self-defence. The priests, he contended, used threats and force to get the Copper Inuit to haul their sleds.

The case proceeded slowly, as translators had to render comprehensible linguistically and conceptually foreign legal terms and ideas. A few words might take 10 to 15 minutes to translate while the translators debated over exactly what was being said, and how best to convey it to the accused. The jury's deliberation took only a short time, about one hour. And, despite the fact that the jury of the "peers" of the Inuit were six White Edmontonians, they acquitted Sinnisiak.

Crown prosecutor McCaul was incensed, alleging that Edmonton opinion had been inflamed by the local press in favour of the accused and against the priests, who had been subjected to rumours of sexual impropriety with Inuit women. Consequently, he contended, a fair trial in Edmonton was impossible. He demanded a retrial somewhere else. This was granted. A few days later, the Inuit were tried in Calgary. The jury, after deliber-

---

Box 10.1	The Media Mountie: An Unrealistic Picture

The Copper Inuit probably numbered around 1000 people (Stefansson 1919 and Jenness 1922) at the time that the Mounties were pursuing Sinnisiak and Uluksuk. The largest single gathering of Copper Inuit at any time of year would be between 100 and 200 people, and that only when and where sufficient game (e.g., seal or caribou) would be available to sustain such a large group. The Copper Inuit did not fight in large groups of warriors, the biggest conflicts being among only several people. This did not keep the press from magnifying the heroic drama of the Mounties going after their men in Copper Inuit territory, men who came peacefully with not even the slightest hint of reprisal from their friends and family. The following excerpt from an article that appeared in the *Calgary Herald* on August 11, 1917 is a good example:

[H]ere on the rim of the world were a people who knew not the law or the law bringers—by the slightest error the patrol would bring upon itself the fury of a thousand warriors—warriors who could send with their mighty arms the copper tip birch arrow through the body of a Caribou at a hundred paces. Warriors who knew no fear in battle. (Robin, 1976: 177)

The Mounties were brave in facing the harsh climate of the Arctic and the unknown reaction of the people they were chasing. But they would have no reason to fear the Hollywood image of "the fury of a thousand warriors." Such was how the reputation of the Mounties in the North was built: a combination of real heroism and grossly exaggerated storytelling.

ating for 45 minutes, returned with the following verdict: "'We find the prisoners guilty of murder, with the strongest recommendation possible to mercy that the Jury can give'" (Moyles, 1989: 80). The death sentence that went with being guilty of murder was commuted by the Governor General to life imprisonment. For almost two years, the two men spent their time in minimum-security detention at the Fort Resolution police guardroom, where they were termed "model prisoners," working willingly at whatever tasks the police set for them. On May 15, 1919, they were released from custody. That year they would help the NWMP set up a police station in Copper Inuit home territory. A few years later, an Inuk killed a Mountie constable and was hanged for the offence. Denny La Nauze would rise swiftly through the ranks of the Mounties to become an Assistant Commissioner.

CONTEMPORARY POLICING IN THE TERRITORIES

All policing in Canada's huge, sparsely populated territories is undertaken by the RCMP. There have been initiatives undertaken to involve Native people as officers. On February 4, 1994, the Canadian government and the government of the Northwest Territories signed an agreement to carry out a community constables pilot project in two small Native communities, Fort Good Hope and Coral Harbour. The cost of initiating and running the project was to be shared by the federal government (52%) and the Northwest Territories government (48%). The initiative was not to be in the form of a reserve program but in the creation of an auxiliary service for the local RCMP detachment. Its primary aim was to create a core group of Native people in Fort Good Hope and Coral Harbour who could provide civilian policing and who would be available to assist the local RCMP in cases of emergency or when regular officers were unable to respond immediately to a specific situation. Candidates employed and appointed as temporary civilian employees with the RCMP could eventually apply to become regular members of the force. Thus, the project was aimed at not only providing assistance to local Mountie detachments and fostering better relations between the police and the Native communities, but also at providing more career opportunities for Aboriginals within the police force (Solicitor General Canada, 1995: 4 and 5).

The community constables in the two communities were selected by the RCMP, in consultation with the band councils, to be temporary civilian employees of the RCMP, and are appointed by the force as peace officers under Section 7(1) of the *Royal Canadian Mounted Police Act*. In Fort Good Hope, a selection committee comprising five members of the band council, members of the community as a whole, and the local RCMP detachment commander was developed to try to ensure impartiality during the hiring process. The committee began by developing and distributing an application form for candidates interested in the project. Then they developed interview questions and met with the 19 interested candidates. Of these, six were selected and three others placed on standby in case any of the chosen candidates were unable to continue in the program. In Coral Harbour, the same process was used, except that the band council decided that it would make the initial candidate selection and that it was up to the local RCMP detachment to give the final approval after conducting appropriate safety clearances on the selected candidates. Thus, the force and each of the committees chose a maximum of six candidates.

The community constables have essentially the same mandate as regular members of the force but work under the detachment members' supervision on a part-time basis. They work 16 to 30 predetermined hours a month and can be called in by the local RCMP detachment to assist regular personnel with a range of general and specific community policing duties. They are able to enforce all federal laws, including the *Criminal Code*, as well as all Northwest Territories laws, albeit their tasks and responsibilities are subject to the limits established at the time of their hiring. Put another way, community constables have the same powers as regular RCMP officers, but cannot intervene unless asked to or authorized to by the local RCMP detachment commander. Working under direct local Mountie supervision, they wear the RCMP uniform and are subject to the rules and regulations governing regular members of the force. Their jurisdictional territory is restricted to the two communities involved. They do not usually carry firearms but may use available RCMP-issue shotguns and .308 calibre rifles, provided they meet certain qualifications.

CONTEMPORARY POLICING IN NUNAVUT

The RCMP are responsible for policing Canada's newest territory, created on April 1, 1999. The Nunavut government pays 70 percent of the cost and the federal government the balance. As of March 2001, there were 87 Mounties serving in the territory. Of these, there were 23 in the capital of Iqaluit, seven in Rankin Inlet, five in Cambridge Bay, and one each in Coral Harbour, Kimmirut, Kugaaruk, and Grise Fiord. Some communities, such as Chesterfield Inlet, Whale Cove, and Repulse Bay, have no resident RCMP officers (*Nunatsiaq News,* March 23, 2001).

Policing in Nunavut presents its own unique challenges. The territory is immense, encompassing 1 235 200 square kilometres. To appreciate how truly large this is, picture Nunavut as being larger than the combined states of California and Alaska, the latter of which is the largest state in the American union. Occupying this huge territory are fewer than 30 000 people, living in only 28 towns and hamlets. There is just about an equal number of kilometres of highway. This means that most travel of any distance in Nunavut is done by airplane. Eighty-five percent of Nunavut's population is Inuit, and Inuktitut is the day-to-day language of many (see Box 10.2 for a discussion of how the meaning of the term "police" has evolved in Inuktitut).

Winters are exceedingly cold in Nunavut, and there is 24-hour darkness and twilight for many days. On the other hand, summer days receive almost continuous light. The extreme contrast in temperature and duration of sunlight can have serious implications for

Box 10.2	The Changing Meaning of "Police" in Inuktitut

H. Finkler wrote in *Inuit and the Administration of Criminal Justice in the Northwest Territories: The Case of Frobisher Bay* about the changing nature of the Inuit's perception of the RCMP. He wrote that the original term for police in the dialect of Inuktitut spoken at Frobisher Bay (now called Iqaluit) was "someone who helps out," but that once the RCMP became more of a regular and regulatory part of Inuit life there, the term for police meant "one who maintains order" (cited in Depew, 1986: 31).

people's behaviour, and, in turn, policing. Seasonal Affective Disorder is a valid Arctic malady. Likewise, with endless sunlight during the brief summer, people are out and about more at night, potentially resulting in more need for a police presence.

A remote northern environment has its own special policing considerations. Many people still hunt for their meat. This means that there is a greater percentage of firearms in Nunavut than in the south, which means that there is a greater potential for accidental (and deliberate) shootings. As well, there is a great potential for people getting lost out on the land, for hunting accidents, drownings, snowmobile and boating accidents, and so on. These concerns are not limited to civilians. In 1979, two RCMP officers, Constable Gordon Brooks and Special Constable Ningeoseak Etidloi, drowned during a walrus hunt outside Cape Dorset.

The Shooting of Constable Jurgen Seewald

Cape Dorset is a hamlet of 1118 people in Nunavut. It is located on Dorset Island, off Baffin Island's Foxe Peninsula, and is 395 kilometres west of Iqaluit and 2050 kilometres north of Montreal. Traditionally, of course, the people were hunters, relying on 20 species of marine and land animals for food. Today, while people still hunt for subsistence, a large number of people in Cape Dorset are artists, in particular soapstone carvers and printmakers. The Dorset school of printmaking has become world famous. In recent years, however, Cape Dorset has also gained a more local reputation for violence and alcohol abuse. In March 2001, an incident occurred that did nothing to assuage that reputation.

There are normally four RCMP officers stationed at Cape Dorset. On Monday, March 5, 2001, however, one officer was on holiday, and another was on duty outside the community. Constable Jurgen Seewald, a veteran with 26 years' service with the Mounties, was one of the officers in town that day. Like many Canadians, he was an immigrant. Born in Germany, he moved to Canada when he was two years old, and grew up in Brantford, Ontario. He joined the RCMP in February 1975 and served four years in the Northwest Territories, later serving more than twenty years mainly at three detachments in Nova Scotia. Seewald was a well-respected police officer. In 1993, he had spent six months with a United Nations peacekeeping mission in the former Yugoslavia, earning the UN Peacekeeping Medal and the Canadian Peacekeeping Medal in the process. He was known by friends and colleagues alike as a "gentle giant" who "abhorred violence and liked to joke around" (www.canoe.ca, consulted March 7, 2001). A long-time friend and colleague said that despite his imposing size (6 feet 4 inches and 240 pounds), he did not throw his weight around and claimed that he "didn't have a mean bone in his body." His father, Helmut, observed that although his son was a "crack shot," he hated using his gun.

Seewald had been married for 25 years and was the father of a 23-year-old son and a 20-year-old daughter. At the age of 47, he could have retired, but he had passed up the opportunity the previous October in order to take a posting in Cape Dorset. His father said that he had decided to stay on with the force and go north because "he loved the work, loved the Northwest Territories" (CBC Radio, March 6, 2001, quoted at www.north-van.rcmp-grc.gc.ca). Northern postings are voluntary, so Constable Seewald's choice to go to Nunavut was his alone. According to his father, his wife and children had stayed behind in Nova Scotia because of work commitments.

Constable Seewald responded to a domestic dispute at about 2 a.m. on March 5, 2001. There he encountered Salomonie Jaw, 46, an artist and employee of the Northwest Company store in Cape Dorset. Details are scarce in terms of exactly what happened after the officer arrived at the scene. According to one account, after Seewald arrived there was a struggle with the accused man, with a single shot being fired and hitting the officer (www.nunatsiaq.com, consulted March 9, 2001 and March 16, 2001). Another version of the events claims that he was hit with a shotgun blast from four to seven metres away (www.north-van.rcmp-grc.gc.ca, consulted March 5, 2001).

The other officer in town that day was called. He took Constable Seewald to the nursing station, where he died a short time later. The police then had to deal with the suspect, who had fled the scene, and also ensure the safety of the other residents of Cape Dorset.

A 15-person RCMP containment team flew in from Iqaluit to deal with the tense situation. The team, which included Inuktitut-speaking negotiators, arrived at about six-thirty in the morning, four and one-half hours after the shooting. Police feared for the safety of the public, so residents were ordered to stay in their homes. Municipal offices, schools, businesses, and the medical centre were closed while the manhunt was conducted for the suspect. He was quickly found, barricaded in a house.

A lengthy standoff followed. Fifteen Mounties surrounded the building while the Inuktitut-speaking negotiators tried to speak to the man. At the same time, the community radio station also tried to get the man to surrender. There was no response from the suspect. Finally, at about 6:30 p.m., 16 hours after the shooting, Salomonie Jaw walked out of the house and surrendered peacefully. The RCMP tactical squad rushed him as he lay down on the snow to surrender (www.canoe.ca, consulted March 7, 2001).

Such a tragedy in a small Nunavut community affects everybody. One resident noted how the officer's death and the taking away of Salomonie Jaw would affect "everyone in the community because everybody's related to everybody" (www.north-van.rcmp.grc.gc.ca, consulted March 5, 2001). The authorities recognized the impact that such an event would have on the community. Government mental health officials were flown to Cape Dorset the day after the shooting to help the community cope.

John Vander Veld, a specialist in such situations, said that such an event shakes up an isolated, tightly knit community more than it would towns and cities in southern Canada. Several factors might make this so: the isolation, with no roads connecting the hamlet to any other community, and the history of traumatic events that such communities all have experienced in their relatively short period of being collected together in what, for traditional Inuit, would be large groups of people (*Canadian Press*, www.canoe.ca/CNEWSLaw0103/07_mountie-cp.html, consulted September 4, 2001).

At Sam Pudlat Elementary School, a counsellor dealt with the children individually. Consistent with traditional Inuit culture, community Elders also went to the classrooms to talk to the children. The RCMP sent a police force psychologist to help the distraught officers deal with the loss of their colleague. In a four-member detachment, such a loss would especially be felt strongly.

Because of inclement weather preventing a flight to Iqaluit, Salomonie Jaw was arraigned via teleconference. He was then held for four days in Cape Dorset, pending an investigation. On Friday, March 9, he appeared in court and was charged with first-degree murder.

Seewald's death had an impact throughout Nunavut. A funeral service was held for him in Iqaluit, before his body was taken to Nova Scotia. Nunavut's Justice Minister, Paul Akalik, speaking on behalf of the government, expressed condolences to Constable Seewald's family, friends, and colleagues. The territorial legislature ended its session early, as many members were too upset to continue. Flags throughout the territory were flown at half-mast.

Before the month ended, Premier Paul Okalik announced that plans for a review of Nunavut's policing needs were underway (www.nunatsiaq.com, consulted March 23, 2001).

While Constable Seewald's death was the first murder of a Mountie in the territories in forty years (Constable Colin Lelliott was shot to death in Cambridge Bay in 1960), two other RCMP officers had been shot and wounded in Nunavut in the short period since the territory was created.

The RCMP were expected to request at least eight new constables to serve the territory. At the time of the premier's announcement, Coral Harbour was already slated to receive a second constable who would also serve Repulse Bay. Staff Sergeant Mike O'Malley, of the Iqaluit detachment, said that the force was looking at it from the standpoint of member safety, suggesting that those four communities presently being served by only one officer should have two. In addition, he hoped to have a pool of officers in Iqaluit whose members would be available to fill in for absent RCMP constables in the territory's smaller communities.

KEY TERMS

customary law (p. 142)   weregild (p. 142)

REVIEW QUESTIONS

1. Outline the principles of Kaska customary law.
2. Identify the measures used in Netsilik traditional justice.
3. Compare how mainstream Canadians and Native people might perceive legendary RCMP officer Sam Steele.
4. Set into a cultural and historical context why Sinnisiak and Uluksuk killed Father Guillaume Le Roux and Father Jean-Baptiste Rouviere.
5. Identify the unique challenges of policing in Nunavut.

chapter eleven

Experiences in the Field

LEARNING OBJECTIVES

After completing this chapter, students should be able to:

1. Identify some of the challenges placed on both a Native and a non-Native officer policing a reserve.
2. Outline several strategies for a non-Native officer policing a reserve.

CASE STUDY: THREE OFFICERS POLICING AN ABORIGINAL COMMUNITY

Three officers from a policing service that works closely with the Ontario Provincial Police (OPP) were interviewed. They work in an Aboriginal community beside a mid-sized city. A large number of non-Natives come to the community on a regular basis because of a very successful casino that exists there.

Leslie is the acting chief of police at the policing service and an OPP officer. She is non-Native, but has thirteen years experience, including two where she is presently working. She transferred into the Aboriginal policing service as a sergeant. Her education consists of Ontario grade 13, plus a two-year diploma in Law and Security from a community college. Her initial posting with the OPP was in northern Ontario, where she spent four years policing a Native community. When she was hired for her current position, the board did not ask her questions about her training or police work per se, but about her experiences working with First Nations people. It would seem that, given her considerable experience, her qualities as a police officer were apparent. As representatives of a Native community, the board considered her ability to deal effectively in a cross-cultural environment as being of the utmost importance.

The board wanted Leslie to serve as chief of police for three years, but the OPP was opposed because she lacked the accreditation. The board did not find this a matter of concern, believing that the standard rules for the posting of the position of chief of police should not apply to their community. As there is a mix of Native and non-Native people in the community, the people she deals with often feel that, as she is the chief of police, she must be Native. She feels that because people are a little uncertain of her status, they are hesitant to "tell her off."

Leslie finds that the younger people in the community are more accepting of her as a non-Native individual than are some of the older people. However, she has never felt that she was not accepted. She has discovered that her present posting entails being far more involved in community activities than in previous postings. Overall, she has enjoyed her experiences to date (summer 2000), and she has made some lifelong friends. She finds that much of her work requires her to assume a teaching role. Because this is a new police service, all of the other officers have relatively little experience, requiring her to assume a mentoring position.

As a non-Native officer, Leslie has discovered, as other non-Native officers have, that Native perceptions of time (the famous "Indian time") are different from those of Euro-Canadians. Thus, to use her expression, a non-Native cannot afford to be "high strung" when working in a Native environment. She has yet to attend a meeting that started on time. In her words, a non-Native officer has to learn to "go with the flow."

Leslie sees the need for officers to have specialized training in order to deal with alcohol abuse and sexual abuse, which, along with excessive gambling, offer policing challenges in the community. The first, she says, is the number one difficulty on her particular reserve. She feels that about 80 percent of the calls her detachment receives are alcohol-related[1].

The community has a sentencing circle and a healing circle. The latter follows the renowned Hollow Water model (see Box 6.1 in Chapter 6). Leslie sat in on the first case, which dealt with the improper sexual touching of children. She had spent her first four years as an officer specializing in sexual assault cases, but she found this initial experience in a healing circle "unreal" (in a positive sense). This was particularly true when she heard a man publicly admit to his deeds, and to hear every woman in the circle speak as a victim of sexual abuse.

Robin is another non-Native officer working for the force. He has a business diploma from a community college. He is from the local town. His father is an officer with the OPP. Rather than waiting an extra year to get hired by the OPP, he applied for the Aboriginal policing service and was hired right away. He had at the time of the interview been in the community for two and one-half years, and he feels that he "has been welcomed with open arms." In the time that he has been there, he has learned a lot about Native culture both from the job and from a First Nations course that he had taken. He has never felt disadvantaged being a non-Native officer policing a Native community. He speaks of the "brotherhood" that exists on the force and feels that he can ask any questions of his fellow officers, Native or non-Native.

"Community" is important to Robin. He believes that it is essential to be a good community person to be a good officer. He does work in the schools, and he finds that since he started doing this, the children are more willing to approach him. Before he started visiting the schools, he felt the children were "scared" of him, but no longer. He feels that playing hockey in the community has helped him to make connections as well. Robin has also been working with the Special Olympics, which adds to his positive community profile.

Robin speaks of the good working relationship that the Aboriginal policing service has with the OPP. He noted one case in which his force had to make a pursuit into the neighbouring town, and says there was close cooperation between the two police forces. This fits in with general practice among First Nations policing services. In the First Nations Chiefs of Police Association (FNCPA) study published on the Web in 2001, over 75 percent of all police officers working in First Nations self-administered police services claimed that they provided assistance on a weekly basis to other police services (FNCPA, 2001, 6.7, "Supporting External Services"). In Murphy and Clairmont's study, 29 percent of the officers surveyed strongly agreed and 58 percent agreed that they had good working relations with nearby policing organizations (Murphy and Clairmont, 1996).

At the same time, Robin noted that local band politics are unavoidable and inevitable. In one case, he had to charge a band councillor's wife. He felt that he had to work extra hard on the report. Despite these concerns, he speaks of the community as a "great reserve."

Frank is from the community. He completed high school and then studied marketing at a local college. Prior to joining the force, he had been the manager of a sports complex. Feeling he needed a change, he joined the police force, where he has been for about two years. The force has given him the "structure" that he wanted in professional life. Being Native and a local person, he feels that he was "not walking in blind" to the community, and can relate more "in good ways and bad ways" to the people with whom he is involved. He generally feels that his background makes it easier for him to deal with the people. However, he finds it difficult having to deal with relatives and then seeing them the next day. Overall, though, he has found that if the people are shown respect, they return respect back to him. He has found this to be particularly true of the Elders. Frank stresses the importance of showing respect to them.

Frank enjoys being a role model for younger people and providing a model to which they can relate. He feels that he has a good rapport with the youth of the community. One of the ways in which he develops and maintains this relationship is as a hockey coach. Like his colleagues, he sees the need for community involvement. He noted the enthusiasm with which the Elders respond to community participation.

Interestingly, he feels that while a "stand-alone" police force might be a good idea, he does not feel that it would really make much of a difference to policing on his reserve. As the situation stands, they can and do make good use of OPP resources. He feels that it is neither a great advantage nor disadvantage being a Native police officer in a Native community. As he says, "You're a police officer doing the same job." He feels a sense of unity with the OPP, observing how the two forces help each other when the situation warrants it.

TWO RCMP STORIES

In the area of Aboriginal policing, damaging stereotypes abound. The stereotype of the racist non-Native cop is a powerful one. As with all stereotypes, all you have to do is read or experience in some way someone acting like the stereotype and it is confirmed. We have seen in this book so far a good number of stories that may be doing just that. It is easy to collect such stories. The newspapers and books written by journalists abound with such tales. As the majority of students reading this book will probably be non-Native, it is important for them to see that there are "good cops" out there doing good work in the field of Aboriginal policing. The following are two such stories, both about Royal Canadian Mounted Police (RCMP) officers. The names are pseudonyms.

Corporal Ship

Corporal Ship has been an RCMP officer for almost 12 years, having joined the force when he was 23 years old. He served ten years, including three different postings, in northern Manitoba. One of these postings was in The Pas, a community that borders a First Nations reserve, a community that was discussed in the chapter on Manitoba in relation to the Helen Betty Osborne case. His second posting was in a non-Native community with a large Native population, while the third was on a reserve with a population of between 1000 and 1200 people.

Corporal Ship speaks with candour and insight regarding his experiences, both of which help the reader feel what it was like to be in his shoes.

He spoke of what it was like to be a non-Native officer among a Native majority population. One of his biggest early challenges was in not understanding the language spoken by the local Native community. He felt lost being the only non-speaker in a group. However, he quickly picked up a few words such as "go," "come," "stop," and, of course, "police officer."

There are a good number of Native communities across northern Canada, where the dominant or at least a significant language on the street and at home is a Native language (e.g., Cree, Inuktitut, or a Dene or Athabaskan language). Elders in many communities are still monolingual or have their speech dominated by their Native tongue. Learning at least a few words of the local language is important, even when most of the people speak English or French. In the First Nations Chief of Police Association study, it was discovered that of the police officers surveyed who worked for First Nations self-administered police services (90% of whom were status Indians), 45 percent spoke a Native language (54% did in the Murphy and Clairmont study, 1996), and another 10 percent understood at least some of the local language (FNCPA, 2001, 6.5, "Language").

Corporal Ship spoke about feeling like "a minority" in his own country. His positive attitude helped him work his way through that feeling. He wanted to learn about a different culture, so he worked hard at learning about the people with whom he had to work.

Corporal Ship found that Aboriginal officers working on reserves had some advantages and disadvantages relative to their non-Native colleagues. Their fluency in the language of the community and their familiarity with the culture were definite advantages. In addition, they could generally calm situations down more effectively and quickly than could most non-Native officers in the same situation. Also, when making arrests they are less likely to be subjected to the charge that, "You are arresting me because I am Native," a charge sometimes levelled at non-Native officers. At the same time, however, they could be seen as being part of the local "establishment" and therefore subject to insults.

Corporal Ship speaks about how one officer's work has an impact on the next officer to be involved with the community. As he puts it, "You know the prejudice of yesterday's officer." In other words, police officers arriving in a new posting will be judged by how the people were treated by the officers who preceded them. The lack of support or confidence that the community felt toward a belligerent police officer will carry over to his or her replacement.

In addition, Corporal Ship learned to not always take at face value what officers might say about how bad a community might be. He found that there is sometimes a cyclical nature to crime in the North. Once all the "bad guys" were arrested, sentenced and imprisoned, the community could become peaceful again. As is the case everywhere, a relatively small number of people are responsible for the vast majority of offences.

Corporal Ship wanted his legacy to be a proud one. "I wanted them to speak highly of me," he says. And, "I wanted the uniform to be thought of highly." He did this by creating a positive, friendly environment. He early developed a practice of stopping to talk with the children and teenagers on the reserve, introducing himself by his first name and telling them that they did not have to tell him their names. On the next encounter, he would just say "Hi," and drive away. As time went by, he found that he could talk to them and they would respond. This, he found, created rapport. Equally important, it created a good foundation at the beginning. Later, when he needed the help of the local people, they were there. If he needed something from people he had gotten to know in this way, or from their friends and family, they would come back and talk, rather than closing themselves off and protecting themselves. Such a strategy is very useful in a small, closely knit community where an act of friendship to one person gets known through extensive networks of family and friends. What was very apparent to the interviewers, and must have been equally obvious to the people, is that that Corporal Ship was genuinely interested in the people with whom he worked.

He learned never to lie. In small communities, he says, if you "burn one person, you burn everybody." A lie, he says, will come back to haunt you. If he had to take somebody to jail, he would tell them so. He would not say that he was simply driving the person home, and then take him to the cell.

Corporal Ship believes that policing on-reserve or in communities with large Native populations can best be accomplished by "acting normal" (i.e., not in a superior or condescending manner). In this way, the people treat you in a regular manner in return. Behaving in a condescending manner does not bring about positive results, and the police officer will not be successful in his or her work. The community will close itself off and will not cooperate with the police.

Corporal Ship is a great believer in the importance of non-Native officers having and showing respect for members of the Native community they police. He feels that this respect entails viewing people as "equal individuals with different experiences." Another, related quality that Corporal Ship feels helps the non-Native officer policing a Native community is curiosity about the culture of the people. Demonstrating an eagerness to learn about Native culture is an important element in being accepted in a Native community, and also in enjoying an assignment on a reserve.

Sports, including baseball, hockey and soccer, are very popular community activities on reserves. Corporal Ship would watch for a while and then be invited to join in. Eventually, people would ask him his name. Inevitably, because of his friendly, open manner, the response would be "I've heard about you. I will talk to you." As he says, being friendly and approachable, "pays dividends." Ultimately, this style of policing helped him with cases. He makes the very important point that the people "don't care what you do, or that you are a police officer; they just like you."

As both a police officer and as a single man in the North, Corporal Ship would go to local bars in both a professional and a social context. As a police officer, he would do "walk throughs," and off-duty he would go to socialize. Perhaps because of his reputation as a solid, professional Mountie, he was never challenged when out of uniform and in a bar. He used discretion to the point that, in one community where he had been for three or four years, friends with whom he had played baseball and socialized asked him upon his departure what he did for a living.

Corporal Ship suggests that it is important for non-Native police officers to live on the reserve, and that police services that have jurisdiction over Native communities should try to encourage this. He believes that if the police are stationed outside the community, and just do drive throughs or are responding to calls, rapport is not established. In his opinion, it creates a negative image that is hard to overcome. The people feel that the officer is acting as if he or she is better than them, thus making effective policing difficult.

Corporal Ship is proud of the fact that five to six years after he left a particular reserve in which he was working, somebody told him that "you were a good officer." This came from a jail guard who had been told this by an inmate who knew Corporal Ship. Such praise from an inmate is commendable indeed. It came to a large extent from his community-policing style. When he entered a community, he would learn who the "bad guys" were and go out of his way to make contact and talk with them before having anything official to do with them. That way, they knew him as an individual, rather than as a police officer whose job it was to arrest them. This paid off. It would provide an answer to a question he asks concerning, "If somebody already has committed a major crime for which they will be punished, what would stop them from doing something to a police officer?" If Corporal Ship was sent to arrest the "bad guy," that individual might then hesitate to resist violently because they knew Corporal Ship and liked him. Had he not taken the time to get to know these people as individuals, they would be less inclined to give themselves up peacefully.

Corporal Ship finds a number of rewards come from working in a Native community, including the sense that he was affecting lives positively by how he handled situations. To the extent possible, he would try to handle situations by trying to resolve problems, rather than just arresting someone. This process, he feels, takes much longer to accomplish but is ultimately more effective.

He tried to keep first-time offenders out of the judicial system. For example, in one case, he applied a form of restorative justice. An offender had shot a BB gun, breaking some windows. Rather than going through the formal system, the offender was put to work building up the winter wood supply for the victim. Solutions like this, he suggests, make more sense than the traditional way of dealing with offenders. In part, he thinks this way because of his belief that fear of the judicial system is a more effective deterrent than the judicial system itself. He feels that once a Native person is caught up in the White judicial system with incarceration, probation, and so on, it is "one band-aid over another."

Corporal Ship never felt like he was "in prison" or "stuck in the North." He enjoyed his work there, made friends, and tried to learn from the experience. He remarked that often officers who complained about their northern and reserve postings wanted to return to them after they had been away from the community for a few years.

Judgment calls are an important aspect of a police officer's work. Corporal Ship noted that other officers were engaged in what he termed "preventative policing" with respect to Native people. If they saw a Native person walking down the street drunk, they would arrest that person. Often, this is a good decision as the officers know from experience that the individual is prone to violence. Corporal Ship often would see somebody drunk and then, later on, would have to arrest that person for a crime committed in that state. However, he felt that this "preventative policing" was sometimes wrong. He put himself in the other person's shoes: "If I am walking down the street drunk, I wouldn't want to be arrested." He was aware that there was often a double standard at play, whereby Native people were more likely to be arrested when intoxicated than were non-Native people in the same situation. He was uncomfortable with this double standard.

One instance of a judgment call made by Corporal Ship has a happy ending of a type rarely reported in the news. The suspect had assaulted somebody with a baseball bat and was walking through the community firing a rifle. There were rumours that he had taken a hostage. Corporal Ship and another officer, from off the reserve, arrived at the scene. The other officer had 14 years experience and had emergency response team training. They approached the suspect, with the other officer assuming a position behind a relatively large police vehicle (a Suburban), his rifle aimed at the suspect. Corporal Ship stood in front, exposing himself to the suspect. He believed that he had time to seek cover behind the vehicle, should the man begin to lift his rifle.

A dialogue ensued between the suspect and Corporal Ship. The man claimed that he did not do the deed for which he was being arrested. Corporal Ship replied, "Give me a chance to prove your innocence." The suspect was, in the officer's words, "irrational." This irrationality was due to his intoxication at the time.

The situation was very tense. Twice during the dialogue, Corporal Ship had very real reasons to believe that he could be killed. The suspect said that he "was going to kill" the officer. Eventually, however, the man gave himself up without any violence or additional problems. Corporal Ship's partner afterwards commented that he had saved the suspect's life at least twice during the confrontation. These situations occurred when the man, in his intoxicated and angry state, had begun to lift his rifle. The officer, with his gun trained on the suspect, had come very close to shooting him out of fear for his colleague's life. Corporal Ship's calm, cool, and professional behaviour had prevented a tragedy. The other officer commended him in his report of the incident.

Corporal Boisvert

Corporal Boisvert joined the RCMP in the late 1970s, after having spent six years with a regional police force in Ontario. Much of his experience with First Nations policing occurred in a Saulteaux community in southern Manitoba, where he set up a satellite detachment. There were three Native officers and himself. Corporal Boisvert was the officer in charge. The experience taught him a lot about Aboriginal policing, and about First Nations communities in general.

Corporal Boisvert worked with the people "one on one," trying to make them feel comfortable and to establish mutual respect between himself and the people. It was important to him as an individual and as a representative of the RCMP to talk to the people outside of a policing context. Corporal Boisvert generally adopted the attitude that when policing a Native community, once you walk onto somebody's "turf," you should treat the people as you want to be treated. He found that if he talked to people first, they would feel more comfortable going to him later because they knew him and would therefore tend to trust him.

Corporal Boisvert's advice for young constables would be that attitude is 99 percent of the job. "Compassion" is a key word with Corporal Boisvert and it is fundamental to the way he does his job. He found that he could defuse volatile situations by talking, not reacting aggressively or forcefully. Following up on a call afterward is an important aspect of showing compassion. For example, he would go back to a house a couple of weeks after a domestic incident to see how things were progressing. It was important not only that he followed up on a case, but that people were aware that the police cared about them and their situation.

One of the keys to Corporal Boisvert's success was that he came to have what he termed a "vast appreciation" of Native culture. He saw that the people had genuine awareness of who they were as a people. In fact, he was "envious" of their culture because he wasn't all that sure of what his own was. He attended all the cultural and social functions that he could, both on and off duty, to show his respect for the people, their community, and their culture.

When asked what he perceived to be the biggest challenge facing non-Native officers policing a Native community, Corporal Boisvert replied that it is trying to understand the culture and why people do what they do. He referred to the first arrest he made. He was told that the suspect wanted to "smudge" before being taken away. Corporal Boisvert did not understand what that meant. Smudging is a purification ceremony that involves burning **sweetgrass**.[2] He asked the suspect whether the police could be there while he smudged. The man agreed that they could. Corporal Boisvert did not understand at first the importance of the smudging ritual but realized that it was important for the man. He appreciated that the people did not object to the police presence while the suspect participated in the ritual.

The community Elders played a large role in the community and in the cultivation of Corporal Boisvert's own role in the community. He knew that he had to be accepted by the Elders, because if they accepted him, so would the rest of the community. As he went about the town, he always carried tobacco[3] and other gifts that he would share. The Elders would be quiet and reticent at first, until they were offered a gift in a traditional way, and then everything would change.

The degree to which Corporal Boisvert was accepted is reflected in the name they gave him. They called him Wapanaoksis, which contains the meaning "until dawn." An Elder told him that this was because, "[You're] up all night protecting us." This is a profound statement of the respect that they had for him.

He showed respect for the traditions of "Treaty Day." He would dress up in the traditional red serge for the presentation of the treaty annuity payment of five dollars. While it might be easy for an outsider to dismiss the celebration and the payment as trivial, Corporal Boisvert learned from an Elder that, "It is not the five dollars; it is to remind us that we have an agreement."

There were a number of cultural differences to which Corporal Boisvert had to adapt. One of these was the informality that characterizes Native communities. One major way in which he adapted to this informality was by familiarizing himself with his new posting. He would walk around the village saying that he was just dropping in, that he was new to the reserve and wanted to meet people.

Corporal Boisvert also learned of the value placed on sharing in Native culture. On one occasion, he was showing a non-Native auxiliary constable what life was like on the reserve. Having spent a lot of time getting to know people, he knew who would be up late and who wouldn't be. He asked his partner whether he was hungry. When the answer was yes, they went to a woman's house. He knew that she often made bannock[4] late at night. It was 11:30 p.m., but he knew she would be up. Arriving at her house, he asked, "Are you making bannock?" She replied in the affirmative, and the three of them sat down to a midnight snack. The auxiliary officer learned an important lesson about community policing in a Native community, and the importance of getting to know the people you serve.

Corporal Boisvert early exhibited the value of sharing. He said to those he met going door to door that they should not be afraid to drop in to see him at the detachment office, and that he always had the coffee on. People would take this invitation to heart, frequently dropping by and having a cup of coffee. He eventually mentioned to his boss that as a result of all the visitors, he felt that he couldn't get anything done. His boss, in turn, told him not to worry, that the visiting was important work and that eventually everything would get accomplished.

His open-door policy would teach Corporal Boisvert something about the Native notion of respect. A man came to see him when he was trying to catch up on some paperwork. The man said to him, "You know when you are talking about respect? That's not very respectful. You shouldn't do that [i.e., be working at his desk] when someone is visiting you."

He also learned the cultural differences in perception of time. He quickly got used to setting up meetings and having people not show up when he felt they should. He learned that there is a value to what is known as "Native time." Native communities often take a long time to accomplish things because of the need to build a consensus on what gets decided. Where that consensus exists, there are fewer problems implementing a decision. An Elder, watching him trying to do many things at once, said to him "You're in a hurry to meet your destiny." In retrospect, Corporal Boisvert feels that he used to be impatient.

While attending his first funeral, Corporal Boisvert was exposed to a different way of acknowledging and mourning the dead. The deceased was a cousin of one of the band constables. Corporal Boisvert was surprised to see the officer in jeans and a tee-shirt, as opposed to a suit or other formal attire. When asked, the man said that he was wearing these clothes because that was what he wore when he saw his cousin when that person was alive. This wasn't necessarily a standard cultural practice, per se, but Corporal Boisvert learned that respect for the dead can take a number of different forms in Native culture. The funeral was followed by an all-night wake in the reception hall, with people drinking copious amounts of coffee and smoking cigarettes.

In order to foster cross-cultural awareness among his fellow non-Native officers in the area, Corporal Boisvert organized an "Indian Cultural Awareness—Sleep in a Tipi" course. It was a three- to four-day program and a number of people in the community got involved, preparing food and organizing activities. The Elders related stories from the community's past.

The programme did not start off well. Some police officers assumed a skeptical position, questioning why they had to be there. Initially, the non-Native community and the First Nation people were visibly divided, with Native people on one side and the police officers on the other. This gradually changed. The pipe was smoked, and the tipis were erected. The Elders explained the meanings of the colours and the symbols that were painted on the tipis. The atmosphere became more relaxed when the people played Native games and had a sweat (see the chapter on Saskatchewan) in the lodge. There was a certain amount of humour at the officer's expense as people joked, "Hey, Mountie, we're going to melt that hair off your back."

The degree of respect that Corporal Boisvert had developed for the people is reflected in his handling of the media. When contacted by the press regarding coverage of the event, Corporal Boisvert advised them that they should contact the Native community, not him, for permission, saying "I am not the one you should be speaking to." The Elders wanted to hold onto their culture, without exposing it unduly or making a sideshow of it. They said "no" to any press coverage.

One of the pieces of advice Corporal Boisvert has for those training non-Native offi-cers to work with Aboriginals is to be aware that there is diversity in Native cultures; don't train recruits in the ways of a Blood or Piegan community if they are going to be working with the Cree. As he learned at the Indian Awareness Days, seemingly little things, such as the local culture's interpretations of the colours on a tipi, can mean a lot to a people.

Even though he became aware of cultural differences, Corporal Boisvert quickly learned that the similarities were important too. In his words, "The more I searched for our differences, the more I found that things were alike." For example, he learned that, like people everywhere, Native people were concerned about keeping a roof over their heads, about the health and well-being of their families, and so on.

Corporal Boisvert's respect for the people as people was key to his success at his job. One of the more memorable and successful of his experiences in the community came from this. He was involved with providing security for a powwow. The security volunteers had not been accorded much respect up until that time, so he got them jackets with "Security" writ-ten on them. He also acquired a mobile home that he used as a command post for the vol-unteers. The security volunteers were treated with much more respect, and they were able to solve a crime. Box 6.1 shows that the community also has respect for the RCMP.

Box 11.1	**The Mountie's Role in the Community**

Corporal Boisvert found that the people in the Saulteaux community where he worked had a genuine respect for the Mounties, and that they still wanted the RCMP there. The community did not join up with the Dakota Ojibway Police Services, as had some of their neighbour First Nation communities. The history of the RCMP played a large part in Corporal Boisvert's duties as an officer.

He had taken a mandatory history of the police force and, at first, had questioned its value. Later, however, he realized its importance when he saw a copy of the First Nation's treaty rights on the wall of somebody's house. He was told that peo-ple "wanted a White man" in charge of the detachment because the First Nation had "made [our] treaty with the White man." It was a profound moment for him.

Individual Cases

There are several incidents and people that remain fresh in Corporal Boisvert's memory and illustrate the distinctive nature of policing on reserves. One of those people is a man whom we will call "Bert." Bert was about 35 years old when Corporal Boisvert met him, and he had a bad reputation. Corporal Boisvert visited his mother first. There he encountered Bert, and approached him saying, "You must be Bert. I'm new in the community. I'm meeting people on the reserve." He noticed that Bert had "Loser" tattooed on his forehead. He had had it done when he was 16 years old, because that is how he saw himself at the time.

Corporal Boisvert's strategy of going to meet Bert paid off in the end. They became friends, spending a lot of time together. Their relationship was treated as a bit of a joke by other police officers, because Bert would always ask for Corporal Boisvert when he had to go to the detachment office. However, in the Mountie's eyes, this was "preventative medicine." The time that he spent socially with Bert was less time the man would spend in jail. As well, when the officer needed information, he always went to Bert first. If the Native man did not have the information, he could get others to provide it for the officer. Corporal Boisvert never let Bert think that he was afraid of him, saying "Don't make me do my job." And, when Bert did end up in prison, Corporal Boisvert made a point of visiting him so that Bert knew that there would still be a bond between them when he was released.

Another case that Corporal Boisvert remembers vividly was a case of abduction. One of the band constables reported that a 25-year-old man who had had a relationship with a 17-year-old woman had allegedly "abducted" her. The Native officer in question was related to the people making the allegations. Corporal Boisvert knew the man in question and had spoken with him often. He saw the two riding in a truck, so he pulled the truck over and spoke with each one of them separately. Corporal Boisvert felt that he should ask the same type of questions that a prosecutor would ask. He asked her whether she was okay. She replied that she was. He then asked if she were in the vehicle against her will, and she said that she wasn't.

Corporal Boisvert had doubts about the allegation that the man had "broken into" the woman's house. It seemed more likely that the young woman had let him in through the back window. It seemed that rather than a case of abduction, the man was simply having difficulty letting go of his relationship with the younger woman. The man broke down emotionally, so Corporal Boisvert took him to the hospital. Although he thought that the young man might be suicidal, the physician who took on the case let him go, claiming that there was nothing wrong with the young man.

Eventually, the man was charged under the then recently introduced stalking law. The case in question was on the fringe of the new law, so the man was given probation (with no trial) and advised to seek counselling. Corporal Boisvert felt that this was a case in which neither jail time nor a fine would be of any practical value.

The difficulties of conducting police work in a small community are evident in this case. The family of the young woman complained about the investigation. Because Corporal Boisvert had had coffee with the suspect, they felt that the officer was guilty of "favouritism," a common accusation when a Native officer is involved. They provided specific dates of when the man had gone over for coffee at the detachment office, information that Corporal Boisvert believes had been fed to them by their band constable relative. Corporal Boisvert suggested that they speak to his boss, which they did. He, in turn, essentially repeated what Corporal Boisvert had already told them about the case. It seemed that the family of the young woman felt that they were the suspects, as, during the course of his investigation, Corporal Boisvert had asked them questions with which they were not comfortable.

One case that proved difficult for Corporal Boisvert because of cultural differences involved an older man accused of sexual crimes. The man in question was 73 years old, a **shaman**[5] or "medicine man," who was recognized as having considerable influence in the community. It was alleged that he had been sexually abusing his grandchildren (among others) when they were between eight and ten years old. Corporal Boisvert had two witnesses, but there were also other people who claimed that they could discredit their allegations. Some people in the community would tell, when drinking, things that they would not otherwise dare to relate. There were stories of the old man "casting spells," putting "curses" on people, and causing illness, including a severe rash. Such allegations were sometimes traditionally used to control someone thought to be acting in an anti-social manner. More seriously, it was related that a family member (either a son or grandson) had been killed in a hunting accident. People claimed that happened because he was going to come forward and tell what he knew about the old man's alleged crimes.

Corporal Boisvert was left with a difficult situation. His dilemma was this. He knew that he would not be able to obtain a conviction. Likewise, he was aware that if the old man were charged, he might go into the woods and hang himself. The loss of face and of his reputation in the community would be too much for the old man to bear. Corporal Boisvert finally decided to speak to the man about what he had heard. He asked the man to come to his office. When the suspect did not ask why he was being summoned, Corporal Boisvert knew that the man was aware of why he was being asked to come see the officer. He asked the man, "Do you know why you are here?" and received in reply, "I think so." Corporal Boisvert then said, "I don't care who you are, how old you are, or what you are. If I get a hint that you are doing anything wrong, I will arrest you and you will spend the rest of your life in jail." No public face was lost. No charges had to be proved. And there was no trouble after that.

NOTES

1. Concerning this point, Frank (see below), a community member who belongs to the force, noted that the same percentage also would apply to the neighbouring town.

2. Sweetgrass is considered by many First Nations to be one of the four "medicines," or materials which when burned in sacred ceremony act as a kind of prayer. The other three are tobacco, cedar, and sage. With sweetgrass, the people wave the smoke over their bodies in an act of ritual purification.

3. In the traditional ways of many First Nation cultures in Canada, tobacco is given to Elders if you wish to learn from them or in other ways are asking a favour of them (e.g., if you want to receive a Native name). The Elders do not necessarily smoke the tobacco. They may put it in a fire as part of a prayer to the Creator.

4. Bannock is a form of flat bread made without yeast, often baked in the form of scones.

5. The anthropological term "shaman" comes from a Tungus (a Siberian language) word meaning "one who knows." In Lehmann and Myers' *Magic, Witchcraft, and Religion: An Anthropological Study of the Supernatural,* shaman is defined as, "A religious specialist and healer with powers derived directly from supernatural sources" (Lehman and Myers, 1993: 417). The role of the shaman is not inherently good or bad, helpful or harmful to the community. It depends on the individual, the situation, and the culture.

KEY TERMS

shaman (p. 168)   sweetgrass (p. 164)

REVIEW QUESTIONS

1. What advantages come from a police officer being able to speak even a few words in the local Native language?
2. According to Corporal Ship, what are the advantages and disadvantages of being a Native officer on reserve?
3. How might one officer's attitudes and behaviours towards Natives affect those officers who follow him or her into a Native community?
4. Identify what Corporal Boisvert believes are three keys to successful policing on reserve.
5. According to Corporal Boisvert, what is the biggest challenge facing non-Native officers policing a Native community?

chapter twelve

Conclusions

LEARNING OBJECTIVES

After having completed this chapter, students should be able to:

1. Summarize the findings of the 2000 First Nations Chiefs of Police Association Study.
2. Argue the strengths and weaknesses of Option 3 (a).
3. Distinguish between the "law enforcement" and "peacekeeper" models of policing.

Long before Europeans arrived on this continent, First Nations had their own finely developed notions of justice and social control. Several examples of these have been discussed in this book. Not long after contact, however, traditional Native ways were being supplanted by those of the newcomers. Through various means, primarily codification of policies that dictated how First Nations should be governed by Britain, and then by Canada, Native peoples had the fundamental right to police themselves taken away from them. In this process, they were often subjected to policing and legal processes that made little sense to them. As well, because of systemic and, in some cases, personal racism on the part of individual officers and justice officials, policing experienced by Aboriginals was generally inferior to that experienced by non-Aboriginals.

Happily, much of the negative character of Aboriginal policing in the first century following Confederation in 1867 has begun to disappear over the last three decades. A number of initiatives, from the federal to the community level, have brought about dramatic change in how Native peoples are policed and police themselves. While there have been some "growing pains" that have limited the effectiveness of some of these changes, and further change is needed, no one can deny that the policies and practices that existed earlier were far more detrimental than what is in place today.

First Nations are moving toward greater self-government. Inherent in this is the right to police themselves and to administer their own systems of justice. While the change may not ever come full circle, Native peoples are coming much closer to making the circle complete again. May they prosper.

The most recent and comprehensive study of Native-run policing services is discussed below.

THE FIRST NATIONS CHIEFS OF POLICE ASSOCIATION STUDY

From April to September 2000, the First Nations Chiefs of Police Association (FNCPA) surveyed the chiefs of police, police officers, civilian staff, police governance authorities and community stakeholders in communities which had "First Nations Self-Administered Police Services." The results of this study were posted on the Web in 2001 (FNCPA, 2001).

The Numbers

They reported that there were at that time 49 First Nations Self-Administered Police Services (FNSAPS), providing services to over 184 communities. This included 377 First Nations police officers. Ninety percent of these officers were status Indians, and about 70 percent were band members of the First Nation that employed them. Approximately 90 percent of the officers were male (a statistic similar to other police services in Canada; see Seagrave, 1997: 95). Approximately 60 percent of the officers had a high school diploma, with a higher percentage of women having a college diploma (about 33%) than did their male colleagues (20%). When Murphy and Clairmont did their research of people engaged in Aboriginal policing (90% of which were Native), 80 percent had a high school diploma or better (Murphy and Clairmont 1996). In both studies, the education level was found to be significantly less than that of their non-Aboriginal colleagues. Of course, Native people generally are less well-educated than the Canadian population, there being a complex mixture of reasons why: the legacy of their abusive experiences at residential schools (see Steckley and Cummins, 2001: 107, 189–93, 251), poverty, low self-esteem, the institutional racism of a school system in which Aboriginals are not a significant part of the curriculum in teaching history. This is one reason why training is such an important issue.

In terms of policing experience, most of the chiefs of police had over 20 years of policing service, the average length being just over 23 years and 3 months. Their average length of service in their current police service was just over 9.5 years. Seventy percent of the chiefs of police had worked for other police services prior to their employment with their current police service, and a majority had worked their way up through the ranks. It was noted, however, that "not many of them had the management experience that a Chief of Police must deliver to the organization" (FNCPA, 2001: 3.6, "Experience Mix").

Given the newness of the FNSAPS, it is not surprising that the policing experience of the police officers is considerably less than that of the chiefs of police. The average length of service in police services is just over 7.5 years, and for their current police service, just under 5 years. Only 40 percent of the police officers had worked for other police services, although most of the corporals and sergeants had had such experience.

The Police Governance Authority

The authors of the study are somewhat critical of the boards or commissions that govern the policing services, particularly regarding the fact that, "The functionality and actual operation of the Police Boards is very much dictated by the local politics in most cases" (FNCPA, 2001: 2.4, "Governing Boards"). They note that there are no apparent specific qualifications required of board members. While membership differs widely from service to service, most boards have a mixture of both elected council members and members of the community at large.

One of the sources of conflict concerning the police boards is that in many instances, the chief of police was on the job prior to the formation of the police board:

> Thus the Board had nothing to do with the hiring of the key management position in the organization and this is a very definite factor in the lack of effectiveness of the Board and the First Nations Self-Administered Police Services structure overall. *Another example of how politics has a detrimental impact on the organization.* (FNCPA, 2001: 5.4, "Recruitment and Hiring"; emphasis in original)

The authors of the study also see a need for the police board to receive training in order for them to better hold the respect of the police officers. In their words,

> The first step once a recruit is hired by a Board is to send that new recruit for training. The Board members themselves get little or no training in the area of governance and due diligence and thus the employees end up being better trained and more knowledgeable than the Board. Once again there is a structural problem where the employees believe that they know more than the boss (i.e., the Board Member), while the Board believes the same way.

This situation could be dealt with quite easily by developing mandatory "training" for Police Governance Authority members (FNCPA, 2001: 5.4, "Recruitment and Hiring").

The Culture of Policing

The authors of the study have a lot to say about the culture of policing. To begin with, they feel that owing to a lack of resources, training, and adequate staffing, the FNSAPS follow a more mainstream **"law enforcement" model of policing** than what they feel is a more culturally appropriate and ultimately more effective **"peacekeeper," or crime prevention, model of policing**.

This notion comes strongly from the people being studied, particularly concerning training needs. Their findings in this regard are as follows: 60 percent of police chiefs and 60 percent of police officers felt that the training being delivered did not respond to the cultural aspects of the job; 75 percent of police chiefs and almost 70 percent of police officers felt that the training offered did not prepare officers for the role of peacekeeper as opposed to law enforcer; and 60 percent of police chiefs and over 65 percent of police officers said that the training offered did not ensure that community values were reflected in the entire formal and field training process (FNCPA, 2001: 9.9, "Training—What the First Nations Police Chiefs Say" and 9.10, "Training—What the First Nations Officers Say"). When the "community stakeholders" were questioned, 90 percent felt that their local police service would benefit from Native-awareness training, and 75 percent felt that the police training the recruits received did not ensure that First Nation community values were reflected throughout the formal and field training process.

This inadequacy of training to meet the needs of Native communities in the development of their own culture of policing has for years been identified as a problem. In 1994, Wally McKay, then Chairperson of the Ontario First Nations Police Commission, wrote the following:

> I ask you to consider the training our constables receive. Glaringly absent are studies of First Nations community dynamics, organization and development, or mediation and conflict-resolution techniques—all skills that will be required, along with investigative procedures, but even more so if our own peacekeepers-peacemakers are to become relevant, effective and legitimized on our territories in the twenty-first century. (McKay, 1994: 353)

The authors of the study also identified how much the police chiefs desired to diversify their staff in order to better serve culturally defined community policing needs:

> At the more senior levels of the First Nations Self-Administered Police Services there is an identified desire to have more personnel and have trained "speciality" officers employed and deployed within the communities they serve. These desires are very basic for the most part in terms of wanting officers who can deliver services in the areas of crime prevention and other community focused areas of need. First Nation Police Services would very much like to target youth and schools, provide more assistance to Elders as well as focus on family related issues, all growing concerns within most communities (FNCPA, 2001: 3.1, "Occupational Mix").

It should be noted that youth are a special policing concern in Native communities because of the high proportion of youth in these communities. Frideres (1998) notes, using projected figures for 2001, that

> well over one-third of the Aboriginal population is younger than 15 and over half are younger than 25. Of the total population, only about one-fifth of the population is under 15 and about one-third are under 25 years of age. When on-reserve Indians and Inuit are singled out of the status Indian population, greater discrepancies are evident. Thirty-seven percent of on-reserve Indians and Inuit are under age 15, while nearly two-thirds of them are under the age of 25. (Frideres, 1998: 119)

Another element of the culture of policing discussed in the study concerned Elders. The authors noted the disparity between the claim made by 70 percent of police chiefs that they used Elders and community members in an advisory capacity, and information generated by the field study that little consulting of Elders actually took place. They felt that the police chiefs (and the 50 percent of the police officers who felt that their service used Elders and community members in an advisory capacity) were giving the "socially acceptable" answer rather than one that accurately reflected actual practice. Still, they optimistically felt that as a distinctly Native culture of policing developed, the role of the Elder would grow.

Murphy and Clairmont title the conclusion to their study "The Evolving Model of Aboriginal Policing: The Two Path Model." In their conclusion, they discuss how Aboriginal policing officers are pulled in two directions, toward the "urban (suburban) crime focused, technology based and legalistic approach to policing" of modern conventional mainstream policing (one of the two paths) and toward a not yet clearly defined alternative Aboriginal model of policing:

> On one path the officers in our sample suggest that they need more conventional police training in order to enhance their basic policing skills and also to be confident in their interactions with [the] non-aboriginal criminal justice community.

The other path, though less defined, is a desire for alternative and somehow more community compatible policing strategies, that would assist them to more effectively meet the unique policing needs of First Nations communities. Developing both of these paths and harmonizing them within one unique Aboriginal policing model would seem to be a difficult but worthwhile destination (Murphy and Clairmont, 1996).

The Community Focus of a Career in Policing

The authors of the study noted that the main reason given by Natives for embarking on a policing career is that "it's a chance to contribute to the betterment of my own community" (FNCPA, 2001: 5.1, "A Career in First Nations Policing"). They went on to discuss that with the strong connections to family that Natives have, as well as the close links that exist to community, a strong motivating factor for young people wanting to work as police officers in a First Nations police force is that they can work in their home community. In the Murphy and Clairmont study, advantages of working in one's own community included a better understanding of local culture and tradition, that "People trust you more, will listen to you before listening to a stranger, are willing to approach you in confidence and will help out" (Murphy and Clairmont, 1996).

Not investigated, but of concern, is how well this desire to work in one's own community will mesh with the family and other political pressures put on officers when they have to police their own community. In Murphy and Clairmont's survey, respondents were asked to indicate in their own words what they considered to be the advantages and the special problems of policing in a small community where they grew up. In their study, 47 percent of the officers were then policing their home community. The responses were not unexpected. The most common problem cited was having to deal with family, relatives generally, and friends. Because

> "[T]hey will expect you to take their side" and "people take things personally," the officer has to deal with stresses and pressures related to bias and favouritism and with associated community expectations and perceptions; even if there is no bias, actions may be subject to that definition. (Murphy and Clairmont, 1996)

Band constables were critical of the strong social connections between police officers and community members. One noted that, "everyone expects a break; it becomes harder to be objective in your own view and you tend to get very cynical" (Murphy and Clairmont, 1996). For the officers who worked in stand-alone policing services (i.e., those that would have been featured in the 2001 study of First Nations self-administered police services), reprisal was a special concern: "[T]he reprisal reportedly could be directed at the officers' family members or material property or could be a loss of friendship; small-minded local politicians could be especially vengeful" (Murphy and Clairmont, 1996).

A number felt the stress of not being able to get away from the police role, that their freedom was becoming restricted. As one officer put it, "[A] lot of people I grew up with, I no longer associate with. My life has changed a lot, mostly for the better but there are some things I wish I could still do such as go to social gatherings on the reserve" (Murphy and Clairmont, 1996).

Further, the percentage of officers in stand-alone Aboriginal policing services who agreed with the statement that they felt that there was "Too much community input in the organization" was 37 percent (as compared to 23% for the RCMP Aboriginal policing officers and for their OPP equivalent [Murphy and Clairmont, 1996])[1]. Finally, in the question concerning stress factors in the work, the Aboriginal policing officers listed "political pressures" as the second greatest stress factor (behind "work schedules"), with 19 percent strongly agreeing and 43 percent agreeing (Murphy and Clairmont, 1996).

Exploring Option 3 (a)

It would seem that these problems could be well addressed by serious reconsideration being given to the first part of the third option that the Department of Indian and Northern Affairs (DIAND) came up with in its 1973 *Task Force on Policing on Reserves*. This option was "that a separate Native Provincial Police Force be established to operate on its own, under the authority of the provincial attorney general, with its own form of police commission" (Seagrave, 1997: 255). Such a provincial (or at least regional or treaty-based) body could increase accountability, having the power to investigate band council actions that are suspect; the possible protection of band council members and their relatives who have committed domestic abuse; and the disbanding of Aboriginal police services because they have opposed the band council. The provincial policing body could also increase the Aboriginal accountability of policing services involved in major urban centres by having a member on the police commissions involved in policing major urban centres in the province.

It was noted in the FNCPA study that there were difficulties that the smaller First Nations self-administered police services have: "The very small First Nations Self-Administered Police Service lacks the positive offerings of a larger service and consequently has to manage a constant turnover in all the positions with the Police Service" (FNCPA, 2001: 5.4, "Recruitment and Hiring").

In Murphy and Clairmont's 1996 study, 41 percent of the Aboriginal policing officers agreed with the statement that they had little opportunity for promotion or being hired by another police organization (Murphy and Clairmont, 1996). Having local police services connected to a larger Aboriginal policing agency could reduce those problems. Promotions are more possible, and greater respect on the part of other policing agencies for Aboriginal officers could result.

NOTES

1. Unfortunately, the authors grouped together Sûreté du Québec (SQ) Aboriginal police officers with band constables into an "Other" category. This category had a 48 percent agreement with the statement, which we feel may reflect the latter's contribution more than that of the former, but with the two being grouped together, this cannot be determined.

KEY TERMS

law enforcement model of
   policing (p. 172)

peacekeeper model of
   policing (p. 172)

REVIEW QUESTIONS

1. Why is training such an important issue for Aboriginal police services?
2. What criticisms do the authors of the study have for the boards or commissions that govern the policing services?
3. Distinguish between the "law enforcement" and "peacekeeper" models of policing.
4. Why are youth a special policing concern in Native communities?
5. What was the main reason given by Natives for embarking on a policing career?

Glossary

Band A group of Aboriginals recognized by the federal government as constituting a corporate entity for purposes of land ownership (i.e., a reserve or reserves) and other potential benefits

Band Constable A category of police officer created in 1969 by DIAND and permitted under Section 81 of the *Indian Act* to administer band bylaws.

Band Council A federally mandated, elected body that governs a band.

Circular 55 A federal enactment that in 1971 created "special constables." Aboriginal police officers with limited authority.

Code of Handsome Lake An oral tradition based on the teachings of the Seneca prophet, Handsome Lake (1735–1815).

Cultures of Policing The notion that each culture has, along with other distinctive features, its own cultural method of policing that differs in some ways from that of other cultures.

Customary Law The system of traditional concepts of right and wrong, plus the means of enforcing compliance with what is considered right.

Great Law of Peace An oral tradition of the Haudenosaunee or Iroquois, establishing their government and some significant religious observances and ceremonies.

Haudenosaunee "They build or extend a house." The name that the Iroquois gave to themselves prior to Europeans imposing "Iroquois" on them as a name.

Hickman Report The 1990 report that followed the two-year Royal Commission inquiring into the handling of the Donald Marshall case.

Indian Act The federal act that created the separate legal status "Indian" and that affects virtually every aspect of Native life.

Institutional Racism The form of racism in which beliefs, rules, and structures systematically discriminate against a particular race or races.

Inuit "People, men" (singular "Inuk"), both an ethnic distinction and a legal term (defined slightly differently in different jurisdictions) that typically refers to someone who possesses a disk number, has a certain percentage of "Inuit blood," or is considered an Inuk by the local Inuit community.

James Bay and Northern Quebec Agreement A treaty signed by the Quebec government, the federal government, and the Cree of East James Bay 1975.

Jay Treaty An agreement signed in 1794 between the United States and Britain in which issues were settled that had not been resolved after the end of the American Revolution. It permitted Native people to move freely across the Canada-US border to bring furs for trade and their "goods and effects."

Law Enforcement Model of Policing A model of policing that stresses arresting and punishing offenders.

Lonefighters Society A traditional Peigan warrior society (see Steckley and Cummins, 2001: 95–96) that was reactivated to protest the damming of the sacred Oldman River.

Medicine Bundle A collection of sacred items connecting an individual to his/her vision and the spiritual world.

Métis Both an ethnic or racial group (typically a mixing of Cree and French) and a legal status, defined differently (or not at all) in different jurisdictions.

Option 3 (a)   The policing option put forward by DIAND in 1973 by which separate Native provincial police forces would be established.

Option 3 (b)   The policing option put forward by DIAND in 1973 by which Aboriginal policing would be conducted under the direction and control of existing provincial police forces.

Pass System   Introduced in 1885 and lasting until the 1930s, this system prevented Native people from leaving prairie reserves without a pass issued by their farming instructor or Indian Agent.

Peacekeeper Model of Policing   A model of policing influenced by Native traditions that is based more on crime prevention and community policing than on the apprehension and punishment of criminals.

Potlatch   A traditional ceremony held by Aboriginals living on the West Coast. It was banned from 1884 to 1951.

Racism   Prejudice, discriminatory practices, and the exercise of power, based on the ideology of the superiority of one race over others.

Registered Indian   A Native person who legally bears the status of "Indian" for the purposes of the Indian Act.

Reserve   A plot of land reserved for a band.

Sachem   A term derived from an Algonquian word for "leader" (see saqmaw) and often used to refer to one of the 50 chiefs of the Haudenosaunee.

Sacred Site   A place that is in some way connected to the supernatural or spiritual world (e.g., where religious rituals have been performed, where religious art is depicted, or where people have been buried).

Saqmaw   A Mi'kmaq word for "leader".

Section 35 of the *Indian Act*   A part of the *Indian Act* that states that the federal government can, without band consultation or permission, expropriate reserve land at any time.

Sentencing Circle   A tradition-based restorative Aboriginal justice initiative in which offenders face community members, who discuss how a criminal act will be dealt with.

Shaman   A term that refers to an Aboriginal religious practitioner who is a combination of healer, psychologist, artist, entertainer and visionary.

Special Constables   A category of Aboriginal police officer, created in 1971 by Circular 55, with limited policing authority.

Starlight Tours   The policing practice of driving Native people who have been drinking to the outskirts of town, forcing them to walk back into town.

Sundance   An important sacred ceremony, typically practised by Plains people (see Steckley and Cummins, 2001: 93), that was initiated, sponsored, and presided over by a respected woman. It was banned from 1895 to 1951.

Sweat Lodge   A ceremonial building (and the ceremony itself) in which water is poured over hot rocks, producing steam. An Elder or some other spiritual leader typically leads people in the ceremony.

Sweetgrass   A plant that is burned so that the smoke can ritually purify a place.

Treaty   A legal agreement between a national government and a Native group or groups. It typically involves the surrender of rights to large tracts of land, the allocation of a small piece of land, the placing of money in trust, and promises of future benefits.

Tripartite Agreement   A policing agreement between the federal government, a provincial or territorial government, and a band or a larger group of Native people. The federal government typically bears 52 percent of the costs and the provincial or territorial government 48 percent.

Watchman   A traditionally respected justice figure among the Salishan-speaking Lillooet of British Columbia.

Weregild   In traditional cultures, this is the payment made by the offender (or the offender's family) to compensate an injured or murdered victim (or the victim's family).

References

Alberta Justice. 2000. *Annual Summary of Aboriginal Justice Programs and Initiatives.*

Alfred, Gerald R. 1995. *Heeding the Voices of Our Ancestors: Kahnawake Mohawk Politics and the Rise of Native Nationalism.* Toronto: Oxford University Press.

Augustine, Noah. 2000. *Indian Reserve a Haven from Racism.* Toronto Star. Op-ed page, April 18, 2000.

Balikci, Asen. 1970. *The Netsilik Eskimo.* Prosper Heights, Illinois: Waveland Press Inc.

Barrett, Stanley R. 1987. *Is God a Racist?* Toronto: University of Toronto Press.

Barron, Marcia Hoyle. 1998. *Finding Our Way: Paths to Justice Reform in an Aboriginal Community.* Unpublished Ph.D thesis: Anthropology, McMaster University.

Bock, Philip. 1978. Micmac. *Handbook of North American Indians, Vol. 15. The Northeast.* Washington: Smithsonian Institution, pp. 109–122.

British Columbia Police Commission. 1997. *Stl'atl'imx Tribal Police: Section 42. B.C. Police Act Inspection.*

Brody, Hugh. 1987. *Living Arctic: Hunters of the Canadian North.* Vancouver/Toronto: Douglas and McIntyre.

Burke, James. 1976. *Paper Tomahawks: From Red Tape to Red Power.* Winnipeg: Queenston House Publishing.

Cardinal, Mike. 1998. *First Nations Police Services—Review.* Alberta: Minister of Justice and the Attorney General.

Clairmont Don and Rick Linden. 1998. *Developing & Evaluating Justice Projects in Aboriginal Communities: A Review of the Literature.* Solicitor General Canada. www.sgc.gc.ca/Abocor/e199805/e199805.

Comeau, Pauline and Aldo Santin. 1990. *The First Canadians—A Profile of Canada's Native People Today.* Toronto: James Lorimer and Company.

Cross, Ronald and Hélène Sévigny. 1994. *Lasagna: The Man Behind the Mask.* Vancouver: Talon Books.

Cummins, Bryan and Kirby Whiteduck. 1998. *Towards a Model for the Identification and Recognition of Sacred Sites. In Sacred Lands—Aboriginal World Views, Claims and Conflicts,* edited by Jill Oakes et al. Edmonton: Canadian Circumpolar Institute, University of Alberta.

Delisle, Andrew. 1984. How We Regained Control Over Our Lives And Territories: The Kahnawake Story. In *Pathways to Self-Determination: Canadian Indians and the Canadian State,* edited by Leroy Little Bear, Menno Boldt, and J. Anthony Long. Toronto: University of Toronto Press, pp. 141–147.

Depew, George. 1986. *Native Policing in Canada: A Review of Current Issues.* Ottawa: Solicitor General Canada.

Dickason, Olive. 1997. *Canada's First Nations: A History of Founding Peoples from Earliest Times*, 2nd edition. Toronto: McClelland & Stewart.

——————. 2002. 3rd edition.

Dosman, Edgar J. 1972. *Indians: the Urban Dilemma*. Toronto: McClelland and Stewart.

Edwards, Peter. 2001. OPP Moves to Fire Indian Activist's Killer: Officer was Convicted in 1997 Shooting. *Toronto Star*, May 24, 2001.

Fenton, William N. and Tooker, Elisabeth. 1978. Mohawk. *Handbook of North American Indians, Vol. 15, The Northeast*. Washington: Smithsonian Institution, pp. 466–79.

Finkler, H. 1976. *Inuit and the Administration of Criminal Justice in the Northwest Territories: The Case of Frobisher Bay*. Ottawa: Indian and Northern Affairs.

First Nations Chiefs of Police Association and Human Resources Development Canada. 2001. *A Human Resource Study of First Nations Policing in Canada*. www.soonet.ca/fncpa/hrdc/.

Fleras, Augie and Jean Leonard Elliott. 1999. *Unequal Relations: An Introduction to Race, Ethnic, and Aboriginal Dynamics in Canada*, 3rd edition. Scarborough: Prentice Hall Allyn and Bacon Canada

Forcese, Dennis P. 1992. *Policing Canadian Society*. Scarborough: Prentice-Hall Canada.

Foster, John E. 1986. *The Plains Metis. Native Peoples—the Canadian Experience*, edited by R. Bruce Morrison and C. Roderick Wilson. Toronto: McClelland and Stewart.

Francis, Daniel. 1992. *The Imaginary Indian: The Images of the Indian in Canadian Culture*. Vancouver: Arsenal Pulp Press.

Franz, Donald G. and Norma Jean Russell. 1995. *Blackfoot Dictionary of Stems, Roots, and Affixes*, 2nd edition. Toronto: University of Toronto Press.

Frideres, James S. 1998. *Aboriginal Peoples in Canada: Contemporary Conflicts*, 5th edition. Scarborough: Prentice Hall Allyn and Bacon Canada.

Friesen, John W. 1997. *Rediscovering the First Nations of Canada*. Calgary: Detselig Enterprises Ltd.

Gagné, Marie-Anik. 1994. *A Nation within a Nation: Dependency and the Cree*. Montréal: Black Rose Books.

Garte, Edna. 1981. *Where the Partridge Drums. The Journal of American Indian Education*, 21 (1), October 1981, www.jaie.asu.edu/v21/V21S1whe.html.

George, Doug. 2000. *For Some a Heroic Time*, www.NatNews@egroups.com.

Goodson, Thomas R. 2000. *Report to the Attorney General Public Inquiry*—The Fatality Inquiries Act. Fatality Inquiry into the Deaths of Connie and Ty Jacobs. Alberta Justice.

Grayson, J. Paul. 1983. *Introduction to Sociology: An Alternate Approach*. Toronto: Gage Pub. Ltd.

Green, Gordon. 1998. *Community Sentencing and Mediation in Aboriginal Communities*. Manitoba Law Journal.

Griffiths, Curt T. and J.C. Yerbury. 1984. *Natives and Criminal Justice Policy: The Case of Native Policing*. Canadian Journal of Criminology 26 (2).

Griffiths, Curt T. 1994. Policing Aboriginal Peoples. In *Police Powers in Canada: the Evolution and Practice of Authority*, edited by R.C. Macleod and David Schneiderman. Toronto: University of Toronto Press.

Hall, Anthony J. Don't bury the tragedy at Gustafsen. *Vancouver Sun*, January 21, 2000, p. A19.

Harris, Michael. 1990. *Justice Denied: The Law versus Donald Marshall*, 2nd edition. Toronto: Harper-Collins.

Harrison, Anne, Muriel Meric, and Alan Dixon. 1995. *Justice and Healing in Sheshatshit and Davis Inlet*. Report by Peace Brigades International, November 1995, www.peacebrigades.org/nap/nap95-02.html.

Hickman, Alexander, Lawrence A. Poitras, and Gregory T. Evans. 1990. *The Report of the Royal Commission on the Donald Marshall Jr. Prosecution*.

Honigmann, John. 1949. *Culture and Ethos of Kaska Society*. New Haven: Yale University Publications in Anthropology, no. 40. (Reprinted by Human Relations Area Files Press).

—————. 1964. *The Kaska Indians—An Ethnographic Reconstruction*. New Haven: Yale University Publications in Anthropology, no. 51. (Reprinted by Human Relations Area Files Press).

Hornung, Rick. 1991. *One Nation Under the Gun: Inside the Mohawk Civil War*. Toronto: Stoddart Publishing Co.

Horwood, Harold and Ed Butts. 1984. *Pirates and Outlaws of Canada 1610–1932*. Toronto: Doubleday Canada Ltd.

Jackson, Michael. 1987. *Locking Up Natives in Canada*. Canadian Bar Association.

Jenness, Diamond. 1922. *The Life of the Copper Eskimo: Report of the Canadian Arctic Expedition, 1913–1918*, vol. 12, pt. A. Ottawa: Department of Naval Service, King's Printer.

Johnson, Joyce and Fred. 1993. Community Development, Sobriety and After-Care at Alkali Lake Band. In *The Path to Healing: Report on the National Round Table on Aboriginal Health and Social Issues*. Ottawa: Royal Commission on Aboriginal Peoples.

Kendall, Diana. 1997. *Race, Class and Gender in a Diverse Society: A Text Reader*. Toronto: Allyn and Bacon.

Kerr, Joanna. 2000. *A Triumphant Homecoming: New Constables Return to Their Aboriginal Communities to Fulfil an RCMP Promise*. Pony Express, June-July-August 2000, pp. 14–16

Kulchyski, Peter, ed. 1994. *Unjust Relations: Aboriginal Rights in Canadian Courts*. Toronto: Oxford University Press Canada.

Kulchyski, Peter, Don McCaskill and David Newhouse, eds. 1999. *In the Words of Elders: Aboriginal Cultures in Transition*. Toronto: University of Toronto Press.

Lambert, C. 1978. *Research Priorities in Northern Labrador*. Montreal: McGill University Press.

Lehmann, Arthur C. and James E. Myers. 1993. *Magic, Witchcraft and Religion: an Anthropological Study of the Supernatural*, 3rd edition. Toronto: Mayfield Publishing Company.

Leonardy, Matthias R.J. 1998. *First Nations Criminal Jurisdiction in Canada: The Aboriginal Right to Peacemaking Under Public International and Canadian Constitutional Law*. Regina: Native Law Centre, University of Saskatchewan.

Linder, Les. n.d. *Growth, Knowledge and Acceptance: After 15 years, the Six Nations Police Service Continues its Evolution*. Solicitor General Canada, www.sgc.gc.ca/whoweare/Aboriginal/NewsletterApril2001/ePage3.htm

Lips, Julius. 1937. *Public Opinion and Mutual Assistance among the Montagnais-Naskapi*. American Anthropologist 39: 222–228.

Mackie, Richard. 2001a. Harris Ordered Removal of Natives, Memo Says: Book on Ipperwash Probes George Death. *Globe and Mail*, September 3, 2001, A1.

—————. 2001b. Ipperwash Paramedics Targeted: Native Protester Didn't Receive Treatment after OPP Shot Him, Brother Tells Coroner. *Globe and Mail*, September 10, 2001, A6.

MacEwan, J. W. Grant. 1971. *Portraits from the Plains*. Toronto: McGraw-Hill Company of Canada Ltd.

Maracle, Brian. 1996. *Back on the Rez: Finding The Way Home*. Toronto: Viking Penguin.

Maracle, Lee. 1992. *Sun Dogs*. Penticton, B.C: Theytus Books Ltd.

McGillivray, Anne and Brenda Comasky. 1999. *Black Eyes All of the Time: Intimate Violence, Aboriginal Women and the Justice System*. Toronto: University of Toronto Press.

McKay, Wally. 1994. An Experience with First Nations Policing. In *Continuing Poundmaker and Riel's Quest: Presentations Made at a Conference on Aboriginal Peoples and Justice*, compiled by Richard Gosse, James Youngblood Henderson, and Roger Carter. Saskatoon, Purich Publishing, pp. 350–355.

McKenna, Paul F. 1998. *Foundations of Policing in Canada*. Scarborough: Prentice-Hall Canada.

Miller, Barbara D., Penny Van Esterik and John Van Esterik. 2001. *Cultural Anthropology, Canadian Edition*. Toronto: Allyn and Bacon Canada.

Miller, Virginia P. 1995. The Micmac: A Maritime Woodland Group. In *Native Peoples: The Canadian Experience*, edited by B. Morrison and C.R. Wilson. Toronto: McClelland & Stewart, pp. 347–374.

Minister of Supply and Services. 1991 (and 1996). *First Nations Policing Policy*. Solicitor General Canada.

Mitchell, Michael. 1989. Akwesasne: An Unbroken Assertion of Sovereignty. In *Drumbeat: Anger and Renewal in Indian Country*, edited by Boyce Richardson, Assembly of First Nations. Toronto: Summerhill Press, pp. 105–136.

Monture-Angus, Patricia. 1995. *Thunder in My Soul: A Mohawk Woman Speaks*. Halifax: Fernwood Publishing.

Moyles, R.G. 1989. *British Law and Arctic Men: The Celebrated 1917 Murder Trials of Sinnisiak and Uluksuk, First Inuit Tried Under White Man's Law*. Burnaby: The Northern Justice Society, Simon Fraser University.

Murphy, C.J. and Clairmont, D. 1996. *First Nations Police Officers Survey*. Solicitor General Canada, www.sgc.gc.ca/epub/Abo/e199606/e199606.htm.

Nihmey, John. 1998. *Fireworks and Folly: How We Killed Minnie Sutherland*. Ottawa: Phillip Diamond Books.

O'Meara, John. 1996. *Delaware-English/English-Delaware Dictionary*. Toronto: University of Toronto Press.

Oziewicz, Estanislao. 2001. Harris Met with Police Just Before Assault on Natives: Document Contains "Startling" Admission. *Globe and Mail*, September 4, 2001, A1 and A4.

Peace Brigades International. 1991. Davis Inlet: Progress with Justice. PBI Special Report, October, 1991, www.peacebrigades.orn/nap/nap95-01.html.

Pelletier, Wilfred and Poole, Ted. 1973. *No Foreign Land: The Biography of a North American Indian*. New York: Pantheon Books.

Perreaux, Les. 2000. Officers Admit "Mistake" Leaving Man in -22C. *National Post*, September 18, 2000, A14.

Priest, Lisa. 1989. *Conspiracy of Silence*. Toronto: McClelland and Stewart.

Purich, Donald. 1988. *The Métis*. Toronto: James Lorimer and Company.

Rhodes, Richard. 1985. *Eastern Ojibwa-Chippewa-Ottawa Dictionary*. Amsterdam: Mouton.

Rice, Brian and John Steckley. 1997. Lifelong Learning and Cultural Identity: A Lesson from Canada's Native People. In *Lifelong Learning: Policies, Programs and Practices*, edited by Michael Hatton. Toronto: Asian Pacific Economic Cooperation (APEC Pub.), pp. 216–229.

Richardson, Boyce. 1991. *Strangers Devour the Land*. Vancouver/Toronto: Douglas & McIntyre.

Roberts, Julian and LaPrairie, Carol. 1997. Raising Some Questions about Sentencing Circles. *Criminal Law Quarterly*.

Robin, Martin. 1976. *The Bad and the Lonely: Seven Stories of the Best—and Worst—Canadian Outlaws*. Toronto: James Lorimer & Company.

Rose, Alex. 2000. *Spirit Dance at Meziadin: Chief Joseph Gosnell and the Nisga'a Treaty*. Medeira Park, B.C.: Harbour Publishing.

Ross, Rupert. 1993. *Aboriginal Community Healing in Action: the Hollow Water Approach*. www.usask.ca/nativelaw/jah_ross.html.

Schaefer, Richard T., R.P. Lamm, Penny Biles and Susannah J. Wilson. 1996. *Sociology: An Introduction, First Canadian Edition*. Toronto: McGraw-Hill Ryerson Ltd.

Seagrave, Jayne. 1997. *Introduction to Policing in Canada*. Scarborough: Prentice-Hall Canada.

Sinclair, Gordon Jr. 1999. *Cowboys and Indians: The Shooting of J.J. Harper*. Toronto: McClelland and Stewart.

Smith, Donald. 1974. Le Sauvage. *The Native People in Quebec: Historical Writing on the Heroic Period (1534–1663) of New France*. Ottawa, National Museums of Canada.

Solicitor-General Canada. n.d. (c. 1998). *Crime Prevention in First Nations Communities: An Inventory of Policing Initiatives*.

Spradley, James. 1969. *Guests Never Leave Hungry: The Autobiography of James Sewid, a Kwakiutl Indian*. New Haven and London: Yale University Press.

Stackhouse, John. 2001. Welcome to Harlem on the Prairies. *Globe and Mail*, November 3, 2001, F2–F4.

Steckley, John L. 1997. Aboriginal Peoples. In *Our Society: Human Diversity in Canada*, edited by P. Angelini. Toronto: ITP Nelson, pp. 131–158.

Steckley, John L. and Bryan Cummins. 2001. *Full Circle: Canada's Native People*, Toronto, Pearson Education Canada.

Stefansson, V. 1919. *The Stefansson-Anderson Arctic Expedition: Preliminary Ethnological Report*. New York: Anthropological Papers Vol. 14, American Museum of Natural History.

Stenning, Philip. 1996. *Police Governance in First Nations in Ontario*. Toronto: Centre of Criminology, University of Toronto.

Stewart, Susan. 1996. A Day in the Life of Two Community Police Officers: The Aboriginal Police Directorate Takes a Look at the First Nations Policing Policy in Action. *First Nations Policing Update, March 1966, No. 4*. www.sgc.gc.ca/whoweare/aboriginal/newsletter/no4/no43.htm.

Stymeist. 1975. *Ethnics and Indians: Social Relations in a Northwestern Ontario Town*. Toronto: Peter Martin Associates.

Szabo, Zoltan E. 1997. *The Mohawk Nation of Akwesasne: Who Are the Mohawks?* www.peacetree.com/akwesasne/whoare.htm.

Teichroeb, Ruth. 1998. *Flowers on My Grave: How an Ojibwa Boy's Death Helped Break the Silence on Child Abuse*. Toronto: HarperCollins Pub. Ltd.

Tester, F.J. and Peter Kulchyski. 1994. *Tammarniit (Mistakes): Inuit Relocation in the Eastern Arctic 1939–1963*. Vancouver: University of British Columbia Press.

Thwaites, Reuben G. 1959. *The Jesuit Relations and Allied Documents*. New York: Pageant Book Company.

Tooker, Elisabeth. 1978. The League of the Iroquois: Its History, Politics, and Rituals. In *Handbook of North American Indians, Vol. 15. The Northeast*. Washington: Smithsonian Institution, pp. 418–441.

————. 2000. Micmacs and Colonists: Indian-White Relations. In *The Tribal Council News*, vol. 2, issues 6, 8, and 10.

Wadden, Marie. 1996. *Nitassinan: The Innu Struggle to Reclaim Their Homeland*. Vancouver/Toronto: Douglas & McIntyre.

Wagamese, Richard. 1996. *The Terrible Summer*. Toronto: Warwick Publishing.

Watkins, Mel, ed. 1977. *Dene Nation—The Colony Within*. Toronto: University of Toronto Press.

Wood, Chris, John DeMont, and John Geddes. 1999. Building New Bridges. *Maclean's*, September 27, 1999, pp. 24–30.

Woodbury, Hanni, Reg Henry, and Harry Webster. 1992. *Concerning the League: The Iroquois League Tradition as Dictated in Onondaga by John Arthur Gibson*. Memoir 9. Winnipeg: Algonquian and Iroquoian Linguistics.

Woodward, Rocky. 1990. Lonefighters Roots Date Back to 1700s, and Peigan Council Backs Lonefighters. *Windspeaker*, September 14, 1990, pp. 8–9.

York, Geoffrey. 1990. *The Dispossessed: Life and Death in Native Canada*. London: Vintage U.K.

York, Geoffrey and Loreen Pindera. 1991. *People of the Pines: The Warriors and the Legacy of Oka*. Toronto: Little Brown and Company.

Zakreski, Dan. Police Chief under Siege: Dave Scott Reverses Stance, Calls for Outside Investigation. *Saskatoon Star Phoenix*, February 17, 2000.

Index